Darkness before Daybreak

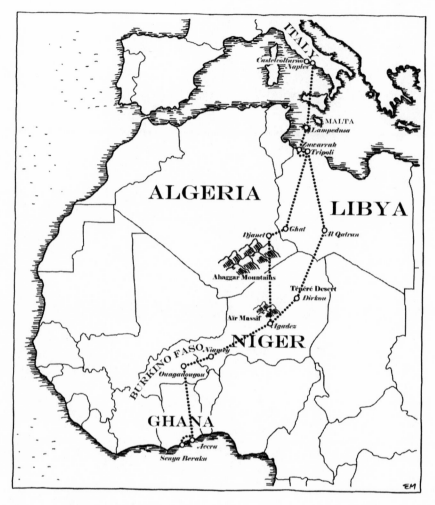

Main routes of the emigrants' journey from Senya Beraku, Ghana, to Naples, Italy.
Map by Eskil Møhl.

Darkness before Daybreak

AFRICAN MIGRANTS LIVING ON
THE MARGINS IN SOUTHERN
ITALY TODAY

HANS LUCHT

UNIVERSITY OF CALIFORNIA PRESS
Berkeley   Los Angeles   London

An earlier version of part 3, pp. 238–252, appeared previously as "Violence and Morality: The Concession of Loss in a Ghanaian Fishing Village" in *Journal of Religious Ethics* 38, no. 3 (2010): 468–77. Reprinted by permission of John Wiley and Sons.

University of California Press, one of the most distinguished university presses in the United States, enriches lives around the world by advancing scholarship in the humanities, social sciences, and natural sciences. Its activities are supported by the UC Press Foundation and by philanthropic contributions from individuals and institutions. For more information, visit www.ucpress.edu.

University of California Press
Berkeley and Los Angeles, California

University of California Press, Ltd.
London, England

Library of Congress Cataloging-in-Publication Data

Lucht, Hans, 1971–
    Darkness before daybreak : African migrants living on the margins in southern Italy today / Hans Lucht.
        p.   cm.
    Includes bibliographical references.
    ISBN 978-0-520-27073-2 (pbk. : alk. paper)
    1. Ghanaians—Italy—Naples—Social conditions.   2. Immigrants—Italy—Naples—Social conditions.   3. Naples (Italy)—Ethnic relations.   4. Fishers—Ghana—Economic conditions. 5. Senya Beraku (Ghana)—Economic conditions. 6. Naples (Italy)—Emigration and immigration. 7. Ghana—Emigration and immigration.   I. Title.
    DG457.G53L83   2012
    305.896′ 67045731—dc22

                                                                2011008230

Manufactured in the United States of America

21 20 19 18 17 16 15 14 13 12
10 9 8 7 6 5 4 3 2 1

In keeping with a commitment to support environmentally responsible and sustainable printing practices, UC Press has printed this book on 50-pound Enterprise, a 30% post-consumer-waste, recycled, deinked fiber that is processed chlorine-free. It is acid-free and meets all ANSI/NISO (Z 39.48) requirements.

In this world, shipmates, sin that pays its way can travel freely, and without a passport; whereas Virtue, if a pauper, is stopped at all frontiers.

Herman Melville, *Moby Dick*

The publisher gratefully acknowledges the generous support of the Anne G. Lipow Endowment Fund for Social Justice and Human Rights of the University of California Press Foundation, which was established by Stephen M. Silberstein.

Contents

Preface

It has become a recurrent image of human distress, prompting concern as well as condemnation, reported by the media from the southern borders of Europe—Italy, Spain, Malta, and in recent years particularly Greece: undocumented immigrants and refugees arriving in overcrowded boats in an attempt to reach Europe. In the summer of 2003 a group of young men from a small Guan fishing village in Ghana's Central Region arrived in just this way. The twelve had crossed the Sahara Desert and then faced the perils of the Mediterranean Sea from Libya to Italy. Presently, they live and work as day laborers in the cutthroat underground economy of Naples. Samuel, my field assistant and translator, is one of them. This book examines their experiences—their lives in the fishing village of Senya Beraku in Ghana, their journey to Europe, and their struggle to gain a foothold on the fringes of Italian society. It explores their precarious attempt to improve their lot in life at a critical moment when local fish stocks are dwindling and canoes have been coming back empty for five years in succession, following a general trend

in the entire West African region. The radical decline in small-scale
fishing has had immediate socioeconomic effects and is also taking its
toll at an existential level, creating a sense among Guan fishermen that
they have lost control over the future. In this view, the fishermen's
attempt to reposition themselves within the circulation of goods both
symbolic and material by traveling illegally to Europe is viewed a strategy of recovering their lives and livelihoods from a discouraging future.
Sammy and his travel companions are not the destitute and defeated
wreckage they may appear to be in television footage the European
public has grown accustomed to—those blank, disorientated faces staring
into the cameras as their shabby boats are dragged to shore by navy
vessels. They are perhaps better viewed, I argue, as people taking action
in the face of almost insurmountable odds in the all-important human
endeavor to strike a balance between, on the one hand, individual and
social expectations and, on the other, the tendencies of the world with
regard to accommodating those expectations (Bourdieu 2000: 222–223;
see also Winnicott 1962: 139). In the same way, the risky, often death-
defying, struggle for a life worth living—or simply the reasons for
being—reflected in the long and dangerous journey to Europe via Libya
may represent not only the desperation caused by the ruin of African
village life but also the human capacity for bringing the new into the
world "in the face of outside forces that act upon lives and livelihoods"
(Jackson 2005: xi).

Traditionally, the sea offered the fishing village of Senya Beraku an
exchange relationship, albeit one contested by the erratic nature of the
fishing work. Local lives and livelihoods were sustained by the environment's responsiveness to the efforts of the fishermen, the sea providing
fish, the material expression of the exchange relationship, in turn for
hard work, magical action, and ritual sacrifice. (Lucht 2003: 43–67). But
since the canoes have begun to return empty, the village has struggled.
As an important source of nutrition, fish are not easily substituted, and
the decline of the village's main industry has meant for the inhabitants
an imminent loss of economic and social agency. This development,
according to the chief fisherman of the village, is the reason behind the
upsurge in child trafficking in Senya Beraku: children are sold to far-off

fishing villages up north on the Volta River, where they work in slavelike conditions. At an existential level, as the outside world fails to sufficiently reciprocate the canoe fishermen's efforts, not only does their sense grow of losing grasp of the direction of their lives, but so does the belief that the decline in local fishing is a sign of the end of the world approaching, as an increasing number of charismatic churches claim. Some even claim that Armageddon will begin in Senya Beraku and spread from there to the rest of the world. But despite the fishermen's increasing concern with their future, they are not passively awaiting the industry's collapse. Caught, like so many young West Africans, in a "seemingly unbridgeable schism between the culturally expected and the socially possible" (Vigh 2009: 95), most direct their attention to strategies for recovering their lives and livelihoods from a depressing future. New fishing technologies for instance, are being put to use, though with disappointing results thus far, and some fishermen are going into farming and trading. But the number-one strategy for improving one's life chances, and the focus of this book, is high-risk emigration to Europe. Migration, of course, is not new to the people of Senya Beraku, but the intensity and extent of the recent wave of high-risk emigration clearly is without precedent.

Although this book contributes to the body of knowledge concerning an important aspect of globalization—the increasing flow of people across national borders—it does so without assuming that the world is converging on a common experience of life in the so-called global world, or indeed that the world is becoming smaller and smaller and is moving toward heterogeneity, good or bad (Giddens 2000: 13). On the contrary, what may be experienced as global connection by some may be experienced as "global disconnect" (Ferguson 2003, 2006) by large parts of the world's populations. Furthermore, this simultaneous global acceleration of inclusion and exclusion should not be mistaken for a heightened exploitation of poor countries by richer countries (poverty and noxious European industries may *not* necessarily attract, as Ulrich Beck gloomily predicts in *The Risk Society*, 1997: 56; see also Beck 2000: 3–4). The reality may be even more disheartening. As French economist Daniel Cohen suggests, the constraints of the globalized world, as seen from West

Africa, for instance, might be understood less as a case of exploitation of the worker within capitalist society than as a case of rich countries having no interest in poor countries, and of people in poor countries, rather than being exploited, finding themselves lost or cut off from the outside world (Cohen 2006: 1). This disconnectedness has consequences on many different levels of life—economic, social, existential. Based on my fieldwork in Naples and the village of Senya Beraku, Ghana, I argue in this book that high-risk immigration from West Africa to Europe is an attempt to revitalize life by *reestablishing connections* between individual and social desires and the many promises and constraints of outside reality, namely, the increasing uncooperativeness of the marine environment and the political economy of the global world.

My task is therefore to address the social and existential longing of the fishermen to reposition themselves within the circulation of symbolic and material goods, within a global context that seems to hinder them on all fronts. To put it more straightforwardly, I seek to develop a vocabulary suitable for describing the relationship between the constraints of the so-called global world and the individual and social aspirations of the new immigrants to Europe. This vocabulary is to be used to address the new immigrants' strategies, rationales, hopes, dreams, and fantasies for being heard, being recognized, having a say, having a hand in choosing their own lives, and enjoying the good life—a life that in a global perspective (and this perspective has to a large degree been adopted by the young West Africans themselves) appears almost antithetical to modern African village life. Staying behind in the village therefore not only risks material and economic privation but also forces one to ask questions about one's social importance and reasons for living.

One day as we were walking home to his house in a bleak Neapolitan suburb, along a dirt road where criminals come by to rob the West African immigrants of their weekly wages and their mobile phones, Samuel was thinking back on his journey, how he almost died in the Niger desert, and the challenges of the new life in Naples. He maintained that though it was a difficult new existence, full of bitterness and disappointment, it was "always better than to rot away in the village in

Ghana." Compared to a slow but inevitable demise in the village, Samuel preferred Naples and the possibility for growth.

To return to the longing to be on the inside of the circulation of material and symbolic goods, the approach here is to work with the classic anthropological notion of reciprocity, but in an expanded framework that encompasses questions of a broader existential nature—reciprocity viewed as a mode of creating connectedness between social and subjective desires and outside reality. I thus outline an *existential reciprocity*, a form of reciprocity rooted in primary intersubjectivity and the social imperative but unbiased toward the ontological status of people and things Reciprocity thus defined does not give precedence to the level of social reality; instead, it is concerned with the *plurality* of human exchange relations as they are experienced and enacted in everyday life, social as well as extrahuman relations. In this sense, reciprocity is an empowering strategy of approaching the outside world, human and extrahuman, local as well as global, and achieving through it a sense of material, social, and ontological security, however contested and frail. Moreover, existential reciprocity, in the tradition of existential anthropology, is concerned with the desire of drawing the world at large into one's domain of influence, by experientially creating expectations and establishing a moral horizon in the outside world, thus taking into one's hands the direction of one's life in the ever-threatening face of uncertainty, arbitrariness, and negation (Jackson 2005: xi, Kleinman 2006: 26). In a way, I explore existential reciprocity by its negation, by the twofold negation the fishermen appear to be facing: first, the growing unresponsiveness of the immediate marine environment, the sea; and second, a disintegration of traditional structures of lives and livelihoods (and the rise of new transnational connections) and confrontation with the structures of the global political economy. As this book shows, however, the desire to become connected is not readily accommodated, if at all, by outside reality as the West Africans slip into the underground economy of Naples.

With regard to the opportunities of the globalized world, the situation of the fishermen is paradoxical. Although they have little or no legal or otherwise legitimate opportunity to get inside the circulation of material and symbolic goods—of becoming connected, so to speak—their skills

and experience as fishermen—skills almost obsolete in Senya Beraku—
have surprisingly come into demand in a far more profitable context.
Libyan human smugglers who organize the transportation of would-be
immigrants to Italy need the fishermen to pilot the boats to Italy. In the
broadest perspective, the very same global forces that undermine local
lives appear to have opened another window of opportunity, full of risk
and suffering, but offering a new beginning in Europe.

   To shed light on this development, let me provide some methodological and empirical background. I did not set out to study high-risk immigration to Europe and its human consequences. My original focus—as
it still is within an expanded global framework—was the decline in
fishing in West Africa, the strategies that members of a small-scale fishing
community implement to deal with the changes in their lives and livelihoods, and the effects of dwindling resources on the perception of the
marine environment. But reality overtook the proposed research as it
soon became evident that the one strategy the young fishermen were not
just talking about but also in many cases pursuing was illegal immigration to Europe. This development became clear when I arrived in Naples
in the spring of 2005 to meet up with Samuel, a former field assistant
whom I had come to know during fieldwork in Senya Beraku in 2002.
One day he called me from Italy and told me in a triumphant tone that
he was now in Europe, living and working in Naples. I was happy for
him, though mystified as to how he had made it there. When he had
called me from Libya some months earlier and suggested the idea of
coming to Europe by paying a clandestine organization for the transportation, I had advised him to be careful and to think twice before trying
anything so dangerous. I was thinking that fishing experience would not
protect him against the reported callousness of the human smugglers
and how they notoriously overcrowd the boats or send people to their
certain deaths by using inadequate or faulty equipment. Calling from
Naples, Samuel explained that he lived with one guy from the village
and that there were a few other young men around too, but he was
always vague and gave few details. He did tell me that they lived in a
rough neighborhood and that "there were a lot of miserable things going
on." When I asked whether I would be in any danger staying with him

in Naples, he paused, surprised at my question, and said, "No, you're white; it's we guys, the blacks, they come for." Then we agreed that I should come down and see for myself.

Although we had agreed he would pick me up at the Naples airport, Samuel was not there when I arrived. Instead, he called me as I was waiting outside the main entrance and instructed me to hand over my mobile phone to a taxi driver, then he would give directions directly to him in Italian. The driver—a cigarette in the corner of his mouth, open shirt, hairy chest—reluctantly took the phone and listened briefly to Sammy. An argument ensued and the driver hung up. Nevertheless, he grabbed my suitcases and was apparently ready to go. As we left the airport, Sammy called back and insisted to talk to the driver again, but this time the driver just grabbed the mobile phone out of my hand and dumped it straight into the front pocket of his shirt, totally uninterested. We drove north on the expressway, up and above the city of Naples, toward Mondragone and the expressway to Rome, while behind us lay Vesuvius. As we drove on, the neighborhood became less like the romantic Naples of postcards and more like the unresolved industrial wasteland at the outskirts of modern European cities, a *terrain vague* that one is happy to speed by, perhaps eyeing the young African and Eastern European prostitutes waiting in the long, yellow grass at the roadside.

After a good half-hour, we parked next to a petrol station. Naturally, and in my preoccupation in seeing Sammy again as he ran toward the car, the Neapolitan driver ripped me off very badly. Laughing as the driver took off with my money, Sammy told me not to worry because everybody who comes to Naples is "burned" sooner or later. He had booked a room at a nearby hotel, but there was no time to check in; we were in a hurry to attend a meeting at a house up the road, the home of several young men from the village, Sammy explained. This was why he hadn't come to the airport. We talked along the way, trying to catch up on the three years that had passed since my first fieldwork in Ghana, Sammy, as always, insisting on carrying my bags. We walked along the highway to Rome, passing the prostitutes, the drug addicts, and the occasional black guys on bicycles moving slowly up and down the side of the road as cars sped ruthlessly by. Turning off the highway onto a dirt road, we came by a group of decrepit caravans; a Romany woman stood in the doorway watching a baby playing on a blanket on the ground, chickens and goats lying under the wagons, resting in the shade of the midday sun. As we approached a cluster of houses, Sammy pointed to one of them. The person next door was flying a huge Italian flag from the fenced gate, and as we advanced, an Alsatian was going mad with rage in the courtyard. On the other side of the houses was a field with a herd of buffalo—the Italians use the milk to make mozzarella cheese. We entered the house through a screen door and stepped into a darkened living room where a big, middle-aged man sat at a table, while twenty to twenty-five young men from the Ghanaian village sat on the floor or stood along the walls listening, as in a classroom. We sat down, and Sammy explained that they were discussing how one could acquire a moped without creating problems for oneself. Some guys had bought a moped on the street without checking if the papers were in order and, when pulled over later by the police in a routine stop, had been detained and fingerprinted.

At the end of the meeting the big man asked Sammy to introduce me and state my business. As Sammy conscientiously did so, I looked around realized that I already knew some of these young men. At the same time, I struggled to come to terms with the unexpected fact that I was seeing them again *here*, in this godforsaken suburb of Naples. After the meeting concluded with a prayer led by Sammy, we approached a couple of the guys and began arranging interviews straightaway. We started with Jonathan, whom I remembered from the village because, one afternoon, we had played football together in a merciless post-fishing match, barefoot on the beach. As the meeting was dissolving, we sat down and Jonathan talked into the tape recorder about his decision to leave the village, about the journey to Libya and across the Mediterranean, and about his situation in Naples. Sammy joined in from time to time, and slowly it became clear that the young men from the village had not been passengers on the boats from Libya but had captained the vessels the Libyan human smugglers used to traffic would-be immigrants to Europe. Indeed, Sammy explained, most of the guys at the meeting had arrived this way. For their services, the young men from the village are given a "free journey"—if they make it. Many had drowned trying. Ironically, the qualifications acquired in West African small-scale fishing, qualifications now almost obsolete due to the rapidly declining fish stocks, had come back into demand on the Mediterranean coasts of North Africa—not to catch fish, but to smuggle people across to Europe. Given that the decline in West African fishing may be a result of, among other things, outside pressure on marine resources by subsidized fishing vessels from the European Union and other industrialized, especially Asian, countries, it appeared that Europe was at the same time both pushing and pulling the West African immigrants.

After checking into the Scalzone Hotel on the Via Domitiana in the evening, Sammy and I made a list of the people at the meeting and began planning our fieldwork. The hotel personnel did nothing to disguise their contempt for what they believed to be some kind of sexual arrangement. "Around here," Sammy said, "why else would a white man take a black person to his room?" I thus included fieldwork in Naples in the research to illuminate this new development as an example of a local strategy the fishermen adopted to deal with changes in their lives and livelihoods; at the same time I sought to fill an ethnographic void with regard to the challenges the young West African men face on arriving in Europe, thereby adding to a much needed "exploration of the life-world" of the new immigrants of Southern Europe (King 2001: 10; see also Anthis & Lazaridis 1999: 6).

After completing the Naples fieldwork, I returned to the village in Ghana not only to assess the current situation in the local fishing industry, as compared to four years before, and the continuing challenges to everyday life caused by the decline in fishing, but also to gather information on how having a member in Europe might alter life conditions for a family. That is, I probed into what kind of social and existential potentials high-risk immigration represented, and of course I talked with relatives of fishermen lost at sea while going to Europe, those who tried to make it but disappeared somewhere and have never been accounted for.

Reflecting the order in which the stages of fieldwork were conducted, the book moves through three overarching empirical themes in a reverse chronology of events, beginning with life in Naples, followed by the journey through the Sahara Desert and across the Mediterranean to Italy, and proceeding finally to the current state of affairs in the migrants' place of departure, the fishing village of Senya Beraku in Ghana's Central Region.

Part 1 opens by introducing the most important field sites in Naples and explains the methodological, thematic, and theoretical aspects of the work. Chapter 2 introduces certain important themes discussed in detail later, including reciprocity, day laboring, and illegal life in Italy. The chapter then describes illegal immigration to Italy and the organization of the Italian labor market for the purpose of discussing the dynamics between, on the one hand, the growing political demands for immigration control and, on the other, the needs of the vast Italian underground economy, continuously attracting unskilled labor to Italy. This is followed by a focus on the three most important migrant work situations and a discussion of immigration from an Italian point of view; that is, the reception of the West African migrants (and the racist forms it sometimes takes) is analyzed as background to a brief overview of certain features of Italian society, culture, and politics. Chapter 3 returns to the life-world of the Guan immigrants to explore some of the typical forms of nullification they encounter on an everyday basis. The chapter then considers the possible reasons for substituting African village life with the difficulties of illegal migrant life in Europe. Next, the concept of existential reciprocity is presented, which, I suggest, is crucial to addressing the disconnectedness entailed in the simultaneous acceleration of inclusion and exclusion in the political economy of the so-called global world. Part 1 concludes by returning to the many losses and the few gains that characterize migrant life in Naples, and the strategies migrants use to establish viable ways of life in sometimes-hostile environments.

Part 2 begins with a background discussion of high-risk immigration from Libya to Italy and the political processes framing it. Chapter 4 then describes the special position of Guan canoe fishermen in Libyan transit migration into Italy and discusses the moral aspects of migrant deaths in the borderlands of European Union (EU) nation-states. Chapter 5 deals with the lesser-known, though equally deadly, part of the migrant journey to Europe—the dangerous route across the Sahara Desert.

Part 3 opens with an introduction to the village of Senya Beraku, followed by some methodological considerations, including the challenge of interviewing families of lost captains. Chapter 6 then assesses the impact of the controversial EU fishing agreements with West African coastal countries and explores, through the case of Senya Beraku, the state of Ghanaian fishing and locally implemented strategies to deal with the decline. Then, I consider how the decline in fishing is affecting people of different strata of village society. The chapter discusses the general economy of Ghana and the lack of opportunities that await fishermen put out of business by the depletion of marine resources, prompting many to turn to high-risk emigration in order to regain a hold on the future. Having examined the organization of illegal immigration in part 2, the book now turns to the impact of migrant deaths on the village of Senya Beraku. Chapter 7 explores the difficulties of obtaining information about a person lost in the desert or on the Mediterranean, focusing especially on spiritual assistance. I then consider the socioeconomic impact of migrant deaths from the point of view of the young widows and explore the existential themes of losing a beloved family member. This chapter also returns to the question of existential reciprocity. The conclusion considers the advances made by migrants in Italy, returning to my main informant, Samuel, and the progress his family is making. The book ends with an epilogue that depicts the current situation of Samuel, having made it out of Naples.

Acknowledgments

This book would not have been possible without the help of a number of individuals and institutions. First, I would like to thank friends and informants in Senya Beraku, Ghana, for sharing their lives and experiences with me. In particular, I am grateful to Chief Kwamena Mortey VI, Papa Kweku Tawaih, and my field assistant, Ebenezer. Also in Senya Beraku I would like to thank John, Godfather, Mercy, Mary, Sebastian, Jane, and all the boys at Fort Good Hope. In Naples, Italy, I would like to thank all the Guan friends and informants in Castelvolturno. I am especially indebted to Sammy, without whom this book would not have been possible. I would also like to thank the following people in Naples: Benjamin, Hope, Jonathan, Junior Teacher, Philip, and Signora Giuliana and Deli. I am also grateful to Bruno Riccio and Salvatore Coluccello for advising me on literature. This book has also benefited greatly from discussions with friends and colleagues at the Department of Anthropology, University of Copenhagen. In this respect, special thanks go to Mark Vacher, who throughout the process of writing has helped me to sharpen and clarify my arguments. I am also grateful to Inger Sjørslev for sharing an interest in exchange theory. I also wish to thank the following friends and colleagues: Mikkel Jes Hansen, Peter Hansen, Charlotte Jacobsen, Kåre Jansbøl, Dorthe B. Kristensen, Karsten Pærregaard, Jonathan Schwartz, Vibeke Steffen, Henrik Vigh, Michael Whyte, and Brian M. Wood. I am also grateful to everybody at "Undergangen"; they make it fun to come to work. I also wish to thank the following people for providing inspiration from their respective fields: Dorte Andersen, Jens Fleischer, Thomas Gammeltoft-Hansen, Nicoletta Isar, Lars Bo Kaspersen, and Chr. Gorm Tortzen. My greatest debt of gratitude is to professor Michael Jackson, whose friendship, insight, and advice have been sources of inspiration and encouragement throughout the process of writing this book. Finally, I wish to acknowledge the Nordic Africa Institute, Torben and Alice Frimodts Fond, Frimodt-Heineke Fonden, and Christian og Ottilia Brorsons Rejselegat For Yngre Videnskabsmænd and Kvinder, which generously funded fieldwork in Italy and Ghana.

PART ONE Losses and Gains in Naples

ONE *Clandestino*

The municipality of Castelvolturno, north of Naples, is a rather bleak and rundown cluster of high-rises, petrol stations, a couple of gated communities set back from the road, small shops, communication centers (where one can use a phone, make photocopies, and browse the Internet), and African supermarkets stretched out along the expressway to Rome. Off the expressway, along the waterfront, lies a string of modest holiday resorts. Standing in stark contrast to the expensive and famous resorts to the south of Naples, toward Sorrento and the Amalfi coast, these are deserted for most of the year except for two busy months in the summer when Neapolitans come to escape the unbearable heat of the city. Unlike the ever busy road to Rome, the back streets of the summerhouse areas and the commercial beaches are usually empty except for packs of wild dogs and occasional West African walkers or cyclists. Sometimes vendors drive slowly down the byroads in small three-wheeled vans with a loud-speaker on the roof advertising chickens, momentarily disturbing the strange silence of the neighborhood. But now some Italians are renting these summerhouses out to immigrants, and some of the formerly closed shops in the area are reopening as Internet cafés or African evangelical churches, and on Sundays the beach strip is bustling with music and chanting and Africans strolling up and down the street in their best Sunday clothes.

This development, however, has not been without problems. West African immigrants are regularly subject to flagrant racism in stores, at their workplaces, in buses, and elsewhere, and racially motivated attacks are not uncommon. Many report having things thrown at them, such as hot coffee, stones, and eggs as they walk along the expressway in Castelvolturno, and some have been attacked by passersby for no obvious reason other than their being black. John, for instance, was waiting at the bus stop when a man passing by on a motorcycle kicked him so violently in the knee that he was barely able to make his way back to his room. And Jonathan was on the bus when a couple of Italian kids sitting behind him set his shirt on fire. Such stories are plentiful in Castelvolturno. In the summer of 2008, the violent state of affairs reached a new high when the Naples Mafia, the Camorra, shot dead six young men from West Africa (three from Ghana, two from Liberia, and one from Togo) in a tailor's shop, allegedly in a turf war over drugs. The incident sparked race riots in the streets of Castelvolturno; cars were overturned and windows smashed as the West African migrants took to the streets, calling for justice and an end to racism. The Berlusconi government responded by deploying four hundred extra policemen and five hundred troops into the streets.

Given these recent experiences, the West African community regards white people—many of whom come to look for prostitutes or drugs or even to rob the immigrants of mobile phones and cash—with an under-standably high level of suspicion. Moreover, the atmosphere of fear and uncertainty is reinforced by the scarcity of jobs and a high rate of unem-ployment among the immigrants. Everybody is trying to find work, and many have little or no money for food and electricity. In December 2005, when I left Naples, most of my informants were suffering badly from the cold because their Neapolitan landlords turn off the power supply during the coldest time of the year, based apparently on the assumption that their West African tenants would build up enormous electricity bills they would never be able to settle. As a consequence, when I visited informants after work in the winter, many were already lying in bed with their jackets and hats on.

Of course, it's not all misery. Some immigrants, as shown in detail later, are nevertheless making a life for themselves, getting ahead little by little. They have secured semiregular work with semiregular wages, and they are putting up houses in Ghana, taking care of their families. One evening as we rode the bus home after interviewing one of these fortunate West African migrants, a man who worked the night shift in a plastics factory, Sammy said, "That's the dream all we guys have."

Farther up the expressway, near a cheese factory, lies Pescopagano, or just Pesco, another modest holiday resort. Between Pesco and the expressway lies a farming area where, according to Sammy, mostly Albanians work the fields. Walking home in the evening along the dirt road from the expressway to Sammy's house, one could sometimes glimpse their faces in the flames of a bonfire. Usually, though, we avoided that dirt road in the evening because of the risk of getting robbed and even knocked about. Especially on Fridays and Saturdays, paydays for the day laborers, criminals would park their cars in the dark at the roadside and wait for the immigrants to come home from work. At the end of this long, dangerous road, with farmland on both sides and no place to hide, stood what looked like a tollgate, separating the farmland from the summerhouse area: reaching that tollgate meant safety. Many of my informants reported being chased toward the tollgate, some making it, others having to give up their wages and mobile phones. Samuel, for instance, had his new mobile phone stolen only weeks after I left. This stretch of dirt road in general was something of a challenge for my project. Whenever we had informants over for interviews in the evenings, it was better for them to leave early. Walking them back to the bus stop, we would, at Sammy's suggestion, carry empty bottles to protect ourselves in case of robbery, our informants hiding their money in their socks, like the seasoned travelers they were.

Clearly, the neighborhood was a bit rough, and when my family arrived a month after I did, we decided to move to an apartment in the center of Naples. Although that decision meant a lot of traveling time, at best one hour in each direction, it also provided a valuable insight into one of the key problems of illegal immigrant life: the difficult and tedious nature of moving anywhere in Naples when relying on public transportation, especially when going to the city to look for work. This theme, explored in chapter 3, was an important reminder of how time and power are closely connected (Bourdieu 2000: 223), and how wasting time—or rather, having one's time wasted—is a central experience for the West African immigrants in Naples.

There is a telling story about the expressway to Rome that every West African immigrant in Castelvolturno appeared to know. In biblical times, when Paul the Apostle came from the Holy Land to preach the gospel, the local Neapolitans captured him and he was beaten and dragged on horseback along the Via Domitiana to Rome, where he was finally executed. In the course of this ordeal St. Paul cursed the road to Rome, declaring that since his blood had been shed on the Via Domitiana, the road should continue to demand blood forever more. And so it does, in a literal as well as symbolic sense. Literally speaking, the road was often the scene of traffic accidents. People on their way to Rome, driving too fast or unable to see because of a lack of adequate streetlights, would hit a pedestrian crossing the street or, more often, a stray dog. (During my stay in Naples work began on installing speed bumps in the most populated areas of Castelvolturno.) Many times, waiting for the bus in the darkness before sunrise, we would see the corpse of a freshly killed dog being torn apart by speeding cars until it ended up in the ditch, and for weeks afterward the foul smell of its swollen carcass would remind everybody of the danger of getting knocked down on the accursed road. "The street is crying for blood tonight," Sammy would sometimes say when we crossed the expressway in the night and cars came uncomfortably close. "You know, in Senya," he once added jokingly, "it would be pacified. They would get a fowl and slaughter it and give the blood to the road." He was referring to the traditional Guan way of dealing with such a powerful interlocutor: presenting it with a symbolic gift in order to draw the object of fear and desire into a relationship of exchange, thus experientially creating obligations and expectations as opposed to a regime of arbitrariness (Lucht 2003: 43–64). In a broader existential understanding, the expressway continually demanded blood in the way that it every so often appeared to constitute a veritable negative zone. Accidents, violence, degradation, and prostitution at times seemed to conform to a one-way street of taking—yet, simultaneously, the dreaded road connected the West African community of Castelvolturno with the city of Naples and the possibilities of growth.

There were several spots from which life on the Via Domitiana could be observed. One of them was the outside terrace of the Scalzone Hotel, only a few meters from the road itself; in fact, the tables were about half a meter below the surface of the street, making the presence of the road particularly strong when cars, their drivers ignoring the newly constructed speed bump, hit it with a loud thump and set sparks flying out from under the car body. Inside, a hotel coffee bar was frequented mostly by drivers stopping at the petrol station that was an extension of the hotel. But West Africans living across the muddy river that ran by the northern walls of the Scalzone also frequented the coffee bar, mostly to buy phone cards and cigarettes. Two dogs, seemingly oblivious of the busy road five meters away, guarded this petrol station as if it was a farmhouse. The animals had a peculiar temperament: whenever a normal-looking automobile pulled in, they would wag their tails and lay down their ears as if their master was coming home, whereas if a strange-looking vehicle such as a dune buggy or tractor pulled in, they would rush toward it and bark fiercely before crawling back into the shade of a parked car. Sometimes horses were exercised in the shallow river that separated the hotel from the migrant high-rises. Their trainers ran them up against the stream, foam coming out of the sides of the their mouths. "It's to make their legs strong for the races," Maurizio, the waiter at the nearby pizza restaurant, explained one evening, as Samuel and I were dining there. As an observation point, the hotel terrace and the coffee bar worked out well; here I would usually meet with Sammy in the evening before going to the West African high-rises.

Another point of participant observation along the expressway was a communication center where a key informant, Junior Teacher, worked as a desk clerk. I had met him during my first fieldwork in Ghana, where he was teaching mathematics and English in the public school. Now he worked fourteen hours every day of the week at the communication center. Usually he would sit outside on the porch in the shade as people entered and left the center and watch the traffic go by.

I moved into Sammy's room in a summerhouse in Pescopagano in September 2005. Sammy gave me his bed and insisted on sleeping on the floor himself. The house was a small white bungalow with a front porch facing the road. The porch offered a view to the north and of the adjacent residential area, which was separated from our house by a stretch of wasteland overgrown with long grass and giant cacti. In the middle of this no-man's-land stood the ruins of a house where stray dogs usually roamed about. The locals used to burn rubbish in this apparently abandoned plot of land.

Across the whole farmland area, the vague roar of the expressway could always be heard. In the distance stood the hills of Mondragone, which appeared to change color every day. One day the hills would be light blue; another day, fog-bound and white; on a clear day they would shine brightly like an oil painting and allow one to study every detail. At such times, on the very tops of the hills it was possible to discern the ruins of a castle or a monastery. The stretch of road that connected the summerhouse area to the expressway was low and swampy, which accounted for the swarms of mosquitoes that would chase us off the porch when darkness fell. The municipality would dispatch small vans with insecticide pumps to take care of the problem, but the spraying seemed to have only minimal effect. The swampy area, and especially the small lakes strewn between the coastline and the expressway, was an attraction to local hunters, who would come by early in the morning, their shots ringing out and echoing against the mountains.

Sammy lived under the roof of a Nigerian landlady, Madam Hope, who was taking care of the house for the Neapolitan owner, a man we saw only when it was time to collect the rent. Apparently he had given possession of the house to Madam Hope for a certain undisclosed price, and she then recruited the West African tenants. Hope had been caught on a railway station in Milan with a quantity of cocaine and was serving four years' house arrest for drug trafficking, which meant she was always home and had to run whatever business she was conducting from the house, except for the two hours a week she was allowed to go and do the shopping. An energetic and outspoken woman, Hope became a valued source of information during my fieldwork. In particular, her criticisms of Italian society seemed to speak to many concerns shared by the West African immigrants, though some of them were a little one-sided and fell under the category of "ethno-Occidentalism" (Carrier 1992: 198; for a discussion of Senegalese street-sellers' essentialized views of Italian society, see Riccio 2002). I clearly remember Madam Hope giving her views of some of the important themes of immigrant life on the very night of my arrival, among many other times during my stay.

Madam Hope: Why do these Italians say we're dirty? We wash two times a day. That's even more than they do. We can't wash off this color. The Father in Heaven gave us this color and he has a plan with that—a plan we can't know anything about. They say we're hungry—but that's not the truth. We have food in Africa, but we don't have any money. Our leaders are corrupt, Hansen. They take everything for themselves; what should we do? Even people who graduate from university drive taxis. Unless you have money or know somebody, you can't do anything. Home is home. Do you think we would be here if we had money? No, home is home. There you don't worry about documents. And if somebody came to my home, to meet my parents, they would be entertained like a prince. Over here we're treated like animals.

Madam Hope had three areas of business. First, there were the tenants. Second, she ran something like a bar, selling beer and sweet, fruity wine from the refrigerator in the kitchen. In the evening, when people came home from work, both her tenants—the ones upstairs, like Sammy and me, and the people crammed together in the small rooms in the basement—as well as other West Africans living in the nearby summer-houses, would come by the house to sit on the porch and have a beer or just hang out. This was an ideal opportunity for meeting people and arranging interviews. For a small consideration, Madam Hope also cooked for Sammy and me. In her third business, Madam Hope basically was a part-time prostitute; when her two regular Italian customers came by, her boyfriend, Martin, a young man from Senya Beraku, would give up the bedroom. One of the customers was a burly but mild-mannered baker named Pasquale who came by very early in the morning, presumably when he got off work, and usually stayed the whole day. He always brought fresh bread, which I greatly appreciated. Sammy, like most other Ghanaians, did not fancy the famous Italian bread tradition at all: "It's too chewy, it'll scratch your mouth and before you know it, your gums are bleeding." Hope and Pasquale argued like a married couple, she usually confronting him with the mistreatment that Africans were receiving in Naples, and the baker sighing, shrugging his shoulders, and going out on the balcony to smoke a cigarette with a dreamy expression on his face. (Madam Hope allowed no smoking in the house.) Pasquale was always available for conversation, though his heavy Neapolitan dialect was difficult to comprehend, and sometimes Sammy or Hope would have to translate. One day, when he woke up from his morning nap on the couch, he came to the porch and told me he had found a job for me down at the harbor. He leaned his elbows on the railings. Since I was so interested in all things concerning the sea—apparently the conclusion he had drawn from the explanation of my project I had given him in poor Italian—he had inquired with some friends who were always looking for a pair of hands in the fishing business. But it was "a job with documents," he added cunningly, watching my reaction out of the corner of his eye.

Although Pasquale was generally unmoved by Hope's continuous rants against the Neapolitans, one theme she would embark upon almost always made him lose his temper. Whenever they watched biblical movies—the dramatic reenactment of the crucifixion of Jesus Christ, for instance—as they frequently did, Hope would take the opportunity to make one of her recurring accusations against the Neapolitans, if not all

Italians: they had abandoned God. Considering that Christ's crucifixion (right there on the television screen) had saved humankind from its sins, such a betrayal appeared thoroughly ungrateful, and Pasquale wouldn't hear of it. He would get up from the sofa, find his cigarettes, and go to the porch. That was rubbish, he said, shaking his head in disgust. "How come, then," Hope would quickly respond, "the Italian churches are all empty on Sundays?"

Hope's other customer was a very old and practically blind man. His son, who led him by the arm all the way into the bedroom, drove him to the house. A long time before, the man had employed Madam Hope as a housemaid, and they had kept in touch since. Sometimes I would talk to his son, who waited in the kitchen with a beer while the father was in the bedroom with Hope, but they never stayed long.

My fieldwork in Naples focused on a group of twenty to twenty-five young men from Senya Beraku. Later, the group was expanded to include young Ghanaian men from the town of Winneba with whom the fishermen of Senya Beraku had close contact and often shared rooms or apartments. Also a Guan fishing community, Winneba is close to and considerably larger than Senya Beraku. The two towns are the only Guan settlements on the coast of Ghana's Central Region, a stretch of coast today inhabited mostly by the Fante people, who belong to the Akan tribe (Buah 1998: 14; Lucht 2003: 10). The testimonies of the Winneba informants were even more relevant because most of them had also arrived as captains on the human smugglers' boats from Libya.

To be precise, when I say "fishermen," I mean only that every Senya person I talked to, except for two, has fishing experience and has at some point worked in the fishing business, regardless of his educational background. For instance, some of those I interviewed had completed high school—including my main informant Sammy—but before, during, and after their studies had helped friends or family in handling a canoe. After completion of high school it is not uncommon for a young man to help out a fishing crew as a clerk, settling the petrol and other bills and handling the business's paperwork. Sammy's step-father, a big-time fisherman in Senya Beraku, disciplined Sammy by allowing him fish in his

castelvolturno
- Senya Beraku
- Ghana
- Guan

soup only if he worked in the canoes when he was not attending school. Although Sammy hated his step-father at the time for that display of authority, and he was teased at school because of it, today he thinks differently about the situation: "It seems the old man unknowingly gave me a chance to go to Europe." But in general, growing up in a Guan coastal community means participating, on some level, in the village's main industry. Traveling on the sea, or commanding a boat across the Mediterranean Sea, for that matter, is therefore considered a risky but not outrageous idea.

The Guan informants in Naples were all men between twenty and forty years of age (except for Senior Teacher, the eldest Senya person in Naples, who headed the Senya Youth Club, established by the young men of the village to deal with the challenges and uncertainties of illegal immigrant life). During my stay in Italy, I met only one young woman from Senya Beraku. That was during a field trip to Udine in the north, where I attended the funeral of Sammy's best friend, Yakubu, who died suddenly after what appeared to be a brain hemorrhage (the diagnosis was never clear to his friends who visited him in the hospital). This woman had traveled to Italy by plane and had overstayed her tourist visa, a costly method of immigration and, as such, not easily pursued by the Senya Beraku would-be migrants. Incidentally, when I returned to the village and asked young women why they did not emigrate, they said the answer was obvious considering the well-known hardships in the desert; it was generally acknowledged that women are raped going through the desert.

Thus I gathered material in Italy solely through interviews of young men, whereas in Ghana, the data come from interviews with both men and women, young and old. There are of course a large number of young West African women in Naples, including Castelvolturno, where I stayed for some time. The ones I managed to talk to, coming and going between Sammy's house and the expressway, came from Nigeria. Sadly, they were all employed in prostitution, some of them pressured into it. Standing along the expressway all day long, every day of the week, they were not easy for me to approach, since I was a white male whom they naturally took for a potential customer and had every reason to be suspicious about—abuse and violence were not unusual. During my stay in Naples I came briefly to know three young Nigerian girls who worked on the dirt road leading to Sammy's house. Sammy used to take pity on them and bring them water on hot days. When they met my wife and daughter, however, the tension between us appeared to subside a little, as if they appreciated this glimpse of ordinary family life, and henceforth we would talk whenever we would meet, in the bus or on the street, though it was mostly small talk. If their situation is anything like that of the Nigerian prostitutes in Palermo, who live tragic and degraded lives on the bottom of the commercial sex industry, and who are trafficked and endure long-term exploitation "by means of intimidation, violence, and debt peonage" (Cole & Booth 2006: 107), then collecting the testimonies of West African women in Naples appears to be a matter of great urgency—though that task is beyond the scope of this book.

How to approach the Guan immigrants was a major consideration from the beginning. Having actively taken part in the smuggling as captains on the boats from Libya, the young men risked expulsion if they were exposed, and they might choose not to talk, even though promised anonymity. Surprisingly, most decided to give interviews. Some needed a little time to think about it, and three of the young men refused to talk to me at all, but in general I was welcomed by almost every potential informant we approached. And most often they took time, carefully and in detail, to share their experiences of the journey and their lives in Naples, expressing hope that if the truth was brought to the fore, something would be done. Eventually, Samuel suggested that we present informants with phone cards in gratitude for their participation in the fieldwork. That solution worked out wonderfully; the phone card had value because it could be used to call home for up to forty-five minutes. And the price was suitable; the small shops in the marketplace would even give discounts for purchases of larger quantities (as low as 4 Euros apiece). "I'll be coming around to get my hands on a phone card one of these days," potential informants would joke with us, after news of gifts got around (informants I had already talked to would come around "to collect their share").

The fact that I had lived in their village in Ghana and knew a few phrases of their language also helped. The main reason for my success in collecting empirical data, however, was the fact that Samuel not only agreed to work for me again but also vouched for me and never gave up calling, locating, and persuading possible informants. This book is thus in many ways the product of my close relationship with Samuel. In fact, as I look back at the time we have spent together, the places our acquaintance and inquiries have taken us, the ethnographic fieldwork appears indistinguishable from the fabric of our own personal lives. Indeed, any account of the way ethnographic inquiry is conducted should simultaneously be an account of the social involvement of the researcher in the field. As William F. Whyte put it more forthrightly, "The researcher, like his informants, is a social animal" and any "real explanation . . . of how the research was done necessarily involves a rather personal account of how the researcher lived during the period of study" (1964: 3–4). Becoming involved, as opposed to maintaining a "convenient scholarly fiction" of detachment between informant and researcher (Ellen & Hicks 1984: 209), is not unwanted: in fact, anthropologists seek these "long-term unquantifiable relationships" with the people they study. Indeed, the anthropologist wants to be *involved* and "violate the canons of positivist research" in order to collect "accurate data" (Bourgois 1995: 11). Ideas, Whyte argued, "grow up in part out of immersion in the data and the whole process of living" and in part as a "logical product growing out of the careful weighing of evidence" (1964: 3–4).

The fieldwork, conducted in two sites (Castelvolturno and Senya Beraku), exemplifies the methodological framework of "multi-sited" fieldwork (Marcus 1995), with its encouragement to "follow the people." But, as mentioned in the preface, some caution is required with regard to the Marxist notion of an integrated "world system," with its modern imagery of a globe interconnected through relationships of exploitation. Such an approach does not fully address the conditions of life in a modern West African village unless it simultaneously demonstrates sensitivity toward the local sense of exclusion from the "world system," or, as Marcus argues, unless it produces ethnographies "both in and out of the world system" (1995: 95). As discussed in the following chapters, whereas some people might oppose globalization on personal, political, or religious grounds, such opposition cannot be taken as the norm when just as many people struggle, even putting their lives at risk, to belong in some way or another to the so-called global world (see Cohen 2006: 6).

So any multi-sited ethnography of the "world system" that recognizes, if only half-heartedly, an intensified degree of global interconnection, or globalization, must also recognize the fact "that while the world may be full of complex mobility and interconnection, there are also quite a number of people and places whose experience is marginal to or excluded from these movements and links . . . and this, too, is the world of globalization" (Inda & Rosaldo 2003: 4). On a more practical level, however, fieldwork conducted among highly mobile youth in a fragmented urban setting like Naples is less a study of abstract global structures than an application of an "extended case method" or "situational analysis," with its focus on the particularity of human existence, social processes, variations, exceptions, and accidents or, more specifically, on "the actions of individuals as individuals, as personalities, and not just as occupants of particular statuses" (van Velsen 1967: 143). In this way the contours of possible global structures might become visible by exploring the lifeworlds of the West African informants, not the other way around. Indeed, as Marcus (1995) maintains, a strategy or design of multi-sited research acknowledges the macro level and the narratives of the globalized world, but does "not rely on them for the contextual architecture framing a set of subjects" (96).

Following the lead of existential anthropology, the empirical focus here is the "critical events" that highlight the question of being as "a dynamic relationship between circumstances over which we have little control . . . and our capacity to live those circumstances in a variety of ways" (Jackson 2005: xi; see also Das 1995: 6). Or, in Arthur Kleinman's words, the focus here is "the always unequal struggle between where the world is taking us and where we aspire to go" (Kleinman 2006: 17). Thus, in examining the plight of the West African immigrants in their effort to secure a desired life, I explore the unceasing struggle of human existence, "struggle for being against nothingness—for whatever will make life worth living, rather than hopeless, profitless, and pointless" (Jackson 2005: x). Kleinman frames this effort as the human need to live a "moral life"—not moral in an ethical sense, but a life in which "what really matters," such as "status, jobs, money, family ties, sexual intimacy, sense of order and self-control, health, life itself, and also religious commitments, political arrangements, and all sorts of culturally and personally specific agendas" are fiercely struggled for. And the struggle is always on unequal terms, entailing a "powerful, enervating anxiety created by the limits of our control over our small worlds and even our inner selves" (Kleinman 2006: 5–6). Consequently, the theoretical direction outlined here echoes one of the main themes of existential phenomenology: to explore being not as a contemplative effort, but as a question of action and constraints on action. As Sartre put it, "To be is to act, and to cease to act is to cease to be" (Sartre 2005: 498; see also Merleau-Ponty 1976: 137).

Acknowledging pragmatism, however, existential anthropology emphasizes the inadequacy of human action and control and, consequently, not only the variety of strategies one pursues to act on the world but also the concessions one has to make in the process (Jackson 2007: 127; Kleinman 2006: 9; see also Biehl et al. 2007: 15). Thus, I probe the life-worlds of the new immigrants in Naples, that is, the lived province of reality that they take for granted, that they engage as human organisms, and in which, existentially, they come "up against obstacles that can be surmounted as well as barriers that are insurmountable" (Schutz & Luckmann 1973: 3). This may not succeed as the ideal migrant study, however, if that is understood as research on three fronts, granting equal attention to the immigrant life-world, the receiving community, and the institutions of the receiving context (Riccio 2002: 177). Nevertheless, important economic and political characteristics of the Italian receiving context will also be discussed in connection with the informants' migration and the social and existential themes they appear to articulate. Employing "critical phenomenology" (Desjarlais 1997: 24), the book explores subjective experiences as informed by socioeconomic and political forces that entail a variety of lives, experiences, and strategies.

In the 1990s, the anthropological study of migration came to focus on transnationalism, and the migrant was transformed into the transmigrant (Glick-Schiller et al. 1995). Anthropologists sought to dissolve obsolete concepts and capture the characteristics of mobility in a globalized world where people move across national borders and create new hybrid identities, making use of new technologies of communication and transportation such as jet planes, mobile phones, and the Internet. These transmigrants are thus agents of change in both their new countries and their countries of origin. However, for at least two reasons, the concepts of transnationalism and the transmigrant appear less relevant in the context of the undocumented Guan immigrants in Naples. First, concerning agency and mobility, the Guan immigrants often appear less as agents of change and travel, working both sides of the border, than as stuck in a negative zone, recognized neither legally nor socially. They seem more concerned with gaining a foothold in Naples and securing "little immediate futures" (Fawzi Mellah, cited in Albahari 2006: 13) centered on the most basic necessities than with becoming "incorporated in the economy and political institutions, localities and patterns of life of the country in which they reside," or with striving to "maintain connections, build institutions, conduct transactions and influence local and national events in the countries from which they emigrated" (Glick-Schiller et al. 1995: 48). Moreover, the supposed counterhegemonic influence of transnationalism and the consequent demise of the nation-state (Kearney 1996: 8, 183) are difficult to identify in the context of illegal immigration to Italy. That is to say, national borders, rather than being contested and transgressed, are being reified in the form of lethal traps from which migrants barely escape alive (cf. Friedman 1999a), as I discuss in part 2. Those who do survive exist in the shadow of the nation-state without legal or political protection but still subject to state power in its most devastating form.

Although one might argue that migrant life in Naples is just a painful prelude to better times ahead, this painful prelude becomes for many the permanent state of affairs. That is to say, for most young Guan migrants in Naples, the day-to-day struggle for work, food, and housing eventually consumes so much of their time that they are forced to postpone their original plans. In this respect, the Guan migrants in Naples are less settled and economically stable than their predominantly Ashanti countrymen in Emilia Romagna (Riccio 2008: 226), not to mention the Senegalese who arrived much earlier and have formed strong, formal social networks and institutions across Italy. (See, for instance, Riccio's work on Senegalese links to their homeland and Sufi brotherhoods, how these links shape everyday lives, and the morphology of their social institutions [Riccio 2001, 2002; Grillo and Riccio 2004].) Perhaps anthropologists have been generally too optimistic regarding the power of human agency in the so-called global world. Arjun Appadurai, for instance, partly in response to criticism of his much quoted book, *Modernity at Large: Cultural Dimensions of Globalization* (1996), now admits to having painted "too rosy a picture of globalization of the early 1990s and as [having been] insufficiently attentive to the darker sides of globalization, such as violence, exclusion, and growing inequality" (Appadurai 2006: ix). In *Fear of Small Numbers* (2006) he proposes "to seek ways to make globalization work for those who need it the most and enjoy it the least, the poor, the dispossessed, the weak, and the marginal populations of the world" (x).

This brings me to the second, empirical and methodological reason for not embracing the concept of the transmigrant. I have used the concept of illegal immigrant throughout the book (rather than transmigrant, or "undocumented" or "irregular immigrant," as suggested by the UN General Assembly to avoid unnecessary stigmatization), because *illegal immigrant* is an empirical category used by the Italian authorities, in public discourse, and by the migrants themselves. It's a legal and discursive category of exclusion, which the migrants are confronted with everywhere they turn (and often regardless of de jure status) and which makes an important difference in an Italian context and in the lives of the immigrants (Hansen 2007: 1). The Italian word for illegal immigrant, *clandestino* (clandestine person or someone displaying somewhat criminal or occult behavior), stands in opposition to *immigrato* (immigrant), which has positive connotations. Especially in the south, most people have themselves, or have relatives who have, traveled abroad to live and work in another country. Most of these are positive stories, some even romantic, about taking on the world and making something good out of a difficult situation. In contrast, the illegal immigrant earns none of this praise but is regarded, rather, as a pariah. (For a discussion of the use of *clandestino* and *immigrato* and the surrounding discursive praxis, see Hansen 2007: 70–73.) The point is that migrant life in Naples and the discursive terms framing it may be less about flow and hybridity than about states and categorizations. In this sense, the empirical and methodological considerations combine with the analytical aim of showing the double nature of globalization in creating both connectedness and disconnectedness at the same time. With regard to African experiences of the globalized world, James Ferguson has recently called "for a new framing of discussions of the global: centered less on transnational flows and images of unfettered connection than on the social relations that *selectively* constitute global society; the statuses and ranks that it comprises; and the relations, rights, and obligations that characterize it" (Ferguson 2006: 23; my italics).

PRAYING FOR RAIN

Senior Teacher was the head of the Senya Youth Club, established by the young men of the village to deal with the challenges of illegal immigrant life. At an early stage in the fieldwork, Samuel and I went to meet him, partly to show respect to the eldest person in the Senya community, partly as a research strategy ("to keep people from getting strange ideas about the work," as Sammy expressed it), and partly because of Teacher's experience in having stayed the longest time in Naples. A brief description of his life's circumstances reveals the critical themes of migrant life on the margins of Italian society, themes I pursue in this and the following two chapters: illegal entry into Italy, the underground labor market and the migrant workforce, and everyday migrant life in Italy.

Senior Teacher worked as a night watchman at a used-car dealership in the center of Naples; he lived in a small shed at the back of the parking lot. When Sammy and I came to the dealership one Saturday morning,

he was sitting in a big wire-fenced shelter in the middle of the lot surrounded by cars, eating lunch with a cousin who was visiting from
Austria. Sammy rang the buzzer on the gate at the road, and Teacher
stood up from the worn-out sofa inside the shelter and walked slowly
to the gate, a bundle of keys in one hand. As he came closer, he recognized Samuel and quickened his pace. He invited us to sit down with
him, casually covering with a T-shirt a half bottle of gin in an armchair.
His cousin didn't say much. He had already finished eating and was
sprawled on the sofa reading a copy of *Watchtower* with an apathetic
frown. Teacher had once taught mathematics and English in Ghana but
had given it up "in search of greener pastures." He traveled to Italy on
a tourist visa and decided to overstay. By now he had been with the
Neapolitan used-car dealership for fifteen years and was content with
the job. He was awaiting his Italian passport: when it arrived, he would
decide what to do—whether to stay in Naples or move on. "When you
get old," Teacher explained, "you always like to be with your family."

Teacher's job was to guard the cars at night. During the week, he got
off at 8:30 in the morning, then went to a nearby pizza place, where he
sat and watched the traffic in order "not to be bothered" by his bosses.
He reported back to the dealership at 1:00 and resumed watching the
cars during the day staff's afternoon break. As a senior Senya person in
Naples in terms of both age and experience, Senior Teacher had followed
the arrival of his fellow Senya immigrants closely.

Senior Teacher: When I came to Naples, there were only two Senya
people in all of Italy. Today, there's so many. That's good. It's an
adventure—you seek your fortune. In Naples, you can get an odd job
without documents, and a cheap place to live. And if you're hungry,
you can go to the Catholic shelter and get free food and clothes. You
can't prevent them from coming, mind you. It's a matter of risk and
reward, of loss and gain. It's not easy staying in Africa, trying to make
ends meet, trying to have three meals a day. Then, one day, one boy
decides to travel to Europe and another one follows him. And soon
enough, if you stay behind, people will say, "Are you crazy? Why
don't you go too?"

We discussed his job for a while, and Teacher mentioned again that he had to "dodge" the owners of the car lot so they could not pile extra work on him. A short buzz at the gate signaled that another young Senya immigrant was coming by to ask Teacher's advice; they excused themselves and withdrew to talk. Teacher returned shortly, and the young man took off. Teacher returned to the question of his work. The problem, he told us, was that a lot of cars were being stolen in Naples. "What they'll do," he explained, "is that they'll steal a car, then they'll send a boy around who knows where the car is parked, maybe carrying a picture of the car on his mobile phone, and if you want the car back, you'll have to pay him." Then the haggling could begin. What kind of demands were the car thieves making, and how much was the car worth to the dealer? The bargaining might go on for some time, offers put forward and rejected, until an agreement was reached and the car was finally handed back to the owner. Calling the police, Teacher said, is not the first option in Naples.

When I asked about migrant life in Naples and the many hardships the young Senya Beraku fishermen were going through, however, Teacher did not encourage such complaints. He agreed that Naples was a hard place, but that was only to be expected, he said.

Teacher: What is life like in Naples? Life here is normal. If you want trouble, you'll find trouble. Most of the Senya boys are law-abiding, you know. . . . They know how to comport themselves. But if you go around the city at midnight, you'll meet bad boys and they will give you trouble. So, it's up to you.

Tired from being on the watch all night, Teacher excused himself. He wanted to go take a nap. It was approaching noon, and the sun was scorching. Walking us to the gate, he pointed out some of the more expensive cars in the lot, a Mercedes and a BMW. The weather had been hot and dry for weeks, and the cars were covered in a fine layer of dust.

Teacher: The director only prays for one thing: rain. He wants the rain to come and wash the dust off the cars. You should see him when it rains. He's very, very happy.

After this visit, I returned to talk with Teacher on several occasions, and the research benefited greatly from his experience and straightforward approach to the challenges of migrant life. The opportunity of a job in the underground economy and a cheap place to live, as Teacher pointed out, is a main attraction that Italy—a relatively new migrant destination—offers to West African immigrants.

ILLEGAL ENTRY INTO ITALY

Although Italy, like the other Mediterranean countries of the European Union (EU) except for France, has a long tradition of emigration, immigration is a recent phenomenon. So-called undocumented immigrants from Eastern Europe and non-European countries, mainly North Africans, have entered Italy only since the late 1980s, with the number of foreign residents, regular and illegal, reaching more than 3 million in 2005, out of a total population of 57 million. Although this figure is relatively small compared to the foreign resident populations of Northern European countries, it is remarkable in that the influx of immigrants was quite sudden; it occurred at a time when Northern European countries were clamping down on the influx of immigrants (possibly as a side-effect of Italy's becoming a "back door" to Europe); and immigration into Italy consisted largely of non-European nationals. In fact, 85 percent of the foreigners residing in Italy in 2000 came from non-European countries, and most of these (according to one report, 75 percent) had come without documents (Calavita 2005: 3; Caritas/Migrantes 2006; Grillo 2002: 5; Reyneri 2001: 2; Venturi & Villosio 2006: 91). As a consequence, Italy has issued five amnesties (1986–1987, 1990, 1995–1996, 1998–1999, 2002—each of which was declared "the final regularisation" [Chaloff 2003: 3]) in order to regularize the status of immigrants, followed in each case by a tightening of the immigration laws. One of the latest legislative revisions is Law 189 of July 2002, also known as the Bossi-Fini Law. Although Law 189 regularized 650,000 migrants—the largest number ever given such amnesty in Italy—it also provided for combating illegal immigration by, among other measures, stepping up deportations.

Simultaneously, the new law made it more difficult to enter Italy legally by changing immigration quotas and employer contracts with immigrants. With regard to the latter, the six-month permit for entering Italy to look for work was abolished, and work permits were made dependent on having a job offer prior to entry, which in practice makes it very difficult, if not impossible, for unskilled migrants to enter. The latest amendments to the law, from July 2009, make undocumented migration punishable by a fine of 5,000 to 10,000 Euros, and those who house undocumented immigrants can face up to three years in prison. The most controversial part of the legislation, however, allows for unarmed citizen guards to patrol the streets (Ammendola et al. 2005: 11; BBC 2009a; Levinson 2005: 3; Venturi & Villosio 2006: 92).

The number of illegal immigrants in Italy varies, according to one estimate, between 200,000 and 500,000 at any one time (Venturi & Villosio 2006: 93). On the whole, more than 100,000 illegal immigrants enter Italy each year. Most cross the Italian-Slovenian border, following routes used by both independent travelers and human smugglers transporting would-be immigrants from Central and Southern Europe, the Middle East, the Indian Subcontinent, and elsewhere in Asia. In contrast, the sea routes from North Africa are used especially by African immigrants. Via this route, predominantly the one taken by the informants in this study, there were 22,939 landings in 2005. This number was almost twice that in 2004, reflecting a controversial tightening of immigration control measures at Ceuta and Melilla, the Spanish enclaves in North Africa (Ammendola et al. 2005: 14).

How do immigrants enter and remain illegally in Italy? There are at least four main ways of illegal enty: (1) crossing a land or sea border without documents, (2) entering the country with a short-term permit and subsequently overstaying, (3) entering with false documents, and (4) entering as an asylum seeker and staying when the application is denied (Reyneri 2001: 18–19). Immigrants who try to enter Italy without valid documents are either rejected, which is common at the land borders, or given an expulsion order (or *folgio di via*). If the immigrant does not comply with the expulsion order, he or she can be forcefully repatriated. Not only is this procedure "very expensive," with costs in some cases reaching "catastrophic figures" (Prefect Anna Maria D'Ascenzo, director of Italy's Department for Citizens' Freedom and Immigration, in a hearing before the Schengen Committee in October 2003, cited in Ammendola et al. 2005: 29), but it also depends, of course, on a positive identification of the immigrant as a national of a particular country and also on a bilateral agreement with that country—neither of which is always obtainable. The Guan informants in this study, for instance, intentionally destroyed their documents prior to the boat trip to Italy, and often claimed a nationality other than Ghanaian. Combining options 1 and 4 above, they entered Italy illegally by sea and subsequently applied for asylum on political or humanitarian grounds.

The regular Italian administrative procedure is then to transport the immigrant asylum seekers to temporary reception centers in Sicily or on the mainland of Italy, where they await the outcome of their applications (though the Berlusconi administration has carried out highly controversial and widely criticized deportations of African immigrants directly to Libya). When an application for asylum is denied, the immigrant is given an expulsion order, which means the person has to leave Italian territory within five days of being discharged from the reception center. In 2005, 65,617 immigrants received such an expulsion order but did not comply, choosing instead to stay and work illegally in Italy (Ammendola et al. 2005: 46). Upon leaving the reception centers, such noncompliant migrants travel to the large cities to look for work, predominantly in the underground economy, though as Senior Teacher explained, "in Naples, you can get an odd job without documents."

THE ITALIAN UNDERGROUND ECONOMY

The immigrants, whether authorized or not, depend on the underground economy and vice versa: in fact, the underground economy's continuous need for undocumented labor, combined with a tightening of the immigration laws that has almost eliminated regular forms of immigration, has a "sizeable pull effect" on illegal immigration into Italy (Reyneri

2001: 53). As Bruno Riccio (2002) puts it, Italy has become "a model case" of the informal economy's power to attract "an unorganized labor force prepared to accept any kind of working conditions" (4). And the well-established underground economy in Italy is, at 28 percent of the country's gross domestic product, "the largest of any advanced capitalistic country" (Calavita 2005: 54; see also Reyneri 2001: 23). The distinctive Italian labor market structure also affects unemployment figures. Although joblessness appears alarmingly high in some places, the figures do not always reflect the reality of the work situation. In the case of Naples, for instance, "only a small proportion of the Neapolitans registered as unemployed are actually out of work" (Pardo 1995: 20); moreover, many unemployed workers receive retirement pensions or other welfare benefits while working in the underground economy and therefore have "no interest in being registered" as looking for work (Reyneri 2001: 23). The unemployment situation, however, *is* disadvantageous in some parts of Italy, especially the South. In Campania, which includes Naples, the unemployment rate reached 22 percent in 2001, comparable to levels in the most impoverished regions of Eastern Europe. Still, there are dramatic regional differences within Italy. In the North in the same year, the unemployment rate dropped to a "historic low" of 3.9 percent (Calavita 2005: 57). In the south, the poverty rate (the percentage of households financially unable to secure a minimum of adequate housing, food, and clothing) rose to 24 percent in 2001, and the extreme poverty rate to 11 percent, the national average being, respectively, 11 and 5 percent. These figures hide the fact that, in the South, the low per capita income is matched by low per capita consumption, and that traditional family and housing structures, especially in the South, allow an entire family to live off one salary or pension. These factors might account for Italy's low internal demographic mobility (Calavita 2005: 58; Venturi & Villosio 2006: 95–96). Another explanation regarding the unwillingness of southerners, unlike the immigrants, to move to the North where there are jobs to be found in factories and money to be made—Cole and Booth (2006) call this "the inexorable pull of the north" (4)—centers on the sociocultural differences between the North and South that have haunted the modern Italian nation-state since its inception. Chapter 2 explores further how the internal north-south division may also influence Italian-migrant relations.

In light of the unemployment situation in parts of Italy, the advent of large numbers of migrant workers in the country's labor market has led to heated debate about competition over jobs and possible downward pressure on wages. However, as one recent study shows, the presence of migrant workers in Italy actually increases wages for unskilled national workers, in part because migrants work in "boom areas" where "competition is unlikely," and in part because Italy has strong labor unions that negotiate general agreements on wages, making these less sensitive to changes in supply and demand. Furthermore, national unemployment does not seem to have worsened because of the intensified immigration (Venturi & Villosio 2006: 91). In fact, the effect of the migrant workers on the labor market is "complementary"; that is, migrant workers engage in work activities, whether regular or illegal, that nonmigrant workers consider less than acceptable, and thus they compete "only" with marginal sections of the national workforce (Reyneri 2001: 55). Which jobs are the migrants taking care of? In Sicily, Cole and Booth (2006) found that migrants do "dirty work"—the jobs that Sicilians themselves have rejected because of their degrading, dead-end, and low-paid nature (1). Along similar lines, Reyneri characterizes these unattractive migrant jobs as "3-D jobs"—dirty, difficult, and dangerous. The occupational sectors where legal and illegal migrants find employment are the same in Italy, Spain, and Greece (the main migrant destinations); namely, "housekeeping, street selling, agriculture, construction, small manufacturing firms, catering and low-level urban services"(Reyneri 2001: 37, 51)—and, one might add, prostitution.

The connection between the underground economy and the migrant workforce is also reflected in the tendency of the former toward "ethnic segregation." Each ethnic group focuses on particular jobs, thus further limiting the available opportunities. In Naples, for instance, the Senegalese and Chinese migrants are the dominant ethnic groups when it comes to street-selling, whereas the Ghanaians dominate in day-laboring. This development is perhaps influenced by the recruitment system, which often relies on networking within the same economic sector; it also reflects employers' preference for certain ethnic groups because they believe them to be "cheaper, more vulnerable and more docile" (Reyneri 2001: 51). I would add that the job preferences of the Ghanaian migrants in this study (their dislike for farmwork, for example) are to a degree influenced by their sociocultural backgrounds, even though of course no one can afford to be particular.

Their strong affiliation with the underground economy has many negative effects on migrant workers. Among the more obvious are employer violations of accident and work safety regulations in allowing dangerous, exhausting, or generally unhealthy working conditions, but also employers' lack of respect for rules regarding working hours, breaks and time off, and night work and their lack of protection for maternity rights and for minors. There are even cases of enslavement (Ammendola et al. 2005: 17). Another negative effect of the link between the underground economy and the migrant workers is that, while the underground economy in some sense provides "a shelter" to migrant workers without which it would be impossible to sustain themselves in Europe, it also appears to have a stigmatizing effect in the sense that the migrants' willingness to take an undesirable job and thus to position themselves in the lowest strata of society seems simultaneously to reveal something negative about their human qualities to the Italians (Reyneri 2001: 53). To explore this point further, the following chapter is devoted to the actual day-to-day experiences of the migrants working in the underground economy—the empirical context, which is absent from many, though not all, of the macro-approach studies cited above (Cole & Booth 2006 being an important exception). Having left the reception centers, the Guan fishermen slip directly into the subproletariat of Italian society by working on small-scale construction projects or in farming. In the words of one informant, Benjamin, "We do the donkey work, the jobs that cannot be done by themselves [the Italians] or by the machines."

TWO Migrant Work Situations

Finding a job that will generate a relatively steady flow of income—thus both sustaining the immigrant while he stays in Europe and allowing him to set money aside for the family in Ghana—appears to be the dream of every young man from the Guan village who comes to Europe, as does, with a view to the future, one day building a house at home. The data here are surprisingly unanimous. There appears to be no ambition to become European or even to belong to European society, possibly because in Naples African illegal immigrants perceive the prospect of becoming Italian as ruled out for them on grounds of social class and skin color. So, when young West African men who can afford to do so apparently imitate European lifestyles—not unlike the Kalela dancers whom Mitchell studied in Northern Rhodesia (now Zambia), who dressed in the style of their colonial masters (cf. Gluckman 1961: 75)—

especially by buying new clothes, stereos, or mobile phones, it is worth remembering that they are most likely striving to associate themselves with an African or African American elite, and not necessarily with their European host society. This lack of ambition to become European or settle permanently in Europe is also reflected in the plans of most migrants to stay only temporarily. Actually, this appears to be a general migration trend; one survey conducted among illegal immigrants in Italy in 2003 suggests that more than 60 percent planned to stay only between three and ten years in Italy before returning home (cited in Ammendola et al. 2005: 29).

However, the reality of migrant life and the fact that money and documents are hard to come by, coupled with the fear of rejection should one return to the village empty-handed, often forces migrants to stay longer than they desire. Some even express regret that they did not stay home and keep the money they used for traveling to Europe, putting it to use in Africa instead. The trend toward lingering in Italy under unfavorable conditions may eventually lead migrants to modify their planned time frame as well as their hopes and dreams.

Very often migrants say they are waiting for "papers" without knowing when, if at all, the "papers" will come. For some this seems to have become a permanent state of affairs, with migrants living hand to mouth, making a little money here and there, and from time to time sending something back to the family. Therefore, finding a job and starting to make money as soon as possible is on everybody's mind; it is the one activity that consumes most of the young fishermen's time and energy, whether they are working, or unemployed and looking for work. The most common form of occupation for the undocumented newcomer is day labor, whereas migrants who have stayed longer in Naples tend to work with a regular master, or *capo*. Migrants given permits to stay or, more rarely, work permits on arrival—and it is a constant source of speculation for the Senya men why some immigrants are given permits and some are not—might be able to find formal work in a local business or industry, though this type of engagement is uncommon: many young West Africans who *have* documents are still working for a *capo* or day-laboring in Naples. This general trend of documented migrants losing their legal status when they work in the underground economy, even though this is often their only job opportunity, has created a vicious circle, as a renewal of their legal status depends on legitimate work experience, which is in practice unobtainable. The now-illegal migrant has no chance, not even theoretical, of finding work outside the underground economy. To make things even more complicated, migrants who were once regularized but have lost this status by working in the underground economy appear to be waiting for a new amnesty so they can apply once again (Reyneri 2001: 53; 2004: 86).

Day-laboring, though scarcely mentioned in the literature on migrant life in Italy, is the most precarious of the informal work situations. In the absence of rules and regulations, it entails a high level of risk and exploitation. Yet it is a form of work not uncommon for West African migrants. En route to Libya, day-laboring can provide the means to continue the journey if one runs out of money and becomes stranded somewhere in North Africa. This quality of day-laboring is echoed in Sammy's imaginative explanation of the word the migrants use for laboring: *califo*. Sammy believes the word reflects how day-laboring can "carry you forward" until you reach your goal (Sammy: "*Ca-li-fo*. Since it originated in Libya we pronounce the *r* as *l* like the Arabs). Another, perhaps more likely explanation is that the word is an adaptation of the French word *carrefour*, meaning "intersection" or "crossroads," referring to a possible pickup point for day-laborers in North Africa.

The second most common type of employment—working with a regular *capo*—seems a more moderate form of exploitation that involves less risk and uncertainty, though here, too, no rules and regulations apply except for the interpersonal forms of exchange and dependency that develop over time and that form the moral horizon of the work situation. The third form of work, the formal position with a pay slip and tax deduction, is rare among the young African men in Naples and here is given only cursory consideration.

On a methodological note, to study day-laboring, we would visit Samuel's old pickup points in Naples early in the morning. Now that he was working with a regular *capo*, he would day-labor only during vacations, mainly in August and September, or when things were slow at work. To reach the pickup points in time, the migrants had to get up at 4 or 4:30 and board the bus in Castelvolturno bound for Naples. This created a problem, as the large number of West Africans looking for work at the same time sometimes made it impossible for everyone to get on a bus—a problem discussed in chapter 3. The pressure on migrant workers at the pickup points was illuminated by an incident in which a young Ghanaian who had been standing a bit apart from our group at the roundabout approached us with a worried frown. He wanted to know what my business might be. When Sammy explained the nature of our research to him, he gave a sigh of relief. To the amusement of most, he had thought we were looking for work, too. "What will happen to us," he said, "when even the whites start going to *califo*?"

DONKEY WORK: DAY-LABORING IN NAPLES

Benjamin: How do I prepare for going to the joint? I pray to God before leaving the room in the morning. Then I focus my attention on the cars, keeping an eye on any car that pulls up, to make sure that I am the first to go near that car.

Migrants from West Africa waiting at intersections and roundabouts and under highway bridges in search of a day's work that might sustain them while struggling to find a foothold in Europe have become a regular feature of the early mornings in the Naples suburbs. The figures of the young West Africans stand out against the dawn light; they watch in silence—faces half hidden under hoods and caps—as the long snake of cars moves toward the city center, ready to make their move if a driver should leave the queue and pull over, looking for a set of hands to mix cement or pick tomatoes. When a car pulls over, everybody rushes helter-skelter to get inside. Fights break out regularly between the immigrants, as when somebody gets to the car first and begins discussing the job with the potential employer, then somebody else just flings open the car door, leaps inside, and shouts, "*Vai, vai!*" (Go, go!). As Benjamin explained, because of his desperation, the person who reaches the car first rarely can take the time to discuss the work or the pay. "You just rush and get inside and move with the car, not knowing were the car is going or what kind of job you're going to do." Every car is studied carefully for details that might indicate an opening; most often this scrutinizing is done in complete silence, almost in resignation—nobody moves until the opportunity reveals itself.

One exception is Richard, Samuel's friend and fellow captain from Libya, who was usually moving up and down the pavement, making jokes and comments to everybody as if he couldn't care less if he found work. But it was only a strategy, a facade—when a car pulled up, he was often the first man to approach it. Talking about his tactics, Richard explained that even though he appeared at first glance to be disinterested, he was alert to any little detail that would reveal a possible employer. "What I am expecting to see is a car that is slowing down as it enters the roundabout, [suggesting] they're coming from afar and they'll be looking for someone, and you'll see them watching us, maybe even doing like this [*makes a small gesture with the hand*]. Some cars also carry equipment, which tells you they're going to work." In the effort to find work, the immigrants are both colleagues and competitors; moving around together in Naples, they feel safe, but at the same time they fight each other to approach cars and land jobs, and usually the stronger or bolder ones push the weaker ones aside. Richard was prepared to do what he had to if someone beat him to an approaching car. "For instance, this morning a car had pulled over and a lot of the guys were standing around the car, discussing with the man. So I said to them: 'This is my man, this is my master. I have been working with him for a long time.' And before they knew it, I was inside the car, moving with the man. This is some of the things you have to do. That gave me the chance to get in there, and I went."

Watching the fishermen at the pickup "joints," how they concentrate on cars passing by in an attempt to figure out which of them might contain an employer about to pull over, is strangely reminiscent of going canoe fishing with residents of the fishing village in Ghana. I was reminded especially of the crucial moment before the net is cast, when the crew sits and waits in silence, the outboard motor switched off, and everybody is watching the fish, the waves, the sea birds, anxious not to get it wrong, while keeping an eye on the competing canoes. Presented with this analogy, Richard laughed.

Richard: It's like that. You have to pay attention to whatever is around you and grab it. If you're studying a fish, you'll always pay attention to the sea and the way it moves in the water and how you'll catch your net around it. You have to be very careful [at the roundabout]; maybe someone will be calling you or inviting you, but because you're not paying attention or looking at the cars, you'll not notice the person calling you, and somebody standing afar will rush to your place. This also happens on the sea. You'll be at a place and there's fish right there—only you wouldn't know it. But somebody will see it, and before you know it, they'll come from afar and drop their net.

Elaborating on this insight, Richard and Samuel discussed how day-laboring also evokes canoe fishing in the choice of metaphors used to describe work events. In Senya, for instance, when the catch is too big for one person to handle, he would say that he has "lifted up the paddle," signaling to others that there's an opening. "We say the same at day-laboring," Richard told me. "When, for instance, you're getting a job and there's another job included, you'll call your friends and tell them that you have lifted up your paddle, that the catch is too big for you to handle alone."

The typical kinds of work are construction and farming. The young Senya men prefer construction work (coming from a fishing village, they generally look down on farmwork as provincial [Lucht 2003]), though nobody can afford to be particular. Wages vary between 25 and 45 Euros for ten to twelve hours of work, with the average day's wage hovering closer to the bottom of that range. The illegal immigrants are not always popular with the local community and are accustomed to harassment when they offer themselves for work. Benjamin, for example, recounts going to a joint at Alzano and having the local Neapolitans throw stones at them from the high-rises. "They'd be at the windows when we came in the morning—even old men and women. One day we also gathered stones, and when they began stoning us, we retaliated. Then they stopped doing that." For their part, the West African immigrants are not enthusiastic about the prospect of day-laboring, either, but they see it as their only opportunity for income. Most of the young men find it degrading to stand at the roadside waiting to be picked up, and some express concern that pictures of them may appear in the newspapers at home, disgracing them. "The Senya boys are embarrassed," Samuel said. "They don't want people at home to know about it. A friend of ours who was expecting a visitor from Ghana changed his phone number so the visitor shouldn't come and find him and tell them at home what was really going on." In general, the work situation that immigrants find themselves in when they come to Europe is, contrary to popular belief, often worse from a "professional or social point of view" than the position they had before they chose to emigrate to Europe (Reyneri 2001: 12).

But apart from being economically and socially disadvantageous, day-laboring is also unsafe work, and accidents happen frequently at the workplaces. When undocumented immigrants are injured or abused by the Italian employer, they receive no financial assistance except what their friends and the Catholic shelters can do for them.

Benjamin: Sometimes you meet people who are very rough, and before you realize it, you'll get hurt and there's nobody to care for you. I have this one [a scar across his knee]: we were transporting potatoes, handing them over to shops in the city, and normally when we get into traffic, you cannot park outside the stores, so you hang off the side of the car and remove the crates. So I was hanging off the side of the car, not knowing the metal bar wasn't probably fixed, and I fell down and hurt myself. There was nothing I could do. I had to go home and stay in the house for almost a month. I went to the Caritas [a Catholic shelter] for food and drugs. Then I joined the man again when I was feeling better. I had no other option. This time we were moving crates with potatoes from one car to another when a car hit me from behind and really hurt my waist [lower back]. For that one, too, I had to come home again—this time for three weeks.

Accidents aside, in the absence of rules and regulations, the job situation for the illegal immigrant is generally fraught with uncertainty. Managing to fight off competition at the joint, landing an actual job, and arriving at the workplace on time (and in spite of the inadequate bus system) is no guarantee that the work situation is under control, that things will proceed normally, or that one will be paid on time. In fact, due to a "complete lack of rights immigrants are generally subjected to oppressive exploitation" (Ammendola et al. 2005: 32).

Benjamin: There's no law. Anything can happen at any time. You can be told in the middle of the work to leave and go away. For instance, today the police came to check our papers, and we had to run and hide. Sometimes they come to check out the new buildings to see if everything is in order—if the taxes are being paid and if the people working there have documents. The *capo* gave us a signal, and we knew we had to run. We ran into the bushes; some locked themselves in the bathrooms. When the police had gone, we received a signal from the *capo* and we came back to work. This happened three times on the same day. Tomorrow, they are coming the whole day to take pictures and register everything, so I am not going to work until the *capo* gives me a new signal.

Any disputes at the workplace—and they frequently occur—leave the illegal immigrants in a weak positions, with no ability to prevent employers from going back on their word.

Benjamin: I was hired to carry concrete. They were putting up a building, about three stories, and the man agreed to pay 30 Euros for two hours, but after the work, he said that he was only willing to pay 20 instead of the 30 Euros he promised. And we said, "No, we have agreed. An agreement is an agreement—so give us the 30 Euros." But before we could know what was going on, he pulled a pistol on us. "Either you get away from here, or I'll shoot you." So we had to run for our lives and leave the money, and the work we had done, gone for nothing.

Sometimes the exploitation reaches Dickensian dimensions.

Francis: A year ago now I was at Afrangola looking for a job when a woman pulled up in a van. Because I was short of money, I couldn't begin to ask what kind of job it was or where we were going, so I just got in the car with her. Her business was some kind of amusement park that's only open for the summer. They wanted me to assemble all the stuff there, and that was very heavy items, like toy cars and merry-go-rounds. They used me very well for almost two weeks. They even told me to sleep there and do some arranging—some cleaning and sweeping—during the evenings. They agreed to pay me 100 Euros a week. And the day they were supposed to pay they gave me some food in the afternoon. Normally, I had to buy my own food. But in less than five minutes [after having finished the meal], I couldn't stand up and began to vomit. The next thing I know is that I'm in the hospital. The doctors told me I was lucky to survive. When I recovered, I went to them to get my money. But they just told me to go away and called their dog to chase me off. I was surprised; I think they tried to poison me in order not to pay the money.

H.L.: *In what way has that experience influenced your view of day-laboring?*
Francis: What I see is that our lives are shaking in the hands of these people. We don't have any kind of security. These people can do bad things any time they want.

In a few cases, however, the illegal immigrant manages to outwit the employer.

Sonny: I was hired to work with this man when I had been only two weeks in Naples. We went around and collected old and used car tires. There's some kind of wire inside the car tire that this man used for something. After two weeks of work the man was supposed to pay me, but he said that he wasn't ready until the following week. But the third week he still wouldn't pay out the money. So I decided to go to his place and I told him that I would give his name to my people back in Africa and they would kill him with juju. He began shaking and took out 100 Euros from his wallet and said, "Here, take that."

Sometimes the prospect of work is a pickup line used by those who pose as would-be employers with the intent of robbing the immigrants, knowing full well that their crime is unlikely to be reported or have any consequences at all. Eric, for instance, was walking along the road when a man stopped him with a job offer. They agreed on a price—35 Euros for the whole day. "But when we got in the car, I was driven to a bushy area, and the man pulled out a gun and demanded that I give up my mobile phone and my money. He took all my money, but he rejected the phone because it wasn't a flashy one." It was no coincidence that Eric was carrying an old mobile phone; those migrants who have money, mobiles, or nice clothes are careful not to carry them around. As Jonathan said: "I always try to find a place to hide my money before going to the joint, like under a rock at the roadside, so that if they get me, they will only get a few coins. Maybe they will kick me around a little bit, but nothing too serious."

Indeed, most immigrants are aware of the risks of robbery and prepare themselves. Apart from not wanting to spoil their good clothes at the workplace, West African immigrants put on worn-out clothes before going to the joints in the morning so as not to look like attractive targets to robbers. But this strategy of dressing down to avoid robbery, many believe, is part of the reason that immigrants are looked down upon by the Italians; they look ragged and dirty, and the Italians get the wrong impression of them as human beings. "They don't know me," Jonathan declared. "When I'm at the joint, I look very dirty in my working clothes, but at home I wear nice clothes; you can't even believe it is the same guy you saw standing at the roadside! When I'm at home, I dress up; I wear nice clothes."

Italian men looking for male prostitutes apparently also frequent the pickup joints. Consequently, in addition to robbery and violence, the African immigrants voice concern over fear of sexual abuse in connection to day-laboring. Many report sexual advances made to them by Italians posing as potential employers. It was difficult to assess the extent of the problem, as homosexuality is a very sensitive subject in a West African context and many shied away from discussing the issue at all. But most, like Benjamin, maintained that "sometimes they do go for our bodies." He found this situation "the most frightening aspect of it all because you don't know what their real intentions are. Suddenly, a man is trying to have an affair with another man with a gun on him. . . . It's bad. Over here, we're exposed to so many risks." In some cases, misunderstandings—possibly due to poor language skills and the West Africans' general mistrust of Neapolitans—affect the situation, making it difficult to determine what is really going on. One time, Samuel went looking for work and was about to return home empty-handed, when an older Italian man driving a Fiat 500 stopped him. The man offered him work in the *campagna* (the countryside), an offer that worried Samuel because the time was approaching noon. "You only go to the *campagna* very early in the morning to farm. Later in the day you'll only go there if somebody wants something bad to happen to you." As Samuel climbed into the car and they took off, he was thinking to himself, "Let me get in the car, and the moment he tries to fuck up, I'm going to hit him, and I don't care if the car will roll over." After some time, driving toward the countryside, the old man suddenly had a change of heart and turned the car around and headed back for the city, bypassing the place where he had picked Sammy up. They drove to a house, and Samuel was told to move some things from one room to another. "It surprised me. At the end of the day he paid me a normal whole day's salary and dropped me off at the place he picked me up in the morning." Although stressful moments occurred for Sammy, in the end the employer had a real job prospect lined up. Yet Samuel still wonders whether the old man really wanted to hurt him but got cold feet, or whether the whole thing was a misunderstanding, a result of the erosion of confidence one suffers when living in a negative zone. A month later, however, the case of sexual abuse was clear when Samuel again found himself in a car with an Italian employer and was confused as to what was going on. This man, also vague about the kind of work he had in mind, only said, "They would see about that when they got to the workplace." Samuel recalled his ride with the old man and his hesitant decision to give it a chance.

Samuel: But then he started feeling my leg and asking me whether I was strong, and his hands kept approaching my groin. I said, "What are you doing?" He said he was only joking and we were really going to work. But we were just driving around. Then he asked me whether I would like to fuck his ass. He would pay me.

At this point, Sammy threatened to cry out, "for people to know that I had been kidnapped." The man began "shaking" and agreed to pull the car over. But as Sammy was getting out of the car, the driver reassembled his composure and asked for a phone number. Sammy shouted, "Waffanculo!" (Fuck you!), and slammed the door. "The next time somebody begins with this stuff, I'll know what's going on."

Incidents like this one and, more generally, the constant risk of abuse, whether of a work-related, violent, or sexual nature leave day-laborers speculating about who can be trusted and who cannot; consequently their general trust in the intentions of the Neapolitans is very low. "Many a time it's up to you to think very fast. If not, you'll fall into trouble," Samuel said, recalling how the other day he was waiting for the bus when an Italian pulled over and asked for a light. "He asks me where I'm going. I say Castelvolturno, and he says he wants to give me a lift. But you could easily see that he was bad. Some of these Neapolitans are very, very bad. So, I just said, 'No thank you.'" Samuel shook his head in disbelief, "Imagine somebody coming with a flashy car and asking you if you'd like a lift—he had something evil in mind."

What worries the West African immigrants appears to be the general uncertainty of it all, the fact that they are at the mercy of whoever picks them up, are left guessing at their intentions, and never know if they're really going to work or are to be abused instead. As Jonathan put it, "We don't know who'll pick us up. Maybe they'll kill us. We don't know." Following Niklas Luhmann (1999), I argue that this relationship of mistrust, continuously fed by new abuses, whether as a firsthand experience or as one of the constantly circulating rumors, paradoxically seems to reduce social complexity in the sense that a sharpening of one's negative expectations reduces the potentialities of the social environment. In other words, when anything bad can happen at any time, nothing the world can throw at you will surprise you. This emotional rearmament, however, comes at a price, as Luhmann argues; such an ever-present readiness to liquidate one's reserves is psychologically difficult to manage (1999: 125). The significant personal resources invested in handling this regime of arbitrariness is perhaps what one report hints at when it concludes: "The lives of illegal immigrants are plagued with great precariousness, which deeply undermines their psychological and physical well-being" (Ammendola et al. 2001: 30). How the migrants keep up their courage in the face of adversity and mistrust is an important theme of life in Naples that is explored later in this chapter and in chapter 3.

Between eight and nine o'clock in the morning, the group of young men at the roundabout begin to scatter: if no job has been secured by then, the opportunity has passed. Some head home to do laundry or watch television; others take the bus downtown to go window-shopping in the Piazza Garabaldi.

Arriving home with Samuel one day, I sat down and talked to Madam Hope in the living room. It was around noon, and Madam Hope's boyfriend, Martin, was busy out in the yard. She had asked him to kill the chickens she had been raising for the past couple of months. She wanted "to fill the freezer up with meat." Martin decapitated the chickens one after another with a kitchen knife and emptied the blood from the neck into a pothole in the dirt, the chicken bodies still kicking and quivering. A summer storm was approaching on the horizon. Sitting at the living room table, Madam Hope had a pile of yellow newspaper clippings in front of her, some up to five years old. They contained the lottery numbers of former drawings. Whenever she had a break from her duties, she studied the numbers, trying to detect a secret pattern that could reveal next week's draws. Martin had told her to let it go—one month, he claimed, she wasted 400 Euros on the lottery—but Madam Hope believed that if she kept playing, scrutinizing these numbers, one day her ship would come in. Examining the numbers that came out the day before, she repeated them carefully to herself rhythmically, as in a piece of music or a chant.

Madam Hope: If I had only known these numbers yesterday, this place would be smelling of money today. Everything is about money, you know. If I had money, they would call me into their office, and they would say, "What would you like, madam?" And I would say, "An Italian passport and a visa to America and Japan." And they would make the call right away, "Madam Hope is going to America—see to it that the paperwork is made in order, *subito* [immediately]."

Madam Hope, suddenly carried away by the idea of winning the lottery, began fantasizing about how she would scold the *carabinieri* (the Italian military police, whom most migrants fear) when they came around to check up on her. "*Carabinieri*, my ass," she would say (now in Italian). "I am much richer than any of you. And I am in command in this house. Now, get yourselves out of here—go, go!" To be sure, this otherwise very levelheaded and resolute woman had great emotion invested in the dream of winning the lottery. When one day a migrant guest, sitting in her kitchen with a beer from the fridge, jokingly remarked that even if she won, the Italians would never ever pay out the money to a black person, she was infuriated and threw him straight out of the house. Her fuming continued long after he left, as if he had somehow touched upon her worst inner fears: actually winning but not being recognized. "That's ridiculous!" she exclaimed. "How can they refuse you the money when you have the ticket?"

Mr. Joe, a middle-aged self-employed Ghanaian salesman from next door who had a small cart with clothes and accessories that he dragged around the streets of Naples, sat down with us, clutching a beer from Madam Hope's kitchen outlet. It had begun raining hard outside, and the streets were now empty. Apart from the shop on wheels, Mr. Joe collected old television sets that he shipped off to Ghana when he had collected enough to fill a whole container. The televisions were piled up against the walls in his dark basement apartment, the empty screens facing outward. Sitting at his kitchen table, you had a strange claustrophobic feeling, as if the walls were moving in on you. After work he often came by Madam Hope's for a chat. He was usually keen to talk about the important decision he had recently made: he was traveling north to establish his little business there—perhaps even as far as Denmark or Germany. Madam Hope dryly remarked that he had been talking about that for years and years, and it would never happen.

The Madam now embarked on another of her recurrent topics, the low morals of African leaders.

Madam Hope: Our leaders are corrupt. They eat all the money themselves. In Africa we have everything. We have a nice climate, minerals, food, oil—everything. God blessed Africa with all these riches. Hansen, do you think we would be here if we had good leadership? No, we would leave this moment.

Mr. Joe nodded in agreement. We now turned to how everybody was looking for money in Naples in order to take care of the family at home, and he joined the conversation.

Mr. Joe: When you go to a hospital in Africa, they won't treat you, even though you're bleeding from a hole in your head. We have mosquitoes that give us malaria. They have mosquitoes here also. But here, you get a bite and scratch it for a while and that's it. In Africa, if you don't have any money, you die—nobody can help you. Here, if you're not lazy, you can get money. Look at the churches in Africa. Every Sunday, they are full of people who pray for help. They pray for up to four hours; they cry and they plead. In Europe, nobody goes to church. If they go, they just [pop in,] do the sign of the cross, and leave again—and look at everything they have. Why? Because God doesn't listen to us!

Madam Hope: You see how it is?

WORKING WITH A REGULAR *CAPO*: MIXING CEMENT

Studying the work situation of the illegal immigrants in Naples posed a methodological problem in that it was difficult to gain access to the migrants' places of work. My research on day-laboring is thus based on narrative and participant observation at the joints, whereas the actual work sites were largely inaccessible. I was myself offered work one day; an old man with an arm in a plaster cast approached me and asked if I wanted work. I am not sure I made the right decision in declining, but it did not feel like the right strategy to pursue. First of all, many others around desperately needed the work. Also, having collected a large number of stories of abuse and exploitation, I didn't feel safe going alone with someone in a manner I had little control over. Recalling the situation even now, an uncomfortable feeling comes over me, the uncanny sensation of being under threat, having one's person, or rather one's body, being sought after—combined with a curiosity as to what could be accomplished by pursuing such a strategy. The same feeling, though somehow less tempting, engulfed me one night sometime later when I was waiting for the bus in Castelvolturno, ready to go back to Naples after work. A car passed slowly by and parked fifty meters from the bus stop. The driver opened the door and waited. The person inside, watching me in the rear-view mirror in the darkness of the car's interior, created this eerie sensation, mixed with feelings of anger and fear, of being singled out for an undisclosed purpose. Maybe this is what Elias Canetti is talking about when he opens *Crowds and Power* with the assertion "There's nothing that man fears more than the touch of the unknown" (1984: 15). Yet not only do human beings depend on those close to them and their familiar worlds, but "the *things* of greatest power and value always lie beyond one's ken, outside one's circle" (Jackson 1998: 45; italics in the original).

Concerning methodology, when Samuel rejoined his *capo* after the summer break, we began planning how to access his workplace in order to carry out participant observation. This proved to be more difficult than expected. Sammy's bosses, Alessandro and Marco, ran a small company off the books, and they were not too keen on having a researcher around, though Sammy talked to them several times. I first met them outside a gas station in a suburb of Naples. Sammy was going to pick up his weekly wages. They drove a beat-up Fiat; the back seat was filled with dirty work clothes and mason's tools. The first thing they wanted to know was whether we were gay lovers. Sammy dismissed that idea and pointed to my wedding ring, at which they nodded, but were clearly unconvinced. Alessandro then opened a brown envelope containing money bills. He began counting them and the days that Sammy had worked. Sammy leaned his elbows on the window frame to follow the settling of the account. Alessandro, displeased with Sammy for sticking his head halfway inside the car, stopped counting every now and then and threatened to smack Sammy in the back of the head. Samuel nonetheless expressed his contentedness with working for Alessandro. "He pays without making stories. When they begin making stories, you can forget about it. That's when they start robbing you." Months passed and the possibility of going to work with Samuel appeared more and more unlikely, as his Italian bosses kept turning down the requests for all sorts of reasons. Then, one day after work, Sammy suddenly came to my apartment in Chiaia and told me, "We have been given a green light" to join Alessandro and Marco the next morning. They were laying tiles on a rooftop in the center of Naples and had finally approved my presence.

Sammy picked me up at a roundabout in Naples at around six o'clock the following morning. The place was called La Belle Époque and was unusually stylish. Inside, no more than five waiters in black trousers and burgundy vests served the guests, mostly groups of small entrepreneurs who would pull in for a quick *macchiato,* the normal Neapolitan way of commencing a workday. The glittering café stood in striking contrast to the cold and rainy street outside and the grayish trail of cars and buses that moved toward the city center in the early hours before sunrise. Under the café's neon sign (featuring a French lady in a long evening gown, presumably at a soiree in the late nineteenth century) a group of young African men were gathering, some with umbrellas, to wait and hope for work. When Samuel arrived, we walked to the next roundabout to meet up with Marco. Daylight broke as we were walking, and it resumed raining heavily. My shoes began to leak and Sammy had the same problem, so we stopped and stuffed them with a couple of plastic bags from my rucksack before we carried on. At the next roundabout another group of young African men had formed, one of them a Senya person, but because of the hard rain we greeted him only briefly and went inside a smaller and more traditional coffee bar. Here, we waited under an extended roof, safe from the rain, for Sammy's bosses to come pick us up. A man riding by on a moped shouted a greeting through the sheets of rain and waved at Samuel. "This guy came with me on my boat," Sammy explained.

At seven o'clock, the junior of the bosses, Marco, parked at the curb and flung open the door. He was a short, muscular guy with a small arrow-shaped beard below the lip. Initially he appeared surprised that Sammy had company, but we quickly began discussing football and the fact that Denmark had not qualified for the 2006 World Cup, whereas both Ghana and Italy had not only qualified but been drawn in the same group—a fact that gave the Ghanaians the hope that they would, for once, come out winning against the Italians. Or as Sammy expressed it, "My guys are really hoping we'll be able to whip these Italians very badly."

We drove from the coffee bar to the apartment complex. Alessandro, Marco informed us, was suffering from a stomachache and would not come to work until later, if at all. The complex was a group of four-story buildings shielded from the street by a high fence; at the entrance stood a small shed with an African watchman. When we arrived, most people appeared to have left for work except for the housewives, *le casalinghe*, who would appear on the balconies from time to time, doing their chores or conversing with other housewives on nearby balconies. We went up the flights of stairs to the third floor of one building, and as we entered the apartment, Marco began arguing with the contractor, Massimo, who was already there waiting. Massimo, a retired cop who had turned to construction, was a strong-looking, white-haired man with big, black eyebrows. "He still carries his police badge in his wallet," Sammy told me later. Such a work situation—an African migrant working for a retired Italian or an Italian with a second job—is typical of places where two otherwise separate worlds converge (Carter 1997: 50). Marco and Massimo were arguing because Massimo felt he was paying Alessandro and Marco too much when, at just the time he needed them most, they wouldn't show up for some cockamamy reason. We waited for a while on a couch while the argument died down and they turned their attention to us.

It soon became clear that Samuel had stretched the truth a bit when he said that we had been given a green light to do the research. The fact of the matter, he later explained, was that, having grown tired of waiting for his *capi* to make a decision, he had invited me along himself. I had the impression that he could do so because they owed him in some way; he knew it and they knew it. Possibly, this was another result of the dependence of the underground economy on the illegal migrant workforce, especially in the South, where the number of migrant workers is higher than the national average. Many jobs would not exist were they not part of the underground economy; by the same token, many small farmers and building contractors would not be able to survive without the availability of an illegal migrant workforce. As Cole and Booth remind us (2006: 5), migrants working as day-laborers, domestic caretakers, and sex-workers support lifestyles that Italians have become accustomed to even as they worry that the migrant presence will change life as they know it. It therefore makes sense to regard the relationship between Samuel and his Neapolitan employers as one of interdependence; without them Samuel would have been on the street day-laboring, whereas his bosses relied heavily on his hard work. This is not to deny, however, that the power distribution is unequal and the working conditions are precarious.

Massimo asked a couple of inquisitorial questions about my being there, but eventually shrugged his shoulders and instructed me to help out Sammy as best I could. To get things going, he picked up his wallet and took out a 20 Euro bill and ordered me to go and fetch coffee and *cornetti,* the sweet Italian pastry. "I am an asshole?" Massimo said, looking at Marco. "You're making me an asshole, because I buy you all coffee and *cornetti,* but when I need you to work you don't show up?"

During the morning, we mixed cement inside the apartment. This was done manually on a piece of cardboard on the floor, while Marco was in the bathroom laying tile. Although Sammy knew very well how to lay tile from experience in Libya, it was the *capo's* privilege to lay them, while mixing the cement was migrant's work. It was hard work, but the morning passed rather quickly and without any problems. At lunchtime we were sent to fetch sandwiches. Then we sat in the living room and talked, Massimo drinking red wine and smoking cigarettes. Alessandro had finally arrived, looking a bit queasy. He was younger than one would have expected and wore baggy jeans and a baseball cap that he put on backwards. Massimo had a go at him, too, for being a no-good lazybones. Then we sat in silence and finished the mozzarella-and-tomato sandwiches. To break the ice, Sammy joked that I should watch out for

Massimo. Since he was an ex-cop, he could easily handcuff me and throw me out of the country. Massimo ignored him, and instead we talked briefly about football and the Danish players in the Italian league. This encouraged Alessandro, somewhat subdued until then, to join the conversation. He mentioned a few Danish footballers he knew, then quickly turned to a theme that appeared to capture his imagination. He wanted to know whether I was aware that all Africans were homosexuals. This was due to their big, curly hair, he explained. He stood to demonstrate how, because of their big hair style, it was impossible for African men to enter a doorway without bending their head forward to push it through the door frame, thus sticking out their behind. Sammy laughed the whole thing off and retaliated by calling him stupid and lazy and a person who didn't know how to perform his job.

Samuel: The gay stuff is their insult. I also insult him. Even if you're not a gay person, they will say that you are, to insult you. They will try to make you nervous or annoyed, but it's just a joke. At first, I didn't understand this too well. I used to become so angry when they insulted me. Later, I found out that it was not so much an insult; it's how they are. Their language is full of insults. At the least thing, they'll blow some kind of insult at you. It isn't really their fault, because it's the behavior they've been used to. So now I just laugh and laugh to prove to Alessandro that I am really not much offended.

After the lunch break we went up on the roof. Alessandro explained that the whole rooftop area had to be tiled. First, we had to mop up all the rainwater, then we began mixing a new batch of cement. I fetched water and poured it into the piles of sand and mortar while Sammy expertly mixed the whole thing with a shovel. The buckets of mixed cement were handed over to Marco, who was on his knees laying the foundation for a floor in one corner of the rooftop, while Alessandro walked around smoking a cigarette. At one point there was a loud noise and a long hiss from a truck down in the yard, and we went to the rail to look down. A dumptruck was off-loading a huge pile of sand in the parking lot. Alessandro, who had earlier thrown together a capstan on the rail, announced that all the sand, about two tons, had to be raised to the fourth-floor rooftop, along with twenty bags of mortar. And it had to be done today, because the residents did not appreciate such a big pile of sand lying around in their parking lot. So we began raising the sand with the rusty, shrieking capstan. Sammy was downstairs loading the buckets and hoisting them up one by one with the rope. The wobbly capstan was all over the place. Alessandro, swearing hard, had to come by every half hour to refasten it to the rail so it wouldn't crash down on Sammy four stories below. My job was to receive the full buckets and immediately lower an empty one. Thus, while Sammy loaded an empty bucket in the parking lot, I carried a full bucket to the place where the sand was being piled up. We worked this way without breaks for seven or eight hours, buckets always going up and buckets going down. It was incredibly hard work. For the first couple of hours, the pile in the parking lot seemed to grow rather than get smaller. The sun had long set before we had finished; in the distance the towering figure of Vesuvius lay in shadows.

Samuel: One thing about myself is that if you put me to work and the work is not done successfully, I feel a little bit sorry about the whole thing. I always feel like doing the work very well. If you give me work, I will do my best to finish everything on time. So, when we were told that the sand couldn't remain down there during the night because of the residents, I forced myself to finish the work like some kind of machine, even though I was very tired. Alessandro knows that putting me in that position is a guarantee that the sand is not going to remain down there, though it was big and heavy work for me.

At times the work is too hard. Every day before I get up, I am always afraid. I have a kind of panic inside me because I think of what kind of work they'll have me doing. Maybe it will be too much and too heavy. So every day when I go to work, I have a fear with me . . . it really kills . . . I don't know how to explain it, it doesn't make me feel too comfortable about the work. You know somebody was saying, "Samuel, ever since you came, I have not seen any change in you; you're not putting on any weight." And I said, "You know, I am working with a Napolitano and he's using me very well." Myself, when I pull off the shirt, I can see that I am becoming very lean and muscular. This shouldn't be the case. When we were living in Africa, and our friends came back from Europe, at least you could see that they had put on weight, their bodies were getting plump.

H.L.: Do you feel safe in the workplace?
Samuel: I feel very unprotected when I am working. I should always be careful, because if something happens, I would have to take care of myself. So I am always with that kind of idea at work, that something might go wrong. They'll sometimes ask me to use this grinding machine to cut tiles into smaller sizes, and this machine can easily chop off your hand. So, when I am using it, I am always thinking that if something should happen, I am on my own.

H.L.: How would you describe your relationship with Alessandro?
Samuel: I know the guy likes me. Sometimes when we're working, he'll just stand and look at me so steadily. I think he himself at times feels that the work is too heavy for me. But he's a Napolitano and he cannot change. Then, the next morning he'll be very nice to me, and he'll try to make me laugh in order to make me forget the behavior they have shown toward me. I think when he goes home and assesses the nature of the work he puts me to, he, as a human being, can see that he's killing me. Then, in the morning, he wants to come back and cool me down with all this funny stuff.

This is one of the reasons I have decided to leave Alessandro, because the work is affecting my health. I don't sleep very well—maximum six hours. Also in the morning I have this fear of what is going to happen, so life here is not all that comfortable.

Samuel was not the only one who felt unsafe and disrespected at work. For migrants working with a regular *capo*, the precariousness of the work situation might be less than that under the regime of arbitrariness associated with day-laboring and might represent a more moderate form of exploitation. But as Norbert, a key informant from Winneba who lived in an all-African high-rise block across the muddy river in Castelvolturno, explained, being with a *capo* for a long time and gaining expertise in your field do not protect the migrant worker from humiliation. "They always pay us, the blacks, less than everybody else," Norbert told me. "A Ukrainian will get 5 to 10 Euros more for the same job. If we're paid 25, he'll receive 30 Euros. That's how it is—even if we work harder than they do. Mr. Hansen, it's very, very bad."

Norbert had "taken" a Nigerian girlfriend, and during the interview his "wife" served us a bowl of pasta. Norbert kept one eye on the wrestling match on television. One beefed-up guy wearing some kind of red and black demon mask had knocked his opponent out cold, and while the other guy was unconscious on the canvas, the demon man went looking for a sledgehammer he had stowed under the ring.

Norbert: One thing I know is that if you're an immigrant and you don't have papers, you're situation is very, very difficult. And even if you get a job, it will not be a normal job, because you're an immigrant. Me, I'm a welder, I have a diploma in welding. So, when I go to the building site, I'm leading the work and they don't know anything. Working there, I'm supposed to get the same money that they give to the citizens—but they won't do it. They don't know anything about welding, so I'm the one saying, "Bring this, bring that," teaching them what to do. But at the end of the month, they'll reduce my money, while they'll get a higher salary. There's a certain Italian boy at our work site; he's an apprentice and he doesn't have any idea of how to do the work. I'm the one taking care of the work. The boy is not strong, he doesn't know how to operate the machines, and he's just standing there. But at the end of the month, the boy will take, say, 900 Euros, and I'll take about 600. This small boy is about sixteen years old! It's very bad, Mr. Hansen. Sometimes, I think about quitting the work, but if I look around, what should I do? How can I get money to pay the house rent? So, I'm supposed to manage.

H.L.: Do you feel respected at work?
Norbert: I will say that they respect me because they know me, the work I can do. But there's a difference. They'll tell me to do any kind of foolish job. When, say, there's too much rubble all around, they'll call me to come and take of care it. They say, "Hey, Joe, come and

throw this stuff away." They don't ask the boy. Any foolish job, they ask me to take care of it. I have been working with them a long time, but they don't care. They just think, he's black, so forget about him.

Concerning safety, Norbert also worried that the construction job would eventually cause him health problems. Already he was beginning to detect little physical problems.

Norbert: They give me this big, heavy machine. They call it a *martello* [demolition hammer]. We use it to break up the concrete. If you don't take care, it will deform you. I don't know how to put it—excuse me—but if you don't take care, your penis will not work anymore. I'm very tired when I come home in the evening; my waist is hurting. Every part of my body is paining me. And if you're my friend and you come to my house, I might insult you or embarrass you. I'm so tired; I'll be using all kind of words. I'm also seeing an effect on my eyes and my ears, because they'll not give you any protection. When I stop working, I'll still hear the machine, only weaker, drrrrr-drrrrr. So, I'm praying that I'll get my documents, stop this work, and get better work.

WORKING THE NIGHT SHIFT

As mentioned earlier, only a few migrants in Naples have a regular job in the sense that they have an employment contract and pay taxes. Among the informants in this book, only three had regular positions, and they were all employed at the same place—working the night shift in a plastics factory. One of them, Francis, became a key informant. He was the one who, while he was day-laboring, as described earlier, almost lost his life from what he believed was a deliberate attempt to poison him by his employer, the owner of an amusement park. By the time we met him, however, Francis was quite established in Naples. Moreover, as one of the few people among the Guan immigrants to hold documents—and to be able to renew them continuously because of his formal job—he was able to rent an apartment himself. (Another way of keeping one's papers valid would be to transfer them to people who had better connections, particularly up North, while staying in Naples and day-laboring or working illegally with one's *capo*.) In a block of high-rise apartments, Francis was the landlord to a large group of Guan immigrants; at one point twenty-one people slept in his three-bedroom apartment. The Ghanaians call the building complex Palazzo Americano because, the story goes, it had once housed American soldiers stationed in Naples. Whether this explanation was historically accurate or reflected the desire to associate oneself with all things (African) American was difficult for me to establish. Samuel and I would usually visit the Palazzo Americano on Sundays, when most of the residents would be at home relaxing or washing their clothes or maybe preparing to go to church.

Incidentally, Sammy and Madam Hope sometimes played a curious trick on his Italian bosses that revealed something about the desired position that African Americans held in the eyes of the West African migrants, a status that meant having all the money and social and cultural capital the migrants were so desperately pursuing in Naples. Sammy had made Alessandro and Marco believe that he had an African American girlfriend, and they were both keen to meet her. He would sometimes call them and hand over the phone to Madam Hope, who then played the role of the American girlfriend, pretending not to understand the two eager Italians in the most amorous and insinuating tone of voice.

The high-rise, across the river from the Scalzone Hotel, was home to between five hundred and one thousand Ghanaian and Nigerian immigrants. Some lived ten or more people to a room, as was typical of the day-laborers and the newly arrived, whereas other migrants, especially those working with a regular *capo*, had a room to themselves. Through the open doors of the apartments would come music, the sound of sizzling hot oil from kitchens, and the smell of food being cooked. Downstairs in the yard, vendors came by with black plastic bags, setting out their contents on the ground for sale: combat boots, baggy jeans, trainers, hooded sweatshirts. A photographer might be walking from floor to floor taking pictures of people posing in their best Sunday outfits, photographs that would be sent home. Occasionally one would hear the odd scream of somebody getting killed in a Nigerian horror movie, and outside the gate, on the cursed road, the bus would regularly pass by without picking up the West African migrants waiting at the stop.

Although Francis came across as a delicate person—a slender and fair-skinned man with long, thin sideburns and a high and melodic voice like that of a natural singer—he was in fact the boss around the house, or the "tycoon" as his fellow immigrants called him. One Sunday, we sat down with Francis in his kitchen while a friend of his fried a fish at the stove. Despite the fact that he considered himself relatively fortunate in terms of work, Francis was always reluctant to rejoice in his position when so many of his friends and flat-mates were struggling, going from joint to joint in the mornings and coming back with nothing.

Francis: I have regular work; I have been registered. But I cannot say that I am okay, because my brothers are still suffering. No, I am not okay. My brother will also need something to help *him*, you see? They'll go to this place to look for work, then they go to that place instead; they'll be cracking their heads day and night, while they end up with nothing. This situation is very frustrating.

Certain issues concerning the factory work he did also worried Francis.

Francis: I begin at midnight and stand on my feet until eight in the morning—without any breaks, my brother. That means I'm on my feet eight hours solid. It's shift work and the machine should never stop. I'll wake up at five o'clock in the afternoon, then in the evening I'll have to take two buses and a train before I arrive at the place. So I am working all right, but I can't get sound sleep.

H.L.: *Are you treated respectfully?*
Francis: I would say that the treatment is normal. The man respects us. He says that we, the blacks, are very hard workers. But there's still a difference; the whites get family allowances, whereas we, the blacks, because we don't have wives here, don't receive that. But there is one

thing that burdens my mind, and I am very worried about it. When a certain machine hurts a black person, it's very hard for them to receive any insurance or compensation.

This machine [the one Francis operates] makes a hard, plastic box that they use to keep their electrical systems inside. We put the hot plastic in the machine, and the machine will stamp it and cut out a piece. I have to handle it with my hands and the material is very hot. When the machine has stamped out the material, it has some very rough edges that you have to smooth out for the job to become neat— you have to file the edges off. But as soon as you start filing, the dust comes from the plastic and you can't stand it. You'll scratch your skin. When the dust enters your skin; it will start itching you. Even if your wear a shirt and the dust goes in, you have to throw it away, because when the dust goes in, you can't wear it anymore, your body will itch; it's very hard. You stand on your feet eight hours doing this, and then another person takes over the machine. See my hands [*displays little scars on the back of his hands*]—when I came from Ghana, my hands never looked like that.

There's not enough evidence here to confidently conclude anything about the formal working conditions. Francis's remains an unusual job situation among the West African informants in Naples, though it seems safe to say that migrants who obtain documents and a regular job do not necessarily have attractive jobs; rather, most still appear to be the so-called "3-D jobs" mentioned above. Nevertheless, though the work might be unattractive, the steady income that such jobs generate seems to transform the lives of the migrants who get them, as well as the welfare of their families at home.

This potential for transformation—economic, social, existential— became the subject of an interview with Bobby, Francis's colleague at the plastics factory. Although Bobby voiced some of the same concerns that Francis did about the tedious nature of the work and the plastic dust that apparently irritates the skin, he quickly turned to the question of progress and how he saw himself moving ahead, into a desirable position. During our interview in his room at the Palazzo Americano, Bobby went to the drawer and pulled out the blueprint of the house he was currently having constructed back home in Ghana.

Bobby: This was sent from Ghana for me to see and approve. It's a big house, five bedrooms, garage, storeroom, a big hall, a toilet, and a bath.

Sammy: Two plots of land?
Bobby: Yes, two plots of land. Maybe next year the building will be finished. When I marry, my family will live there.

So, gradually we're improving here—Rome wasn't built in a day. Every month I can set money aside, send something to my parents. And now, I am getting a bank account. This means that soon I can buy a car and pay in installments, because they know I am working. That's why we're forcing to enter the EU, you see?

Mr. Hans, you have been to Ghana, so you know that we are not totally poor, but we still needed to see an improvement. The difference is too big between the economies of Africa and Europe. Here you work, and even though it's hard work, the little amount you get, you can send it back home. As a young man you're able to buy your own house. Here, if I make 1,000 Euros after tax, I'll be able to send home 700. Out of that my family will receive 200, then 500 will go to the projects I am working on, the house and some other small things. I'll keep 300 Euros aside for myself, to live off here in Naples, for the rent and my expenses.

Let me tell you something, when I was going to school, my parents were not able to pay the fees, and I had to drop out. So, if I had had somebody to help me, like I am helping my nephews, maybe I could have gone to university and become a doctor.

When I was young, I always told my parents and my teacher that I wanted to become a medical doctor. The teacher said it could happen, and I focused very hard on this, but because of financial problems I had to leave school. I didn't get that chance, but in the future I want my children to get into a better position. Being in Italy, I can pay for them to attend expensive international schools in Ghana.

So maybe I was no good to become a doctor, but maybe one day my child will become one.

On the bus going back to Sammy's house in the afternoon, we discussed the interview with Bobby and agreed that it was a relief, for once, to meet an informant who was making real headway in Naples. As Samuel expressed it, referring to the steps that Bobby was taking in life, "That's the dream all we guys have."

However, to obtain a more complete view of the life-world of migrants in Naples—and the "losses and gains" it sometimes boils down to, as Senior Teacher explained—it is necessary to account for the everyday humiliation that counts among the "losses" that migrants have to incur in Naples. Examples of seemingly unmotivated attacks reported along the Via Domitiana have already been mentioned: John, who was kicked in the knee while waiting for the bus; Philip, who had an egg thrown at him from a passing car; and Jerry, who was struck in the chest by a person driving by on a scooter. Apart from these violent attacks, spitting incidents took place practically every day, sometimes carried out by boys on motorcycles racing up and down the Via Domitiana—though many times youth was not the issue. Once, when Samuel and I were walking around in the empty streets of Pescopagano, two men coming toward us on a motorcycle surprised us by leaving a blotch of saliva on my jacket as they passed. Samuel could not believe it. He kept walking in circles around me, checking my jacket, two or three times, to see if they had really spat at me. Sammy eventually concluded that the Neapolitans just didn't like blacks and whites walking together like friends. On a methodological note, this small and insignificant moment in the field provided a glimpse into the difference between being "welcome" and being "unwelcome," a question that makes "all the difference in the world," as Ronald D. Laing remarks (1976: 29).

On another occasion we were going home on the bus, passing the San Paolo football stadium, when an old, apparently crazy lady, toothless and obsessively gnawing her gums, suddenly began screaming at Sammy. She didn't like him sitting on the seat next to her, because, she yelled in his face, he stank and looked ugly. Sammy took out his monthly bus pass and insisted that, having paid the fare, he had the same right to sit as everybody else. The crazy lady wouldn't leave him alone; she spat at his feet, raised her hand, and threatened to slap him if he did not get away from her. The bus driver told her to keep it down, while the other Italian passengers remained passive. Some of the other African migrants on the bus began calling on the crazy lady to shut her mouth, which only wound her up more, and she retorted with horrendous racist remarks. Shortly afterward, the seat next to me became vacant and Sammy switched places, but the argument continued until the old lady reached her stop. In fact, just as she was getting ready to get off, she suddenly changed her mind, turned around, came back, and threatened Samuel with one hand raised, as if intending to give him a blow. Fortunately, other passengers stopped her before she could reach the place we were sitting. To be fair, a young Italian couple, shocked by the woman's behavior, came to Sammy's seat before getting off the bus and apologized to him, saying that he shouldn't mind the ranting and raving of an old person who clearly had a mental problem. Sammy was still fuming with anger and embarrassment as we got off the bus and walked to his house.

Sammy: If you begin to worry about all the miserable things going on, you'll only get confused and lose sight of the reason why you're here. Let them only think that I am a dirty day-laboring bastard. They don't know me. On Sundays, I put on my best clothes and I grab my new mobile phone and go to church.

The discrimination that is the focus of the following chapter, however, was of a more muted, but no less depressing, kind. It consisted chiefly of having one's time and effort wasted when buses drove by without stopping for West African passengers. Although not quite as dramatic as the events described above, it was a form of discrimination that could have dire consequences. Being ignored by the bus driver ruined the migrants' chances of reaching the pickup points in town, or their regular workplaces on time, in which case they would have to return home empty-handed. I had a good opportunity to study this phenomenon closely when my family came to Italy and we found a place in the city.

As I came to depend on the bus system in order to meet up with informants, I was able to glimpse an aspect of immigrant life that caused
much stress and concern. Before exploring this theme, I consider the
complex sociohistorical and political context of Italian-migrant relations
in Italy.

Walking home, Sammy and I passed some Nigerian girls on the dirt
road. They usually slept on an old stained mattress in the shade of a tree
in their skimpy underwear while waiting for business to arrive, but
somebody had apparently torched their mattress, leaving only a smoking
pile of blackened springs. The girls were now squatting in the shade of
the tall rushes that stood along the farmland ditches. When I later told
Madam Hope about the girls' predicament, she said, "You see how they
are? Out of wickedness they won't allow the girls to rest."

THE ITALIAN CONTEXT OF IMMIGRATION

Most West African informants seemed mystified by the abuse and discrimination they experienced in their everyday lives. Some argued that
Italians were not educated; others that Italians did not like to travel and
therefore did not have knowledge of the outside world and the people
living there—an ironic theory considering the history of emigration from
Italy. Still others, in the manner of Madam Hope, maintained simply that
Italians, especially Neapolitans, were "wicked." Although from a migrant
perspective this kind of discourse might be empowering (a question I
will return to shortly), from an analytical and ethical point of view, it is,
of course, not desirable to view Italy or Italians as a homogenous space
and mass (of essentially bad people). Rather, it is more useful to see
immigration in Italy as taking place within the country's complex and
changing sociohistorical structures as this society is altered by transformations that not only inform migrants' experience in Italy but also may
continue to influence representations of immigrants and shape certain
modes of action. As a consequence, while Italian-immigrant relationships
are, of course, influenced by the immigrants' own characteristics—eth-
nicity, gender, livelihood strategies, and the like—they are also largely

formed by processes within Italian society. Indeed, as Jeff Pratt (2002) argues, "We will not understand these relationships, or the racist form they sometimes take, if we treat Italian society as monolithic, pre-formed and immutable" (25).

To begin with, certain important general characteristics of immigration into modern Italy can be identified, especially, as discussed earlier, the sudden influx of mainly non-EU migrants at a time when other EU countries were tightening their immigration controls; the dependence of the underground economy on the migrant workforce, resulting in a pull effect on immigration; and the influence that the structures of the Italian labor market have on not only the lives of the new immigrants but also certain representations of them. But to arrive at a fuller understanding of the migration nexus into which the new immigrants are thrown, certain other, perhaps less material phenomena must be considered.

First, the modern Italian nation-state was an attempt to unify a population characterized by strong class distinctions and strong regional divisions. The building of the Italian nation-state was thus less a question of a homogenous nation coming together and creating an independent state than one of a state creating a nation. Massimo D'Azeglio, one of the architects of the Risorgimento, famously captured this paradox in 1861: "Now we have made Italy, we need to make Italians" (cited in Pratt 2002: 26). However, strong divisions in Italian society persist and give shape and substance to certain discourses and practices. There is not sufficient space here to discuss the many forms these divisions take, but one theme important for contextualizing responses to recent immigration is the division between North and South (Naples being the largest city in southern Italy). The North is characterized in the dominant discourse by "development, rationality, and modernity," whereas the South is characterized as "backward, magical, and archaic." Consequently, one of the central projects of the modern Italian nation-state from the outset has been to make the South more like the North.

This hierarchical division within Italy may entail low self-esteem in the South and affect the Guan migrants to the degree that "self-hatred, and the internalization of the subaltern position," has been detected as a theme in racist practice on the part of southern Italians (Pratt 2002: 29–30, 36). Reflecting this invisible axis, northern Italians have stigmatized southerners by the very same labels that are today deployed to signify immigrants (Mai 2003: 89). Indeed, as Carter (1997) argues, a great deal of the tension concerning the new immigrants stems from the fact that many Italians, having in mind the unresolved issues of southerners' supposed inherent differences, feel that Italy is not "a receiver nation capable of incorporating a permanent migrant community" (213). It could be argued, accordingly, that migrants settle into a well-established North-South dichotomy of difference-making that places them in unfavorable positions as naturally inferior and unwanted and, moreover, that the new immigrants have displaced the dominant discourse; that is, the hierarchical misrepresentation and mistreatment once reserved for southerners is now projected onto immigrants (Mai 2003: 89).

Politically, this theme of North-South difference, and everything symbolically related to the South, such as immigrants, has been part of the agenda of one of the most important political movements in modern Italy, the Lega Nord of Umberto Bossi. The Lega Nord has shaped at least two interrelated political discourses that have substantial backing: first, the idea that northerners are indeed different from southerners, and it is unacceptable that northerners should pay income tax to an external, inefficient if not corrupt, government in Rome, which then "uses the money to support itself and a parasitic South" (Pratt 2002: 37); and second, a normalization of hard rhetoric against immigrants and immigration, sometimes in the form of a crypto-fascist discourse that compares immigration to the Holocaust. In Bossi's words: "Hitler exterminated all the Jews. The communist-masons want to exterminate all the peoples of Europe with immigration. They are true Nazis, red-Nazis" (*La Repubblica*, 13 August 2000, cited in Pratt 2002: 25). The Lega Nord generally encourages supporters in their conviction that "all their problems would be solved by separation from the South, Southerners, and migrants" (Pratt 2002: 36–37). It has not all been rhetoric. During the Berlusconi administration, the Lega Nord succeeded in seeing many of its political views implemented. Umberto Bossi was thus instrumental in tightening the immigration laws. As mentioned earlier, one revision, popularly known as the Bossi-Fini law, bears his name, whereas the latest revision was steered through Parliament by the Lega Nord's interior minister, Roberto Maroni.

In connection with politics, the media debate surrounding immigration into Italy is also worth considering as an aspect of the immigration nexus. One analysis of media representations of immigration in Italy suggests that the 1980s saw the emergence of themes that were elaborated during the 1990s, namely, "the development and institutionalization of an undifferentiated and totalizing notion of 'immigration'; the politicization of the topic; and the thematization of immigration as an area of social conflict." In news articles in the 1990s, the now-established "problem" of immigration became increasingly tied to criminal acts, social deviance, and social disorder (Sciortino and Colombo 2004: 106–108). Without going further into the media aspects of the immigration nexus, it is interesting to note that, while immigrants were increasingly cast in a negative light, the enduring relationship and interdependence between the migrant workforce and the Italian economy received scant attention, as did the conditions of marginality and poverty and the effects these conditions have on migrants' lives (Sciortino and Colombo 2004: 108). Indeed, while the migrants are increasingly seen—both from inside and outside Italy—as "harbingers of disorder and living proof of the incompetence and hypocrisy of southern European governments," they perform an "indispensable service to the Italian economy," taking on all kinds of "dirty work" and thereby helping otherwise unprofitable businesses to survive and supporting Italian living standards (Cole and Booth 2006: 10, 13).

Another theme of the Italian migration nexus is Italy's fascist and colonial past and whether it may continue to shape negative representations and ill-treatment of the new immigrants in Italy. Most researchers, some with more conviction than others, cite this theme as an important factor in explaining the sometimes-hostile responses to immigration in Italy (see, for instance, Daly 1999: 173; Grillo 2002: 11–12; Mai 2003: 90).

According to Mark I. Choate, imperial Italy moved through three stages of expansion in the late nineteenth and early twentieth centuries: (1) as a territorial colonial power occupying what is today Somalia and Eritrea, but shattered by military defeat at the hands of the Ethiopian army in 1896; 2) as an "ethnographic colonial power" boosting the Italian economy by indirectly colonizing North and South America, as when it sponsored development projects for Italian immigrants in South America; and 3) as a territorial colonial power again, as the informal strategy began showing declining returns and could no longer compete with "the grandiose visions, glorious conquests and bloody vengeance promised by the Italian nationalists." This third strategy culminated in the successful wars with Turkey over Libya in 1911 and, during the Mussolini regime, with Ethiopia in 1935–1936, as well as in invasions of the Balkans following the First World War and, again, prior to the Second World War (Choate 2003: 65–72). The Italy of today does not fit easily into a postcolonial context (Grillo 2002: 11), a circumstance reflected, for instance, in the national composition of immigrants, who, aside from Albanians (Italy invaded Albania in 1939), come mainly from countries that have no special relations with Italy, unlike the cases of France and the United Kingdom (Reyneri: 2001: 13). Yet a recurring argument in connection with immigration in Italy is that Italians have yet to come to terms with their fascist and colonial past. Some researchers argue that Italians suffer from "a collective amnesia" (Maher 1996: 162) and falsely appear to nurture somewhat hypocritical images of themselves as "inherently good" or *brava gente,* a line of scholarly argumentation that Robert Ventresca has examined critically (2006: 189).

Indeed, although "something of a consensus emerging among scholars" has formed around the proposition that Italians have yet to come to terms with fascism and the colonial experience, other scholars argue that "Italians have indeed known how to come to terms with their Fascist past, albeit in varied, contradictory, and ambiguous ways" (Ventresca 2006: 189–190). In fact, Ventresca argues, Italy's hastened devotion to a democratic transition in the postwar area itself marked a desire to disassociate itself from the legacy of fascism that arguably paralleled Germany's wish to disassociate itself from Nazism (190). Ironically, not only did this democratic transition, and the later integration into the European

Union, perhaps influence the discourse on migration and migrants positively, as the EU pressured Italy to tighten immigration controls prior to signing the Schengen Accord, but the question of whether Italy could be a full member of the EU hinged both on meeting certain economic standards and on keeping non–EU citizens off the European continent. As a consequence, it seems likely that the demands made by the EU in the early 1990s—and with renewed force in the early twenty-first century, as immigrants continue to enter Italy illegally—have sparked a reemergence of colonial and fascist oppositions between Italians and immigrants, along with the underlying North-South dichotomies discussed above, and thus helped to produce negative stereotyping and mistreatment (Mai 2003: 88).

But the assumption that Italians are in a state of denial should perhaps be scrutinized even further. Robert Ventresca, without wanting to diminish "the obvious and disconcerting omissions in the documentary record and the concomitant weakness in our understandings of, say, Italian Fascism's repressive, racist, and murderous policies, both at home and abroad," argues that "it is hard to imagine a historical question that has animated and dominated contemporary political and social discourse in Italy more than the legacy of Fascism" (Ventresca 2006: 190). However, when it comes to what can be said and done about immigration and immigrants, it appears obvious that the possible absence of a critical postcolonial debate may have affected "the Italian lack of reflection on political correctness" (Riccio 2002: 190; see also Grillo 2002: 11). Nonetheless, the task here is not to decide whether or not Italians have come to terms with their allegedly repressed past—that is, whether the treatment and representation of migrants form a subconscious expression of a colonial past gaining strength in the darkness of national denial. Nor do I seek to question arguments over "how long-lasting have been the effects of the colonial experience, despite its short-lived and disastrous nature" (Grillo 2002: 12), though there certainly are some very interesting observations to be made in this regard. In Naples, for instance, I was surprised to find a Mussolini calendar on a newspaper stand—a phenomenon, mutatis mutandis, impossible to imagine in present-day Germany. Rather, as Grillo points out, there is another, more general issue, one that may be inseparable from the fascist and colonial experience: the much "longer-term, widespread, and diffuse legacy common to many European countries, including those . . . without a history of colonization: the pervasive 'Orientalist' and 'Africanist' conceptions of the Other," a phenomenon especially relevant in the case of Italy, considering the historic cultural and mercantile ties between, for instance, Venetian merchants and the Levant as well as North Africa (Grillo 2002: 12). This consideration, of course, echoes the early anthropological study of how individuals and societies come to terms with people and things that appear strange and unfamiliar, even dangerous—and this could be said for immigrants as well as Italians, despite the power distribution being completely unequal—but is considered somehow crucial to survival (Lévi-Strauss 1969: 54; Jackson 1998: 45). In this sense, an ambiguity might be at play more deep-seated than could possibly be explained by a repressed colonial and fascist past. Nicola Mai has compared the Italian discourse on Albania prior to the fascist invasion of 1939 to that after the collapse of the communist regime in 1991, when Albanians fled in large numbers across the Adriatic Sea to Italy. In identifying two recurring parallel discourses—namely, Albania as the solution to Italy's "demographic, geopolitical, and economic needs," and Albania as "a problem and emergency"—he seems to describe both the possible "subconscious association" between the two countries, grounded in a rejected past of "poverty, dictatorship, and backwardness" (Mai 2003: 86, 88, 90–91), and a general ambiguity surrounding most non-EU immigration into Italy.

To summarize, migrant lives do not unfold against a fixed or essentialized Italian background, but in dynamic relationship with a complex and ever-changing Italian context. Accordingly, when approaching the question of why, in the late eighties and early nineties, migrants in Italy increasingly became the subjects of a "racialized xenophobic political and social discourse, and victims of the reality of xenophobia" (Grillo 2002: 15), a whole range of themes pertaining to the immigration context has to be taken into consideration. But again, these references would benefit from taking into account the immediate context of interdependence between the migrant workforce and the underground economy, and the ambiguity concerning it. As one analysis of the public discourse frames it, "The basic problem does not stem so much from the hostile positions of some political parties, but rather from the more generalized uneasiness in Italy with regard to immigrants, who often feel that they are not treated in a friendly manner and that they are needed but poorly tolerated" (Ammendola et al. 2005: 25). So, while recognizing the importance of engaging critically in the analysis of sociohistorical developments, political discourse, and media representations, and how these inform subjective experience, this book focuses mainly on the everyday empirical context of migrant life: how migrants struggle against unfavorable circumstances, sometimes successfully, to find viable ways of managing their stressful lives. Thus, in accordance with the overall methodological aim, I explore the human capacity to live, in a variety of ways, within circumstances over which one has little control (Jackson 2005: xi). Different methodological approaches yield different results: alongside the macrodynamics of economy, politics, discourse, and so forth, complex microdynamics unfold—most urgently the individuals' own projects as they seek to navigate in an ever-evolving social, political, and historical setting.

So to return to the question of how the Guan migrants experience discrimination on an everyday basis, I now take a closer look at the one place where they came into daily contact, and very often confrontation, with the local Neapolitan community—namely, the public bus system. The buses were a constant source of frustration and anger to the young West African men. Once I moved to the city and thus had to rely on the loathed buses for my daily transportation to the field and back, it was possible to gain a firsthand impression of the situation.

THREE Suffering in a Globalized World

KING GEORGE AND THE CLOWN

Walking, wasting time, and having one's time wasted characterized the experience of migrant life in Castelvolturno. Unlike Italians, West African immigrants walked along the expressway, though some would ride bicycles. The Italians would always drive in cars (sometimes ruthlessly fast), motorcycles, or scooters, unless of course they were looking for companionship or drugs. But stretches of the expressway—around Pescopagano where Sammy lived, for instance—were not intended for pedestrians, and in the hours before daybreak it was especially unsettling to walk there, as the road was unlit and cars drove by at top speed. Samuel would usually walk close to the low fence at the side of the road and wave his hand at approaching cars so they would see us and steer clear. Many times giant trucks, like moving walls of bright lights, would pass by so closely while sounding their horns that it would knock the wind from one's lungs. During the day, the fear of getting "knocked down" was less imminent, though in some stretches the road was a little wider than one would expect and it was not always uncomplicated to reach the other side. At some places along the road were narrow, hidden footpaths connecting one branch of the expressway with another that only the immigrants appeared to know and use.

Farther down the road, in Castelvolturno, the expressway was used for walking up and down. Groups of young men would stand on the sidewalk, talking and shaking hands, while cars passed relentlessly. For the immigrants, these moments of tension and anxiety at the round-abouts, where so much was at stake, were succeeded by moments of unoccupied time, waiting—moments of seemingly aimless strolling up and down the road, running small errands, borrowing a DVD, bumming a cigarette, killing time. In contrast to the perpetual traffic and the busy-ness of the outside world, the sense of being stuck seemed ubiquitous among the immigrants. But if to passersby the expressway was, in the words of Marc Augé, the quintessential example of a "non-place of supermodernity," in representing a liberation from the constraints of the "anthropological place," "a world surrendered to solitary individuality, to the fleeting, the temporary," it simultaneously retained characteristics of the "old anthropological place" to the immigrants living along it, walking along it, having things thrown at them along it. To them the expressway was, rather, part of a relationship, a place formed by bodily engagement, subjective experience, and "the unformulated rules of living know-how" (Augé 1995: 78, 101). Perhaps it is a paradox of late modernity, parallel to the debate on globalization, that inclusion and exclusion both accelerate simultaneously, sometimes in settings shared by those moving and those not moving. In fact, it appears that no matter how close one moves to the centers of mobility—one might even live right on the expressway—inclusion in the circulation of material and symbolic goods always remains at a distance that cannot be bridged, though somehow that fantasy appears to be the very attraction of such places.

I had the opportunity to watch migrant life on the Rome expressway from the porch of an African communication center, where a close informant, Junior Teacher (not be confused with Senior Teacher) worked throughout the week. The center's desk clerk, Junior Teacher would usually sit outside and watch the traffic go by. Whenever he saw fellow immigrants walking up and down the cursed road with expensive new mobile phones, he would shake his head and declare: "They don't even know how to operate it; they'll receive a message, but they can't read it. Around here, you'll never see a black person receiving education, and you'll never see a black policeman." I knew Junior Teacher from the village of Senya Beraku, where he had taught English and Mathematics in a public school prior to leaving. He was one of the few Guan immigrants to have traveled by air to Italy and overstayed his visa. His original plan to pursue a Western education were shattered when he realized his travel documents did not entitle him to study in Italy. Now he was in limbo. Junior Teacher was a skinny, fragile-looking person with a serious frown; he kept mostly to himself, studied the Bible, and played Scrabble on the center's front counter. With the bus stop situated just outside on the street, he would sit in the shade and observe the buses passing by and regularly declining to pick up black people.

Junior Teacher: It's very bad the way the Italians treat us; basically we're second-class citizens. A good example of this is the way we're treated on the bus. When you stand alone at the bus stop, a black person, the bus will just pass. But I don't feel bitter about it. The Italians act out of ignorance, and sometimes you'll get lucky and meet a pleasant one. You know, sometimes they'll stop by here and ask me for the way to Rome—and this *is* the way to Rome! That will tell you that they may never have left Naples. They don't know the outside world.

In the late morning and in the evenings, the bus ride could be quite comfortable. There was no fighting over the seats. Passengers usually included the odd West African going to visit friends along the road; newly arrived immigrants with their belongings in the blue plastic bags handed out at the reception centers; middle-aged Russian ladies going and coming home from their work as housemaids, reading magazines written in Cyrillic. It was possible on such rides to relax while driving through Castelvolturno and sit in silence while passing the fishmonger's store; the dairies where they made buffalo mozzarella; deserted houses with groups of rough-looking people outside; the marble outlet; the African stores advertising Nigerian horror movies; the filling stations; the Romany campsite; a shop yard with religious artifacts in plaster—full-size figures of Jesus, the Virgin Mary, and San Gennaro, the patron saint of Naples. In the early mornings, however, the bus ride was quite another story.

The early-morning bus ride is crucial to the young African men because, if they are unable to board the scheduled ride to the city, they will arrive late at the pickup points in Naples where contractors and farmers hire people to work in the underground economy, and the chance of finding a job for the day will be lost. To the immigrants working with a regular *capo*, the bus ride is equally important, for, more often than not, if a migrant worker arrives late, he'll be told to leave and come back the next day. Usually, the opportunity for day-laboring is over by 7 or 7:30 in the morning, making it necessary to get on the first bus out of Castelvolturno by 5 at the latest. However, there were not enough buses for all the riders, and every morning before the crack of dawn, fights would break out at the bus stops along the expressway among young men pushing hard to board. Among them was Benjamin, the Senya Beraku informant who had lived in Naples for some years but, much to his regret, had never secured contract work with a regular *capo*. Instead, he would be on the expressway every morning in fierce competition with the newly arrived.

Benjamin: It's very bad. People are stepping on your feet; people are pushing, the big ones trying to outweigh the smaller ones. It's like living in the jungle—the strongest survives. Sometimes—no, most of the time—we fight each other. We, the blacks, we fight. You'll be sitting in a seat and somebody will be sleeping on you. You can't complain, because the person can find nowhere to rest. The person is lying on you. In the morning the crowd is too much. We, the immigrants, we don't have places to stay here, so if you see another black person, you'll follow him and stay where he stays. So our places get crowded. And nobody wants to miss the first three buses at 4:30, 5, and 5:30. With those buses it is a big problem. Those who wait for the 6 [or] 6:30 buses, those are the people who have regular jobs, but even then the buses are full too.

Going home in the late afternoon, the bus situation is equally difficult to deal with. Many are tired from hard work at the construction sites and would like to sit and rest for the two-hour ride. One of the strategies is to stand next to a white person.

Benjamin: We know that normally the whites will never go to the last stop, so we try to stand beside the whites, and when they get up, you take their seat because it's a long journey, a two-hour journey. So I'll be standing in front of the white, and another person will be standing behind the white, and when the white gets up, everybody will be making an attempt to take that seat for himself. So, if, let's say, I touch the seat first with my behind, then the next person will also have a leg or a hand in there—who is ready to give in to the other? And it becomes a fight and the strongest survive. This happens every day. We know that the whites won't be going to the end of the line, so we use them as our target to sit down. The journey is two hours, and you have been standing throughout the day and you would like to rest before you get home.

When you come home, you cannot go to sleep straightaway. You have to prepare your food, take your bath, and you prepare for the next day. Maybe change your clothes, wash your socks, do a few things around the house—so when you're in the bus, you would like to sit and relax for those two hours. A little nap, something.

Many, including Sammy, adopted the strategy of moving farther up the expressway to the bus station in Mondragone, from where the bus departed, in order to avoid the morning scramble at stops closer to Castelvolturno. But the immigrants living down the road, closer to Naples, quickly adopted countermeasures. They would get up at 4 and take the bus in the opposite direction, all the way to the station in Mondragone, to get a seat on the first bus heading back to Naples. Such strategies, however, did not protect the immigrants against the brutal fact that many times the bus drivers simply ignored them. As Benjamin described the situation: "They don't respect foreigners—blacks, to be precise. For instance, you'll be standing at the bus stop and the bus will pass by. But if you're standing there, a black together with a white, the bus will stop, no matter how full it is."

Much depended on the inclination of the driver. Sammy directed my attention to a bus driver that I too eventually came to seriously dislike. A short, soft-looking man in his late fifties with brown, curly hair and a wry, self-assured face, he looked like a clown out of makeup, with that same sad face that encapsulates the tragic nature of the clown as he steps into a bucket with his oversize feet. But I never saw him smile or offer a friendly gesture, which of course is the quality that makes a clown enjoyable to watch, even amusing at times. This observation aside, the Clown's most frustrating feature was his idiosyncratic driving. If a passenger pushed the stop button at a point when in the Clown's world it was too late—even if it was well before the bus stop—he drove calmly by, unaffected by the passengers' appeals, and continued to the next stop, though it might be several kilometers ahead. At other times he ignored the ring completely or pretended not to have heard it. He never showed any regret for such incidents; it was as if the West African passengers did not exist for him. Sometimes he shrugged his shoulders without lifting his hands from the wheel, as if he couldn't care less whether a person would have to walk for hours to get home. The Clown also drove deliberately slowly. Sammy pointed this fact out to me, and after a while I began to see what he meant, though I liked this difference to begin with—most drivers drive too fast and take too many chances. But gradually one came to hate the Clown's driving. Approaching an intersection, he would never try to make the green light, instead slowing down to what seemed like a walking pace, as if to make sure the light would change to red so he could again bring the bus to a full, lengthy stop. Stopping the bus seemed to please him, as he rested his elbows on the wheel, gazing indifferently at the road ahead through his weird swollen eyes.

"I hate this man very much," Sammy would often say, and spending a lot of time in buses going back and forth between my place in the city and the field, I eventually understood why. The Clown embodied the whole experience of having one's time wasted, or put another way, his lethargic handling of the bus invited riders to project on him their frustrations over constantly being made to feel worthless—the places where they were going, the things they were involved in, their timetables rendered as of no importance. As Pierre Bourdieu argues, if one's time is the rarest and most personal object of exchange, then what is received in return—that is, the price of one's time on the labor market or the symbolic services associated with one's time, such as eager attentiveness to one's words or needs—is a mark of one's social importance. Conversely, having one's time wasted or negated is a central experience for the subalterns of the world in the sense that "the art of . . . making people wait, of delaying without destroying hope, of adjourning without totally disappointing, which would have the effect of killing the waiting itself, is an integral part of the exercise of power" (Bourdieu 2000: 228).

The West African immigrants in Castelvolturno experienced this relationship between time and power in many different forms: in the time-consuming walk along a road on which others were driving by at expressway speeds; in waiting for the bus, sometimes but not always in vain; in putting up with the moody ways some drivers drove their vehicles. One day a driver drove straight past every stop in Castelvolturno, and Samuel, as always ready to fight for his rights, went to him and complained. The driver explained that at an earlier stop an African passenger had tried to board the bus without a ticket; angered by this, the driver now wouldn't allow any black person on board during the ride. Clearly, such a whimsical dismissal of rules and regulations, and of the waiting passengers' time and, by extension, their objectives and very persons, bespeaks this particular field of social relations and its inherent power discrepancies in a way that cannot be understood unless the temporal dimension is taken into consideration. Paradoxically, following Bourdieu, this time dimension of the social field becomes noticeable only when efforts are thwarted. One is almost unaware of the sense of time and being when one is preoccupied with an "illusio" or a "center of interest"; it passes from unnoticed to noticed only when the connection between one's expectations and the tendencies of the world with regard to accommodating these expectations is broken (Bourdieu 2000: 208). Most of us who have read a book, fished, or been in the company of friends have had the sudden realization that time has passed unnoticed, whereas waiting for the bus and seeing that bus drive by without stopping are time-stopping, and therefore time-exposing, predicaments for migrants in Naples. But this kind of time exposure, when time is either arbitrarily wasted or simply negated, is a form of nontime, a testimony to one's social insignificance, a time that does not unfold in connection with any aim or expectation but marks the end of the possible. As such, it is time to be killed, as in the strolling or the window-shopping that occupies migrants' time (Bourdieu 2000: 223).

Billy provided another example of such time killing. More precisely, he had devised a way of coping with the pain of not moving closer to his goals. He had been without work for a long time and had on several occasions declared that he had stopped looking altogether because he couldn't be bothered anymore. Instead, he would get drunk, put a cigarette in the corner of his mouth, and walk down the expressway looking determined, as if he had somewhere very important to go. "I just like moving," he said when I once asked him about these walks.

The life-world of the migrants, however, contained many surprises, and not only negative ones. In contrast to the detested Clown and his seeming perverse joy in wasting passengers' time was the man the Ghanaians called King George. This tall, long-legged, wild-eyed bus driver was a Moroccan-Italian who, according to migrant legend, had once lived in the cool, green hills of Kumasi, the Ashanti capital of Ghana, where he was employed by an international chain of luxury hotels to drive wealthy American and European holiday visitors around the country to see the sights. King George behaved in keeping with his name (though the migrants appeared unaware of the historical mad English king). Like a madman, he barely watched the road as he blazed through Castelvolturno at full speed while sticking his head out of the driver's cubicle to scream down the aisle in Twi. He demanded that all black passengers come to the driver's seat and kiss the fake diamond ring on his little finger, as one would greet the Ashanti king, and he wouldn't give it a rest until every black person had done so—Ghanaian or not. "Ohene George!" (King George), he would yell down the aisle of the bus; "Nana George!" (King George). "Me nua, me nua, bra, bra" (My brother, my brother, come here, come here"). "Wodin de sen?" (What is your name?). "Ye fre me Nana George, Ohene George" (My name is King George, King George). "Wo shoua! Wo shoua!" ("Your testicles! Your testicles!" The meaning being "King George my ass!"). When a black newcomer stepped on the bus, King George would start afresh: "Bra, bra." Sometimes he would even halt the bus for black people walking along the expressway—with no bus stop anywhere in sight—to inquire whether they might fancy a ride to town. King George, though a well-meaning, if slightly condescending, ally of the immigrants in their ongoing struggle with the bus system and its ways of making them feel small and insignificant, contrasted with the everyday nullification. But the fantastic character that prompted him to do so somehow also reduced the real value of this recognition for the migrants; it was as if only a crazy person would be nice to the immigrants.

Benjamin: Yes, King George. He drives very fast, at top speed. He tries to speak a little bit Ghanaian. You have to kiss his ring as a sign of respect before you get on board. We take it as a joke, and he's one person who keeps us happy on the bus. The rest never talk to you. Sometimes you go to ask a question, but they don't respond.

Except for shops and workplaces, the transportation system is often the only place where West Africans are physically close to Italians, but contact is rarely established. In fact, informal segregation is observable. The few whites sit in the front of the bus, while the blacks sit at the back. Some migrants, including Samuel, disregarded this system, however, and always fought for a place at the front of the bus. Sammy's quarrel with the old woman, described earlier, should be viewed in this light. According to the migrants, another factor that sabotages any contact between the West Africans and the Italians—though they share the same physical space for hours—is the dirty, worn-out, sweaty clothes they are wearing as they come home from a long day at work. Their appearance and odor, they believe, often reduces the chances of engaging in friendly conversation with an Italian passenger.

Benjamin: That is the main reason why the Italian citizens don't want to sit together with us, because the scent is too much; you can't take it. You just imagine, somebody standing on his feet for a good ten hours working—and then that person is coming back wearing the same work attire with all the sweat and the scent sticking to his clothes. The smell that comes out from this person . . . it's not easy.

This problem had encouraged some migrants to carry extra clothes in their rucksacks to enhance chances of meeting Italians, though as yet without any positive results.

Benjamin: Foreigners, especially blacks, are not known in this part of the world. Because when we came [to Italy], we would sit on the bus, and where you would sit there was space all right—but none of the whites would like to sit next to us. Previously, they were complaining about the way we dressed, but now most people have changed the way they dress, and some people even carry perfume in their bags just to give themselves a nice body smell, so that the whites would sit down with us and chat with us, in order for the whites to get used to us, but up until now that is not happening. For example, if people say they have an Italian friend, whether a boy or a girl, man or woman, that means they are getting some kind of services from you, and when that service is over, that is the end of the relationship. So here we don't have any kind of intimate friendship with them, not any kind of closeness. There's a separation. When you get on the bus, you can see for yourself. Always, the blacks are sitting in the back of the bus, and the whites are sitting in the front.

This sense of nullification, not just in connection with the workplace and the transportation system, but as a general failure to create an all-important connection between one's aspirations and where the world takes one is explored later in this chapter, as are the techniques of "re-enchantment" the migrants resort to when real participation is denied.

PERMANENTLY WAITING

During fieldwork, Benjamin, whom I have cited many times already, became almost a second research assistant for me next to Samuel, always taking time to shed light eloquently on the life experiences of the young Guan men in Naples. Since he had not been fortunate enough to secure regular work and still relied on day-laboring, his insights were especially helpful. Benjamin lived under Francis's roof along with about twenty other people. He was a Senya man who had a diploma in agriculture from a Ghanaian university but had been unable to find work. "I didn't have a big man to push me," he explained. Having lost patience, he traveled to Europe in search of brighter opportunities. But, as should be clear by now, coming to Italy and working and living as an illegal immigrant does not guarantee that a the connection between one's expectations and the willingness of the world to accommodate those expectations will necessarily be established. Benjamin gave me three formal interviews, the first one on 5 May and the last one (as follows) on 16 December 2005:

Benjamin: The job situation is worse than when we met initially, because the number of people here has increased. Every morning at 4:30 I leave my house and go to my usual joint and stand at the roadside, and [then] come back empty-handed. That has been the trend for the past three months. Only three jobs in November and December, 80 Euros in three months—after rent, light bill, gas, you're left with nothing. We're living from hand to mouth. We get little support from Caritas, food and clothes, because the money cannot see you through. Normally, I go for rice, oil, and tomatoes [from Caritas]. They also give out cooked meals in the morning and in the afternoon, so those who don't have places can eat there.

I sometimes feel so downhearted when I have to make that journey. That was not my plan coming here, and I don't know what is happening. Sometimes I feel shy about going there because I see that place as for those who have given up. When you go, you see these junkies and drunkards—they come there to eat because they have no other place to go to—and you queue up with them for food, and then you feel like your purpose for coming to Italy has been defeated. So I feel very sorry every time I have to go there; I feel very sorry for myself.

Times were especially difficult for the Guan informants when the Christmas season was approaching. Often they would find themselves with little or no money to take care of basic everyday needs; at the same time, family and friends at home would put them under increasing pressure to send back gifts and money.

Benjamin: The calls keep on coming for Christmas. They start calling you to remind you that they need to get new clothes for Christmas and eat better food, maybe get a chicken or a goat, a change of diet, and you being a brother in Europe—where we all know it's heaven on earth—definitely, you have to send something. And if you don't send it, they'll be saying all kinds things about you; that you've abandoned the family. So, the calls keep coming—I've just received one right now before you came, when I was in the other room. For three months now, they haven't heard anything from me, and Christmas is just around the corner. I have about three friends requesting mobile phones, a junior brother asking for shoes, and my mother is also on the line. She'll not ask, but it's my duty to give her something. But whatever I do, it'll never be enough. The more you send, the more requests you'll receive. People are thinking: so Benjamin sent this brother a mobile telephone; let me also try to call him and see if he'll send me one. I tell them the truth—that I don't have a job. But they don't believe it; they don't believe that I still don't have a permanent job after almost two years in Italy. They're saying that I'm wicked and selfish; they say that everything I have I want to spend on myself. And the African family system is not like that. We have the extended type of family—whoever is successful must reach out to those less privileged. They know it's my duty, and they keep worrying me until I send them something. So the little money I make, I try to save something and send it back to them, however small the amount may be. It makes me angry sometimes, because I already have a lot of problems to deal with and more pressure is coming from home. If you don't look out, you may end up doing things you're not supposed to do. The situation will push a person into crime, for instance, because you need the money. You have promised a lot of people, and you really need to get that money. If you don't get them anything, they'll say that you're useless. They'll say, "All your friends came out here and they're making it, and you alone always keep complaining that you don't have a job. That's why you're useless, and you're selfish, and you're spending your money on women and drinks—you're going to discos and having a good time." Some even say that they wouldn't like to have anything to do with you anymore.

H.L.: How do you keep up your courage?
Benjamin: I keep on hoping. I keep hoping that one day the Lord will smile down on us and we'll get our documents, so that we'll be allowed to find regular work, and change this life-style and the life-style of my family, as I have promised to do. That keeps me going. I have been tempted on so many occasions to say that God has forgotten the Africans. Look at our forefathers who were slaves . . . and the kind of jobs we do and the salaries we make. The hardships are just too much. And here I am praying every morning and every evening, attending church as usual, trying to stay out of trouble and not do anything that is sinful—and yet still I can't break through. Sometimes I don't know whether God is still having his eye on us, because things are tough, really tough.

The hardships of life in Naples are endured because there is no alternative. Returning to Ghana empty-handed is not an option for many illegal immigrants, whose families have invested money in their journeys and have great expectations of those who have gone abroad. These unfulfilled promises and unpaid debts to relatives at home are an added burden amidst the other challenges of migrant life and are a concern for most immigrants in Italy. They are often forced to prolong their stay, though their lives become increasingly difficult—because if they returned home empty-handed, "they would be walking dead men" (Reyneri 2001: 18). One way of dealing with illegal migrant life, especially the difficulties of obtaining documents, is to put on hold the expectations one had upon arriving, put away the sense of failure associated with those expectations, and submerge oneself in the effort to keep one's head above water. Very often, as mentioned earlier, this postponing of plans while struggling to gain a foothold in Italian society and desperately watching one's plans fall apart becomes a permanent state of affairs. Having been disappointed so many times, Junior Teacher, for instance, eventually refused to speculate about obtaining documents, though that had been his original purpose in coming to Italy.

Junior teacher: There's word that's been echoed around that they'll be issuing documents very soon, very soon. But they have been saying this ever since I arrived two years ago. It cannot be predicted. You can't make any meaningful plan; it really makes the heart sink. Myself, I have taken my eyes off the documents. Finding work helps you take your mind off the documents. Now my focus is on the work and on being able to get out with a few thousand Euros.

Another way of viewing this indefinite postponement of one's hopes was expressed by Jonathan, another Senya Beraku captain, whom Samuel and I visited a couple of times during fieldwork. Jonathan held a special position among his fellow Guan migrants. He was a strong, square-shouldered man, a fisherman by trade, and the type who could always make people around him laugh. Samuel used to say that, when he felt down about life in Naples, he would go see Jonathan. On one occasion Jonathan was on the bus without having purchased a ticket when a controller appeared. But when he turned to Jonathan, it so happened that the driver suddenly had to break hard, throwing the controller on the floor of the bus. When he got up, he was so confused that he forgot all about checking Jonathan. "That was the ghost of my father pushing him away," Jonathan exclaimed to the amusement of the rest of the Ghanaian passengers. "He's always with me, protecting me."

Jonathan was also a lady's man and the first of the Senya guys to ever "chase a white lady." In this capacity, he would advise others on how to handle women. One of his more extraordinary tricks involved a toad. "Liberian women love the toad. If you present a Liberian girl with a toad," he claimed, "she'll treat you like some kind of husband." Although he was one to stand us up, when he missed interview appointments, we could always forgive him because of his great spirit. It seemed as if everybody, perhaps for his own sake, needed Jonathan to be this strong, courageous person whom nothing could keep down, not even the miserable state of affairs in Naples. As we stood with him and a group of other informants one evening in the railway station in Rome, waiting for the endless rain to cease, he suddenly cried out, "We're from the beach! Why should we mind a little water?" And he marched out into the street. A moment later, he was instructing an African drunk staggering around in the pouring rain with a bottle of wine to find somewhere private to finish his drink, so that his drunkenness wouldn't reflect badly on all black people. As a man having certain inclinations of his own, Jonathan would characteristically not tell the man to abstain altogether. "You try to carry the cross like Jesus Christ," he said, "but even the Lord himself couldn't do it. He had to have people to come and help him. So really, my brother, the cross is too heavy and it might fall on you and hurt you."

Addressing the need to cope with suffering while postponing expectations, Jonathan came up with an analogy to farmwork. However necessary to survival, farmwork in Senya is commonly considered the most tedious and undignified occupation, and comparing a work situation to it testifies strongly to that situation's undesirability. According to Jonathan, a certain plant grows at the farm, *sason*, that "burns very well."

Jonathan: If it touches your skin, you'll be itching and burning, and there is nothing you can do about it. That's like our life here in Naples. We have already been burnt, yet we have no money and the things we want for ourselves are not coming, so what can we do? We are already in it. We have to wait for the good things to come, and the expectations that we had when we came to be fulfilled, and to endure whatever awaits us. We just have to keep on trying.

It's like if you have bought a drum, but if you play it, your mother will die, and if you don't play it, your mother will die anyway, so why wouldn't you play it?

Benjamin: My brother is right. You feel the pain inside, but there's nothing you can do about it. If you don't go to that pickup joint, you'll go hungry; if you don't go to that place, you'll sleep outside because you don't have money to pay the rent. This thing is paining you all right, but you can't leave, you have no other alternative. You're forced to do it—though inwardly you don't like it.

If this aspect of illegal immigrant life can be described in one word, it might well be "suffering." That is, if, following Arthur Kleinman, we define suffering as involving those critical events in life in which people come up against resistance to their actions and life plans and when "resources are limited, often desperately so," when "vicious cycles of depravation and oppression make misery the routine local condition," or when "people are rendered wretched as a normal, day-to-day condition." In this sense, "suffering" aptly describes this "dark side of experience . . . with all its moral and somatic resonances" (Kleinman 1992: 174).

Benjamin: We know from the Bible that man must sweat to get his daily bread, but this is too much, the sweat is too painful . . . eight to ten hours carrying cement, stones, sand up a six-story building—that, my brother, is not easy. To succeed, you have to suffer—but to me, this is not the kind of suffering that our forefathers were talking about. This is more painful, more hectic. Sometimes I feel the pain, and when I'm alone in my room, I cry. I shed tears because what we heard about Europe in Africa, that's not what I am seeing. If we were treated right, I think we could contribute to the development of the nation. If they would just allow us . . . Most of the blacks can be competitive in so many fields, but, no, here the door is totally shut. They won't allow you, even if you know how to do it. We, the blacks, have all that it takes, and yet we feel so defeated all the time.

Emotionally, it affects your attitude toward other human beings, like when you're ordered to do something by means of a gun, you tend to become fearless and whatever actions you decide to take, you don't think about it twice, you go straight ahead, you also become that brutal. You have no emotional attachment to human beings, because anything can happen at any time. Psychologically, you become some kind of . . . you have no emotions or feelings for your fellow human beings; you can decide to do anything, at any time. We're seeing the effects here, we see our friends doing certain things we don't understand, that are not common with us where we come from. Somebody can just take a bottle and knock you on the head when he's annoyed. So, when you live in this kind of environment, these are some of the influences that you see on your life. If you're not careful, you'll also lose sight of who you are, what you want to do in life, because sometimes you feel like giving up totally.

However, once people have accepted or have become resigned to such a hostile environment—an environment one may describe, following Jackson (2005), as "all-taking"—it also functions as a social and existential relation. In fact, the data presented here suggest that even a place full of suffering and humiliation like Castelvolturno eventually becomes familiar and inhabitable. As Sammy described the phenomenon: "When I first came to Castelvolturno, I hated the place. Now it feels a little bit like home." As with day-laboring, the Guan migrants lower their expectations to a minimum, or below zero, and are therefore never, on the face of it, disappointed when dispossessed materially or emotionally. One might suffer along the way—for an illegal immigrant in Naples, suffering is guaranteed—but one's expectations of misfortune and mistreatment are nevertheless met, however negatively. But again, such a moral rearmament, though it reduces social complexity, is psychologically hard to manage. Becoming "brutal," as Benjamin put it, is a way of toughening up, protecting oneself against an all-taking environment. But, as the data imply, it provides no peace of mind. Existentially, this foretelling of the inevitable unfortunate turn of the world appears to hold a kind of *defeatist agency* for the deprived in the sense that knowing what the world has in store for you is possible only as a result of mastering the circumstances you are thrown into, which again seems almost to border on somehow assisting the outcome. An example of this might be the Neapolitan men driving restlessly up and down the expressway night and day, with almost tragicomic regularity, in search of black girls or eastern European prostitutes. This practice encapsulates for many West African immigrants the essential "wickedness of the whites," which not only black people are powerless against but also to a degree the Neapolitans themselves, as if the latter were brute animals, slaves to their own desires, passive tools in the hands of their own predictable natures.

The winter season came. The Nigerian girls on the dirt road leading to Samuel's house built a small charcoal grill out of scrap metal and gathered around the fire, warming their hands. One day, I met Linda on the bus going home and sat next to her. She was the most provocative of the girls when she was on the street, both in the way she dressed and in the way she addressed the customers who came by. But on the bus she was so timid and quiet that it was hardly possibly to understand a word she said, and she avoided eye contact. When I asked what she was doing for Christmas, she said, "Nothing." She never did anything. When she was not working, she practically whispered, she just stayed at home.

THE GLOBAL DISCONNECT?

The question remains, then, why this suffering in Naples is preferable to life in the village in Ghana with one's friends and family (bearing in mind that while the suffering, or at least its intensity, came as a surprise to most, few regretted having come in the first place). Sammy gave one answer, quoted in the preface, one day while walking the dirt road to his house. Although life in Naples was hard and disappointing, it was "always better than to rot away in the village in Ghana." This likening of life in the village with symbolic death, as if one were a corpse rotting away, may go a long way toward explaining the choices the young Guan men made as they risk their lives coming to Italy and endure the pains of Naples. Perhaps, if one is already dead, socially and existentially, there is not much to lose, whereas there is a whole new life to be gained if one manages to reach the European continent. In this respect, the Guan fishermen's suffering is different from the chronic suffering of North Americans discussed by Arthur Kleinman (2005), in the sense that the

West African emigrants have a geographical place to reach where the pain might be relieved. There is a practical, though difficult and deadly, solution at hand, namely, illegal migration from one continent to another. Accordingly, one way of understanding illegal immigration to Europe is to consider the larger context in which it occurs: the global political economy. (This focus alone, however, cannot provide a satisfying answer. To reach a more comprehensive understanding of the processes that push and pull people toward risking their lives to migrate, regional differences also have to be taken into account—that is, local economic and social transformations and the negative impact these changes can have on individual life-worlds. I explore the question of illegal immigration in local, ethnographic detail in part 3.) Eschewing a causal explanation of these processes, which would seem to presuppose fixed and bounded entities, I prefer, following Norbert Elias (1970), to describe the constantly changing pattern of immigration as a "figuration," consisting of certain "chains of interdependence" (for instance, the complex chains of interdependence between the EU, Italy, Libya, the Italian underground economy, the migrant work force, and the Guan fishing industry); such links are determined by one another, though, of course, some are privileged in terms of power (Elias 1970: 129–132).

Although times are hard in Senya Beraku because of the decline in local fishing, no wars or famines in Ghana have prompted the exodus of young men to Europe. Rather, it appears to be a question of their desiring to move upward socially and economically; as Bobby, the nightshift worker, explained: "We are not totally poor, but we still need to see an improvement." In fact, most immigrants in Italy come from a country with an "intermediate level of development, . . . at a disadvantage but not completely poverty-stricken," and the immigrants themselves "are not the poorest people from these countries, but rather those who are at a relative disadvantage, but possess the material and cultural resources to face the costs and hardships presented by emigration" (Reyneri 2001: 10). Moreover, two surveys conducted in the Milan area show that African migrants, North Africans excluded, have a relatively high educational level, about 40 percent of the respondents stating that they had completed high school (11). These numbers, however, do not directly apply to the Guan migrants, because the educational level of immigrants is higher in the Milan area than in Naples, and many Guan migrants are fishermen and therefore have certain practical skills that allow them to migrate, though their financial and educational resources might be below average. Nevertheless, rather than a group of hungry and desperate people seeking refuge from chaos in their home countries, as in the popular imagination, many African migrants coming to Italy belong to the "elite youth of their own countries, who most intensely feel the gap between expectations and reality" (Reyneri 2001: 12). In contrast, "the poorest tend to migrate less than those who are slightly better off" (de Haas 2008: 832). Although migration as the last means of survival does take place, "most new immigrants are simply escaping from the downfall of their growing expectations caused by the globalization of the Western everyday life models" (Reyneri 2001: 13). Again, the political economy of the globalized world and its inherent polarization—that is, the parallel mechanisms of inclusion and exclusion—appear to play an important role in understanding illegal immigration to Europe and the risks immigrants take. To better grasp the experience of such a gap between one's expectations and where one is taken by the world, a subsequent section explores questions of connectedness and disconnectedness in social and intersubjective life. But first, what are we talking about, when we talk of globalization?

One of the problems, at least for an anthropological understanding of the phenomenon, is that globalization simultaneously entails growing connectedness and increasing disconnectedness in the world. Indeed, while the world becomes intensively interconnected (for some)—people, capital, goods, and images moving rapidly between places; new flows, links, and modes of action developing; social, cultural, and political practices expanding, making long-distance action possible—there are other people and places whose experiences are marginal to or excluded from this allegedly shrinking world—"and this, too, is the world of globalization" (Inda and Rosaldo 2003: 4). Globalization, then, whether one is for or against the universal spread of capitalism, is not the fait accompli of popular Western belief (Beck 2000: 19). Whereas some things may indeed circulate all over the world (for instance, the accelerated worldwide diffusion of images, movies, music, and ideas), jobs, technology, and wealth are not inclined to so circulate but are rather features of "the global disconnect" (Ferguson 2003: 136). Consequently, it is useful to distinguish between a material and economic dimension of globalization on the one hand and an immaterial and cultural dimension on the other. (Of course, this distinction is ideal; in reality it would be difficult to determine which dimension, say, a pair of sneakers falls into). That is to say, globalization may reach all corners of the world, but only as a promise of wealth. To be sure, the desired economic and material resources of the globalized world may move faster and faster, but they appear mainly to follow the same patterns as always (Beck 2000: 20).

Indeed, the discontent that makes the world's poor people lose patience is perhaps best viewed, not as resistance to global capitalism or cultural hegemony, but as a consequence of the *absence* of full-scale material and economic integration, the unfulfilled promise of which might be the only thing really circulating all over the world. (Of course, such integration is in itself no guarantee of happiness and equality; rather, as Amartya Sen argues, it is a question of providing people and societies with "the means to build destinies worthy of their expectations" [cited in Cohen 2006: 166].) As Daniel Cohen (2006) argues, "The new global economy creates an unprecedented rupture between the expectations to which it gives birth and the reality it brings about. Never before have means of communication—the media—created such a global consciousness; never have the economic forces been so far behind the new awareness. For the majority of the poor inhabitants of our planet, globalization is only a fleeting image. What we too often ignore, however, is how strong this image is, how pregnant with promises yet to be fulfilled" (6). In this connection, James Ferguson provocatively advises anthropologists to be careful not to overlook extreme inequality in promoting cultural diversity. When the disconnected embrace real or imagined Western standards and the expectations they engender, this should not be viewed as undesirable "mental colonization or capitulation to cultural imperialism, but an aspiration to overcome categorical subordination" (Ferguson 2006: 20). In this respect, the critical literature on globalization is strangely out of place in an African context. "Most Africans can hardly feel they are being dominated by being forced to take on the goods and forms of homogenizing global culture when those goods and forms are, in fact, largely unavailable to them" (Ferguson 2006: 21). In this way, Ferguson offers a clue for the question posed above as to why the suffering in Naples is preferable to life in the village with friends and family. He reminds us not to assume that family and friends can replace growth and progress, or to assume that the African village's cultural diversity, held so dear by anthropologists, is always better than the homogenization of the globalized world, when in fact modern African village life may be "simply a polite name for poverty" (Ferguson 2006: 21).

To sum up, theorists of globalization look at roughly two different and simultaneous developments: the heightening and intensifying of exchange between the world's richer countries, and the poor countries having less and less business with the world while being spectators of an increasing cultural globalization. Concurrently, there are at least two radically different human experiences of globalization: one an experience of being inside the circulation of material and symbolic goods and having greater freedom of movement to pursue desirable destinations and courses of action (in fact, the psychology of late modernity identifies the endless options open to people in the West as a source of growing stress and concern [Jørgensen 2002: 141]); and the other an experience of being on the outside, of belonging to a geographical place cut off from the globalized world, with little or no possibility of movement and little power to influence one's circumstances. "Some can now move out of the locality—any locality—at will," Zygmunt Bauman argues. "Others watch helplessly the sole locality they inhabit moving away from under their feet" (1998: 18). And there is no reason to believe that these two modes of experience will converge into one global experience; that is, whether one is for globalization, believing that capitalist dynamics can funnel wealth to the poor, or whether one is against globalization because it imposes capitalism on the rest of the world and may, among other things, exploit the less privileged, the presumption that in the end globalization will unite the world in one homogeneous system may be altogether incorrect. However depressing this prospect may be, "it would be better to say," Cohen (2006) argues, "that these [poor] countries suffer from being abandoned to their fate" (1). In this connection it could be added that in their willingness to risk it all, West African migrants may in fact "succeed" in securing so-called "dirty work" in Europe as more or less exploited workers in the underground economy, barely tolerated legally or socially. But for many, the great distance covered and the untold hardships endured have not brought them any closer to the circulation of material and symbolic goods, except in a purely physical way.

This experience of disconnectedness—even after arrival in Europe— is worth keeping in mind when trying to grasp a phenomenon that continually puzzled me during fieldwork in Naples: why immigrants were so passionate about mobile phones. Having left the detention camps, the first thing many would do was to purchase an expensive mobile phone—not just any mobile phone, but often the most "powerful" one they could find. And thereafter they would talk about phones, remain on the lookout for better phones, put money aside for them. There were practical reasons for this. The mobile phone is a necessary tool for arranging work situations with employers and, of course, for keeping in contact with family members at home, especially since documents are required to access the Internet in Italy. But, of course, the mobile phone is also the quintessential symbol of having connections to the world, to another social and political reality. It contains the promise or potentiality of connectedness, while emphasizing the very lack of these forces in one's life by reminding one, as does all new technology in a West African context, of "the existence of better times and places" (Vigh 2009: 103). As such, the acquisition of a "powerful" mobile phone may be viewed as a kind of magical reversal of one's exclusion from the circulation of material and symbolic goods or, perhaps, as one of "the avenues to re-enchantment" that thrives in circumstances in which real participation is denied (Jackson 2005: xxv).

Viewed from this perspective, it is striking that the immigrants gather every day around the shopwindows in the Piazza Garibaldi to admire, discuss, and fantasize about the newest mobile phones on display. And bargains are struck outside these stores too. Farther down the street, outside the main Naples train station where groups of junkies and homeless people gather in the evening to sleep on cardboard boxes, one can watch the ever-busy mafia infantry trying to persuade passersby to buy stolen mobile phones at amazingly low prices. At the other end of the square lies the marketplace, which has a special area reserved for the sale of used mobile phones. On most Saturdays it is almost impossible to enter this area, so packed is it with immigrants seeking a look at the mobile phones. Here, it is relatively safe to buy a phone; you get what you pay for, and you're allowed to test the phone with your own SIM card before putting the money down, which is not always the case with mafia salesmen. Their offer is too good to be true. Unfortunately, this is a lesson one learns only after spending time in Naples. Newcomers are often tempted by the sudden chance to acquire an expensive mobile, of the finest quality and design, for next to nothing.

One informant, Eric, gave in to temptation and bought an expensive mobile phone at less than half price, but when he got it home, the wrapping contained a bottle of mineral water instead. He went back to complain, but his objections were not welcome. A goon appeared from out of nowhere and slapped him so hard across the face that it knocked him off his feet and he rolled on the sidewalk. But there were also rumors about effective strategies to pursue in handling the mafia. Samuel, together with a colleague, had acquired a Motorola V1, the most sought-after phone at the time. One of them tested the phone, the other handed over the money, and when they were then offered a phone wrapped in its original box, it was politely declined. "The trick is never to let go of the phone once you have tested it and you know it is working."

Even if there are ways of handling the mafia, this kind of business is morally problematic. A phone obtained in this way is likely to have been stolen from a fellow immigrant. Coming home in the evening, Samuel knew very well that criminals could be waiting in cars parked with their headlights off on the dirt road leading to his house, and the first thing they would look for, apart from money, was a mobile phone. In fact, only a short time after my departure for Denmark, Samuel had his new phone stolen in this very manner, after having invested in a new Motorola V1 a large portion of the money he had earned translating. This risk of being robbed was one reason that many migrants, if they could afford to, had two mobile phones—an old worn-out model for the workplace and for moving around Naples, and a nice Sunday phone for church and social situations. The point here is that nobody seemed to take so great an interest in the mobile phone as the illegal immigrants. The design, the screen displays, the features, the ring tones, the accessories—everything was indulged in with great passion.

Sonny: The phone really disturbs us guys a lot. We came here with the aim of bringing something back with us to Africa. So this buying of new phones regularly upsets our money situation. Instead of saving money, we're going for new phones.

In contrast, people privileged in terms of connections and power do not seem to share this passionate relationship with the mobile phone. Rather, among them, the tendency is to restrict its use, as by prohibiting mobile phone use in certain places. Some even regard it as a vulgar instrument, use of which should be kept to a minimum, just as those whose families have had great wealth for generations consider the nouveaux riches unfit to handle money. Like the *sapeurs* of Congo who, by acquiring French and Italian haute couture, are ritually transformed from ordinary, powerless youth into great men (even posing danger to the people in power), the Guan migrants gain potentiality through mobile phone acquisition, based on the fantasy "that one can reach the 'top' without passing through the accepted channels of education and 'work'" (Friedman 1999b: 184). Thus the phone speaks of the person who possesses it, not only of his lavishness in spending a considerable amount of money on a mobile phone (while otherwise fighting by hook or by crook to secure basic needs) but also of the connections he might have. In this way, the possessor perhaps hopes that through acquisition of a symbolic object, essence and appearance may be confused (Friedman 1999b: 182).

Sonny: If a child and an older person are crying at a funeral, they will both be taking their dues [their part of the feast]. But the difference is that the child cries without any good information, whereas the older person cries with good information; the things she'll say show her connection to the dead person. In the same way, the cry of the 30 Euro phone and 200 Euro phone is not the same, though they, by crying, show they are both mobile phones. The small phone cries like the child [imitates a monotone ring tone], whereas the bigger phone cries like the old woman [imitates a polyphonic ring tone].

Given that migrants are denied real participation, the mobile phone may represent their fantasy of becoming connected, an avenue to re-enchantment, which of course will have to yield to real obstacles; and this is why people are constantly looking for new forms of expression through symbolic action (Friedman 1999b: 168). Perhaps it is not so difficult to understand why this "enchanted" world of mobile phones, however fragile it may appear, holds such attraction for the Guan migrants. As in the case of the *sapeurs,* the acquisition of symbolic goods "simultaneously rehabilitates the self and inverts the structure of power" (185). Conversely, sporting an older, larger phone with no camera or radio, a "cassava stick," is to call into question not only one's financial capacity but also one's very existence. Samuel was coming home one day on the bus, having borrowed an old phone from a friend because his new phone had been stolen, when his friend remarked, "So, Samuel, have you come to the end of your life?"

In another case of magical re-enchantment in the form of reinventing the self, a newly arrived West African migrant in Italy, regardless of legal status, would be called a *burger* (most likely from the German word for "citizen"), whereas a migrant who had stayed longer in Italy and mastered the dos and the don'ts would earn the title of *tycoon,* a person who has connections and could make things happen (this metamorphosis is discussed further later in this chapter). But, on an individual and social level, what does it entail to experience a gap between one's expectations and where one is taken by the world?

To be sure, the experience of being disconnected, or being "excluded from the game" (to use Pierre Bourdieu's expression), always presupposes a lack of power—defined as a certain minimum of economic and cultural capital to invest in the game—and the objective chances it opens up in connection with the game (Bourdieu 2000: 222). Bourdieu's game metaphor is especially useful here, but not because it describes the world as it is (it is not a sensitive category, as it were), but because it describes the world as it is not. The game analogy is rather a mockery, a caricature, or perhaps best, a vehicle of alienation. But this inversion of reality created by the metaphor is always, to follow Hegel (quoted in Zizek 1994: 10), a double inversion, in the sense that we return from this world turned upside-down to the "first" world with a more radical alertness; but this is a return that the practice of mimesis is paradoxically denied. In this way, Bourdieu's choice of words appears to be a deliberate vehicle of alienation designed to produce *Verfremdung*, to borrow a term from Berthold Brecht's epic theater.

Without the power to influence the game in their favor, the dispossessed refrain from making investments at all (or entertain unobtainable fantasies), instead filling up their time with pseudo-events such as the lottery. Or they may try to shake their feelings of being the "plaything[s] of external constraints" by, for example, engaging in violence and death-defying games, "as a desperate way of existing in the eyes of others, for others, of achieving a recognized form of social existence, or, quite simply, of making something happen rather than nothing" (Bourdieu 2000: 223). Michael Jackson (2005) has described this existential imperative, which may take a destructive course, as the human need "to transform the world into which one is thrown into a world one has a hand in making—to strike a balance between being an actor and being acted upon" (x). Spending time with Sammy, I was constantly reminded of this desire to clear obstacles that could stand in the way of his taking matters into his own hands, though much of the time he remained a victim of the arbitrariness that characterized migrant life. Around his neck, for instance, Samuel carried a golden key given to him by his sister—the key to unlock the doors of opportunity, supposed to provide him with a fair shot at taking his life in a desired direction.

This central need to choose one's life course instead of being the plaything of circumstance became a focal point of an interview with

Jonathan about the death of his brother-in-law, who had disappeared on the Mediterranean Sea while captaining a boat to Italy. As it happened, Jonathan considered the act of taking matters into one's own hands through illegal migration to be worth risking one's life for, or to put it perhaps even more strongly, to be one of the few things really worth dying for. "I feel very sorry for him," Jonathan told me. "But the aim of this journey is to look for something to help us in Africa. So, if somebody decides to take this journey to Europe, it is not a bad thing, it is a very good thing. It is about the way a person wants his future and his life to be." In a similar vein, Michael Jackson (2006), writing about the young Kuranko men of Firawa who are faced with disillusionment in postcolonial Sierra Leone, finds a corresponding longing to regain a sense of direction in their lives: "There was no one word for what these young people craved. Perhaps power comes closest, if we allow that the word covers a vast array of imperatives, any one of which an individual may consider vital to his or her existence: wealth, worth, work, status, strength, renown, knowledge, recognition" (161). Indeed, the power to take charge of one's life and direct it toward desired goals—in time building one's own house, driving one's own car, sending one's children to better schools—seemed a matter of the greatest importance to the Guan informants—possibly more important than could be explained by the acquisition of material rewards alone. If there is symbolic death in a dead-end village life, there is happiness to be found in activity, a happiness, as Bourdieu writes,

which exceeds the visible profits—wage, prize, or reward—and which consists in the fact of emerging from indifference (or depression), being occupied, projected toward goals, and feeling oneself objectively, and therefore subjectively, endowed with a social mission. To be expected, solicited, overwhelmed with obligations and commitments is not only to be snatched from solitude or insignificance, but also to experience, in the most continuous and concrete way, the feeling of counting for others, being *important* for them, and therefore in oneself, and finding in the permanent plebiscite of testimonies of interest—requests, expectation, invitations—a kind of continuous justification for existing. (2000: 240, italics in original)

At stake in illegal immigration is empowerment or agency: this undertaking is an attempt to regain direction in one's life—even at the risk of that life—by positioning oneself within the circulation of material and symbolic goods. However, being on the inside of that circulation (and I have questioned whether that really happens for the migrants) does not mean eliminating risk and uncertainty from one's life-world. Although the willingness of the world to give what is desired (bearing in mind "that expectations tend universally to be roughly adjusted to the objective chances" [Bourdieu 2000: 216]) may appear to be a causal relationship, it is in fact no such thing—even for someone possessing the power to influence the game in his or her favor; rather this is a relationship of exchange with the essential constituents of one's life-world. In this sense, experientially if in no other way, any desired effect is what one *receives* by putting forward action in a given environment while waiting and expecting (Ingold 1992: 46). The desired effect of such an effort put forward, however cyclical and regular the outcome may appear, is thus a *quasi-perfect coincidence* between subjective efforts and the objective tendencies of the world; in other words, "nothing must be absolutely sure, but not everything must be possible" (Bourdieu 2000: 213, 234).

The notion of reciprocity developed in the following section—that is, the connectedness between one's aspirations and the world's willingness to accommodate them, which may at times supersede the rewards themselves—cannot be restricted to a sociological level, that is, solely in connection with the development, function, and morphology of social institutions in the tradition of Marcel Mauss (1990 [1924]). Rather, the classic anthropological notion of reciprocity is expanded here to encompass questions of a broader existential nature. (This may, at least implicitly, be the suggestion in Mauss's *Essai sur le don,* in which he mentions, for instance, the obligation to give to nature and the gods as a fourth theme in the moral system of gift giving [after the themes of giving, receiving, and reciprocating within the social world], but then regrets that "we have not undertaken the general study that would be necessary to bring out its importance" [1990 (1924): 14]). This form of reciprocity is concerned with the *plurality* of human exchange relations as they are

experienced and enacted in everyday life; with social as well as extrahuman relations; with real as well as imaginary, articulated as well as unarticulated, conscious as well as unconscious relations.

The whole dynamic field of intersubjective exchange relations that
sustain a person or a group of persons is involved here—the symbolic
exchange relations whereby a sense of "ontological security" may be
achieved, to adopt a famous phrase coined by psychiatrist Ronald D.
Laing. The phenomenon Laing addresses is a taken-for-granted security
that a person experiences as "a sense of his presence in the world as real,
alive, whole, and in a temporal sense continuous," as well as a feeling
"of the permanency of things, of the reliability of natural processes, of
the substantiality of natural processes" (Laing 1973: 39). To put it differently, following Anthony Giddens, humans beings stand in a continuous
relationship with "a shared—but unproven and unprovable—framework of reality" that precedes engagement with the world at large, a
framework "simultaneously sturdy and fragile," but whose very taken-
for-granted nature makes it possible to venture confidently into the
world at all. In fact, "to answer even the simplest everyday query, or
respond to the most cursory remark, demands the bracketing of a potentially almost infinite range of possibilities open to the individual"
(Giddens 1992: 36). Thus exploring connectedness as a relationship of
exchange with the essential constituents of the life-world through which
a sense of ontological security might be achieved is at the same time a
study of this basic trust in the existence of an external reality that exists
apart from oneself and in which everything is grounded. As Giddens
reminds us, referring to the phenomenology of Husserl, this belief, so
fundamental to human practice (and even to the positive sciences, as
Heidegger has argued [1999: 61]), conforms to a "natural attitude"
toward the world—an *as if* environment, produced and reproduced by
practical knowledge so that human beings can "get on with the affairs
of day-to-day life" (Giddens 1992: 36, 40), keeping the endless possibilities and uncertainties at bay. The shattering of this framework may result
in chaos and even a loss of reality. Moreover, what is surprising is that,
in Kleinman's words, "given the manifest shakiness of our lives, . . . we
act, think, and write as if we were in control of ourselves and our world"

(2006: 7). In fact, existential control is produced by the success of reciprocal encounters, or quasi-perfect coincidences, obtained in the environments that one is sustained by, and by the measure of leverage one is
thereafter able to exercise regarding the direction of one's life.

The analysis up to this point has revolved around the legal, economic, and social perspectives of undocumented immigration to Europe.
I have focused on the relationship between the underground economy
and the migrant workforce, the political reception of and discourse on
immigration in Italy, and the social context of southern Italy that the
immigrants settle into. To better understand why West African immigrants risk it all for Europe, I now move to a perhaps more abstract,
yet empirically immediate, level of analysis by exploring illegal immigration from West Africa to Europe as a means of reconnecting with
one's aspirations, thereby, one hopes, regaining a sense of direction and
recovering one's life from a discouraging future. Understanding the
social and existential importance of being connected, or disconnected,
I argue, requires inquiring into the primary intersubjective world of
reciprocity and how this experience continues to play a central role in
the human life-world.

THE THREE GRACES:
NOTES ON EXISTENTIAL RECIPROCITY

There is a certain, purely incidental symmetry in writing on the question
of reciprocity and its place in human life when doing fieldwork in Naples.
Among the artwork excavated from Pompeii and Herculaneum at the
National Archaeological Museum, the pink baroque palace fronted by
palm trees at the foot of the hill of Santa Teresa, is a fresco painting from
the house of T. Dentatus Panthera portraying the Three Graces. In
Seneca's famous interpretation of the Greco-Roman image (they have no
independent mythology [Tortzen 2004: 287]), these three sister god-
desses, Agleae, Euphrosyne, and Thalia, symbolize not only eroticism,
elegance, and beauty but also sharing and gift-giving and the central
position of such virtues in human life. During the Renaissance, when

Seneca's work *On Benefits*, his major moral philosophical work (Sørensen 1995: 221), was rediscovered and translated into French and English, the dance of the Three Graces was made available to a wider, European audience and the image itself was reproduced numerous times (Davis 2000: 13). The Pompeii fresco (a mosaic of the Graces is also to be found in the Naples museum) depicts the young nude maidens with white flowers in their hair, standing in a circle against a rocky landscape, their hands on one another's shoulders. One sister is seen from behind, and the other two turn to each side in a mirror image. This popular classical tableau prompts Seneca to ask: "Why do the sisters dance hand in hand in a ring which returns upon itself?" His response: "For the reason that a benefit passing in its course from hand to hand returns nevertheless to the giver; the beauty of the whole thing destroyed if the course is anywhere broken, and it has most beauty if it continues and maintains an uninterrupted succession" (Seneca 1964: 13).

But if the Graces are of another world, a realm of the gods, so is this "uninterrupted succession" of benefits passing from hand to hand in a perfect circle. In fact, the image is not well suited to illuminating the challenges that reciprocity poses in human life—and, to be sure, this is not Seneca's purpose. Rather, he evokes a moral ideal tellingly unfolded in mythical time. Apart from the uncertainty, negation, and even exclusion that mar exchange in the social world of human beings, exchanging symbolically with members of one's close family only (here from sister to sister) appears to go against the very grain of the social by violating the universal incest taboo. According to the principle of exogamous exchange, one social group gives up a woman in the expectation that it will in turn receive a replacement from the outside (Lévi-Strauss 1967: 51). But this universal rule of reciprocity based on the incest taboo not only contains the seeds of alliances but also places people categorically under "the tyranny of others" (Cohen 2006: 21). Lévi-Strauss discusses this ambiguous secondary effect at the very end of *The Elementary Structures of Kinship* (1967). Having placed the norm of reciprocity, with all it perils and ambiguities, at the center of social formation, he finds, in myths of future happiness or golden times long past, that human beings have longed repeatedly for a place where the obligation to exchange with outside forces beyond one's control can be eradicated from the social world, a place "eternally denied social man, . . . a world in which one might keep to oneself" (Lévi-Strauss 1967: 497).

This paradise lost, however—the uninterrupted succession of benefits between close kin that may symbolically take on an incestuous character—is not altogether strange to the human condition. The image of the Three Graces may represent the lost world of the child all entangled in the mother or primary caregiver, a primordial stage of exchange with no clear boundaries of self and Other, which, though perpetually unobtainable, remains at the center of human life and has continuous ramifications. In discussing the central question of connectedness and disconnectedness beyond the level of sociology, I scrutinize the give-and-take of early infancy a bit further: how this all-important stage of reciprocity continues to inform one's dealings with the constituents of the human life-world; how it allows not only the social world but also the world at large to appear to the individual to be susceptible to exchange, regardless of ontological status; and how, by being susceptible to exchange, the outside world is experientially dragged into the sphere of individual and social influence, however fragile and contested this connection may be.

In primary intersubjectivity, according to D. W. Winnicott, creating a sense of uninterrupted succession with the outside world is precisely the all-important outcome of the mother's or primary caregiver's symbiosis with the infant. By presenting the baby with the breast every time the need is felt a thousand times before weaning, motherly care introduces the child to external reality through the caregiver's body, which, imbued with a sense of omnipotence and the illusion that what is needed can be created, represents the outside world to the child. "From this develops a belief that the world can contain what is wanted and needed, with the result that the baby has hope that there is a live relationship between inner reality and external reality, between innate primary creativity and the world at large which is shared by all" (Winnicott 1962: 138–139). This extreme form of reciprocity blurs the boundaries even between self and Other ("a baby cannot exist alone, but is essentially part of a relationship" [137]). Marshall Sahlins has described it as "generalized reciprocity," a one-way flow of giving that may never be reciprocated ("all-giving" in Jackson's terminology [2005: 43]). Opposite to this form stands "negative reciprocity," or the attempt to get something for nothing ("all-taking," Jackson calls it [2005: 43]), and the middle point is "balanced reciprocity," a direct exchange that "stipulates returns of commensurate worth or utility within a finite and narrow period" (Sahlins 1972: 194–195).

To return to the "live relationship between inner reality and external reality": the baby's caregiver is not done once a sense of general reciprocity, this belief in the readiness and willingness of the world to provide what is desired, is instilled in the child. On the contrary, gradually the caregiver now has to accustom the child to the realities of the world—the lack of immediate response, waiting, and sometimes disappointment. "The mother enables the child to allow that though the world can provide something like what is needed and wanted, and what could therefore be created, it will not do so automatically, nor at the very moment the mood arises or the wish felt" (Winnicott 1962: 140). The project of raising a mature human being, according to Winnicott, thus entails cultivating the capacity to deal with loss, as when an action put forward is not reciprocated, while retaining in the infant the fundamental belief that a "live relationship between inner reality and external reality" may, at some point, be established. Seneca's depiction of uninterrupted succession may have an empirical existence in primary intersubjectivity, if only to be dismissed in the process of becoming accustomed to the realities of the outside world. The point is that, under normal conditions, a basic sense of security with regard to one's being successfully develops, and the normal circumstances of life with its ups and downs do not disrupt this feeling of ontological security (Laing 1973: 41–42).

Of course, as Lévi-Strauss argues in his famous example of an exchange of wine from a low-price restaurant in southern France, social distance, when maintained, is never trivial: "Even if it is not accompanied by any sign of disdain, insolence, or aggression, it is in itself a matter of sufferance in that any social contact entails an appeal, an appeal which is a hope for response" (Lévi-Strauss 1969: 59). In fact, the negation of symbolic exchange is a critical moment for any human being. George Devereux finds that infants denied "social response" suffer immensely and either wither away or, if they survive, lack the ability to develop basic human traits and become "psychologically crippled for life"; "the organism's need for a response is a fact," he concludes (Devereux 1967: 32). This response dependency does not disappear with psychological maturity, but is a dominant theme in the human life-world. Indeed, "unresponsiveness, or even diminished responsiveness, is neurotically interpreted either as a regression to an inanimate (= inorganic) state, or else as an intimidating power manoeuvre. . . . Hence, cynically deliberate non-responsiveness is sometimes a means of intimidation, and a cold rage [is] often more frightening than a boiling rage, perhaps because the hotly angry person 'telegraphs his punches,' whereas the coldly angry man does not" (Devereux 1967: 34). But for Devereux, the problem of response dependency pertains not exclusively to the social world— though it originates in primary intersubjectivity and the social imperative ("the prototype of all panic caused by a lack of response is the reaction of the infant in the absence, or temporary unresponsiveness, of its mother" [1967: 33])—but to all the constituents of the human life-world, whether social or not. Thus, according to Devereux, the (positively) nonresponsive surroundings that are part and parcel of the human life-world is at the root of human beings' "cosmic anxiety." "No matter what poets or mystics say, the stars do *not* look down either upon the astronomer or upon the lover who scans the skies" (Devereux 1967: 18, emphasis in original). Instead, according to Devereux, human beings panic whenever they are faced with the silence of the object world. To reduce this anxiety caused by the "unresponsiveness of matter," we animistically interpret physical occurrences as substitutes for a response (32). Even logical and scientific thought is really a defense system, Devereux radically argues, another way of reducing "cosmic anxiety," which is to say that the intolerable fact that the object world is unresponsive implies that any solid data produced are epiphenomenal to the study of the researcher himself and his anxieties (19, xix).

Although one may disagree with the anachronistic and pathological dimensions of Devereux's argument—as when, for instance, he compares animistic and anthropomorphic thinking with puerility, primitivism, and mental derangement—I would like to extract two important suggestions from the argument above. First is the central position of (symbolic) exchange in human life, as discussed by Seneca, Winnicott, and Lévi-Strauss. (One could also add Aristotle, thus locating exchange theory in the earliest texts of European intellectual life; in *Nicomachean Ethics*, he argues that exchange keeps people and the polis together, for which reason the temple of the Three Graces was placed on the main road [Aristoteles (Aristotle) 1995: 101–102]). Second is the absence of a clear categorical break between the social world and the nonsocial world in terms of reciprocal engagement.

Under what circumstances does the positively nonresponsive external reality appear responsive? Following the phenomenological approach, it may prove productive to bracket out questions pertaining to the positive validity of the experience of connectedness—not to abandon the investigation of external reality, however, but to explore the modes in which that reality may appear to us. In this way, we may illuminate the transcendence of subjecthood, or more plainly, show how human beings are not distant observers of external reality so much as mediums through which external reality comes into appearance at all (Zahavi 2003: 21–22). So, instead of seeing symbolic exchange relations with an animate and anthropomorphized extrahuman world as a relic of less mature stages of human development, as some kind of cognitive survival mechanism prompting us to take mistaken precautions on the principle of "better safe than sorry" (Guthrie 1995: 5), it may be more useful to explore this sense of reciprocal connectedness with all the constituents of the life-world while disregarding ontological status, as a mode of appearance shaped by the primordial exchange encounters of primary intersubjectivity. Consequently, a human environment characterized by the politics of give-and-take is perhaps better viewed as *authentically anthropomorphic* (Lucht 2003: 52). Or as Michael Jackson frames the issue in discussing anthropomorphism, technology, and the experience of the object world as saturated with intentions: "It is not even that we project human consciousness and will onto machines, or try to imagine machines as persons, for inter-subjectivity so shapes our experience from early infancy that it constitutes a 'natural' attitude towards the world into which we are thrown—a world that includes persons, machines, words, ideas, and other creatures" (Jackson 2002: 341).

Tim Ingold, while dismissing the idea that humans, for whatever reason, impose life or spirit onto the object world, shares this view of the human life-world. The animacy of the life-world, he argues, "is not a property of persons imaginatively projected onto the things with which they perceive themselves to be surrounded. Rather . . . it is the dynamic, transformative potential of the entire field of relations within which beings of all kinds, more or less person-like or thing-like, continually and reciprocally bring one another into existence" (Ingold 2006: 10). Following this line of thought, _existential reciprocity_ is a form of connectedness that concerns the entire field of symbolic exchange relations among the constituents of the human life-world, sustaining individuals and bringing them into existence. Reciprocal engagement with the environment, it could be argued, is not confined to social and existential matters, but in a physical and biological sense, too, we seem to rely on responses from our surroundings to maintain day-to-day existence. Take, for instance, the gift of sight. Although we talk about vision as penetration—a gaze can be searching, piercing, probing—it is really we who are penetrated, as light is reflected from our surroundings and received at the back of the eye, where images are composed. In this sense, we are _receivers_ more than we are producers of light; we are not the creators or conquerors of what we see, but subjects to the available light in which something might appear. The same could be argued with regard to sound, smell, taste, or touch, though these involve different impulses.

What kind of organization of the human life-world does existential reciprocity entail? As already suggested, it inevitably implies a practical understanding of reality as a coherent and external whole that both underwrites the possibilities for action and is produced and reproduced in action. Moreover, this framework of reality is not only a passive backdrop to human actions but, in experience, also a moral entity— potentially both provider and depriver—that can be approached and negotiated with. Indeed, the idea that there is an ethos to human environments is beautifully captured in Ralph Waldo Emerson's essay "Gifts," which begins with the following playful remark: "It is said that the world is in a state of bankruptcy, that the world owes the world more than the world can pay, and ought to go into chancery, and be sold" (Emerson 1997 [1844]: 25). Emerson here underscores some interesting features of existential reciprocity: the tendency toward authentic anthropomorphic thinking (the world is depriving its inhabitants); the moral nature of any given human environment (it can be determined what one owes and is owed); and gift exchange as a strategy of empowerment in the face of the relentless arbitrariness of given circumstances (measures can be taken, or the world dismissed, if it doesn't repay what it owes). In other words, the gift of one's time, effort, attention, and hard work obliges the world at large to repay one, or at least to refrain from certain unfortunate modes of behavior. This conception offers a mechanism not only for reducing complexity but also for transforming the given world into a world one has a hand in choosing, even creating (Jackson 2005: xi). Moreover, having to give up something cherished — as when misfortune strikes — also conforms to a kind of giving that, since the thing has been taken morally, should be repaid.

Perhaps this helps explain the suffering of the illegal migrants, for whom enduring the hardships of Naples is an accumulation of good things waiting to happen. As George expressed it when talking about his tribulations in Naples, "There is always darkness before daybreak." Suffering viewed in this way, rather than being a passive state of affairs, is transformed into active engagement. One carries on with vulnerability—giving up what there is no certainty of getting back, in the manner of a saint or a hero—thereby creating in the outside world the very moral normativeness that is missing, and thus dragging the unresponsive world into one's own sphere of influence (Luhmann 1999: 88). But again, as Zygmunt Bauman explains, inclusion within the moral universe of obligations is not readily granted to the less privileged. The link between poverty and crime that inheres, for instance, in the term *illegal immigrant* seems to eliminate the very substance of morality, to negate "the impulse of responsibility for the integrity and well-being of other people who are weak, unfortunate, and suffering" (Bauman 1998: 77). Bauman, drawing on medieval scholastic debates, has termed this critical phenomenon *adiaphorization*, a process whereby an action becomes morally neutral, "subject to assessment by other than moral criteria while being exempt from moral evaluation." At this point, Bauman continues, "there is no more a moral question of defending the poor against the cruelty of their fate; instead, there is the ethical question of defending right and proper lives of decent people against the assaults likely to be plotted in mean streets, ghettos, and no-go areas" (78).

How is an understanding of the empirical context furthered by this theoretical expansion of the notion of reciprocity? To begin with, one can perhaps better appreciate the effort to create connections, to gain access to the circulation of goods, in a globally disconnected world by keeping in mind the existential dimensions of symbolic exchange. Having connectedness to the powers that sustain life, however fragile those connections may be (and however "dirty" the forms they take), not only supports material and social needs but also reduces the devastating feeling of insignificance, of being the plaything of external constraints, that so many of the world's immigrants are consigned to "by accident of birth" (Cole and Booth 2006: 2). Indeed, I have introduced the notion of existential reciprocity upon which ontological security is ultimately based in order not to leave unexplored, or perhaps self-evident, what it means—what the gravity of the experience is—when people "intensively feel the gap between expectations and reality" (Reyneri 2001: 12), when they feel so cut off and "abandoned to their fate" (Cohen 2006: 1) that they undertake risky, even death-defying courses of action, such as illegal immigration. What the empirical context of Naples reveals, with few exceptions, is a number of uncompleted attempts to achieve this all-important connectedness. Having crossed the Sahara and the Mediterranean Sea, the migrants still have not accessed the circulation of material and symbolic goods, but have drifted into the Italian subproletariat and found that, in the context of extremely unequal distribution of power, the world does not present itself as one of opportunity. Whereas some can enter social fields holding, because of their capital, "preemptive rights over the future," others find a "signposted universe, full of injunctions and prohibitions, signs of appropriation and exclusion, obligatory routes or impassable barriers" (Bourdieu 2000: 225). As Benjamin put it: "Most of the blacks can be competitive in so many fields, but, no, here the door is totally shut. They won't allow you, even if you know how to do it. We, the blacks, have all that it takes, and yet we feel so defeated all the time." Moreover, whereas those who find in the "permanent plebiscite of testimonies of interest—requests, expectation, invitations—a kind of continuous justification for existing" (Bourdieu 2000: 240), those who are disconnected from the fields of power, may find this especially hard to bear when they are so close to what they imagined would be the turning point of their lives, and may start to question the reasons for going on, the reasons for existing. Benjamin, in talking about the disappointments of life in Naples, expressed this well: "If you're not careful, you'll also lose sight of who you are, what you want to do in life, because sometimes you feel like giving up totally."

LOSSES AND GAINS (REPRISE)

So far, I have argued that the migrant life-world, instead of facilitating connectedness or existential reciprocity, seemed to generate failed attempts at connectedness between migrant aspirations and the promises of the outside world. In addition to this everyday experience of nullification and disorientation, or perhaps as its inevitable outcome, the migrant social imaginary produced certain negative trade-offs of its own, which not only revealed the reciprocal logic fundamental to human experience but also the "minatory power" of environments that refuse social and reciprocal recognition (Jackson 2007: 126). Keeping in mind Devereux's analysis of how, in many cultural contexts (Anglo-Saxon, Chinese, and Plains Indian), a person's aloofness indicates his or her social prominence, power, and even aggressive disposition (Devereux 1967: 34; see also Lévi-Strauss 1969: 59), one cannot be too surprised at finding Guan migrants concerned with the workings of the Italian health care system and preoccupied with the secret motives of the doctors who treated them—to the extent that they chose to go to hospital at all. Why, indeed, would medical treatment be given out freely when all other advances in Naples entailed so many losses? Although basic health care was at the time free for everyone in Italy, including illegal immigrants (since 2009 doctors have been compelled by law to contact the police if patients have invalid documents or none at all), and no reports were subsequently filed with the police (Ammendola et al. 2005: 24), most migrants agreed that medical treatment was governed by an "occult economy" (Comaroff and Comaroff 1999) centered on stealing patients' blood.

That prolonged reduced, or negative, existential reciprocity gives rise to bodily metaphors has been widely recorded among those relatively deprived of money and power in the globalized world, especially, though not exclusively, in a postcolonial context along a north-south axis (see Comaroff and Comaroff 1999 for an African perspective, and Scheper-Hughes 1996 for a Latin American perspective). In Naples, too, the precarious position of migrants in an all-taking environment appeared to produce a sense of the body being under attack, thus bringing *the weight of the world* into the most immediate and intimate sphere of human experience. "They want to use us up," Sammy would often say of the Neapolitans, as if migrant strength and vitality were something the Neapolitans could somehow suck out and use for their own ends. "They tried to kill me today," Sammy told me when his two employers had again piled too much work on him, as if the enormity of the workload was a direct attempt on his life. In this connection, Michael Jackson (2007) writes concerning the mild forms of paranoia that Sierra Leonean migrants experience in London: "One readily falls prey to the fears that forces, named or unknown, are conspiring against one when, in reality, it is simply one's own powerlessness and estrangement that produces this erosion of self-confidence" (126).

The blood-stealing rumors appeared to have originated from the fact that some migrants had had blood samples taken when they visited the hospital for treatment. Among others, this happened to Richard, who had been "knocked down" by a car while day-laboring in Naples. He was, as usual, chasing a car driven by a potential employer when he was suddenly struck by another car, coming from out of nowhere. When he woke up, he was in the hospital having his forehead, elbow, and leg stitched and his broken ankle put in a plaster cast. The medical team then took a sample of his blood. Richard knew beforehand that this might happen in the hospital, that the doctors might "go for his blood." Although he allowed it, in case "they needed to do some testing," when the nurses returned shortly after taking the first sample "to fill another bottle," without informing him as to what had happened to the first sample or showing him the results of the test, he refused. "They had already taken one bottle away, and now they came around for a second; I would not allow that." Richard believed that they were interested only in keeping him long enough to steal his blood, "over and over again until you die."

Richard: They check if the blood is clean, and then they give it to their old people, who are weak and can't move around. They see our blood as very strong, and as soon as it has been given to the old ones, it will make them strong too and prolong their life a couple of years. They see us as illegal immigrants and Africans, and they don't care whether we live or die. We help them make money, yet they don't respect us. If a white person is dying, they'll come for our blood—even though they say we smell—and give the blood to heal the white person.

When the medical personnel learned that Richard would not allow them to take any more blood, it was, he felt, as if he were being thrown out, though with a broken ankle he was barely able to walk. An Italian woman took pity on him and gave him a lift. "I refused to let them do what they wanted. They were annoyed with me and wanted to kick me out. But I did that to protect my life." Moreover, the migrants' sense of isolation in the hospital, without a family to take care of them, and their friends too busy finding work and money, made them even more likely targets for sinister plans. As Eric explained: "If a white person has been hospitalized, the family will be around that person day and night, whereas if a black person is hospitalized, no one will come. So the doctors will see that this person is not an important person because no one comes to visit him, and they'll think of any other thing that they feel like doing. They see us as worth nothing, and stealing our blood is one of the ways

in which they humiliate us." Samuel stressed the unacceptable economics underlying the situation: "They steal our blood because we can't pay
for the treatment. They want to suck us like mosquitoes, or vampires,
because they believe black blood is powerful."

The blood-stealing rumors appeared to be a bodily correlate of the
experience of living in a disconnected globalized world, one in which
the everyday experience of nullification produces minatory environments that drain one's strength and vitality and put at risk one's bodily
integrity and well-being. As such, these rumors belong to the accounts
coming in from across the globe "of how the rich and powerful use
monstrous means and freakish familiars to appropriate the life force of
their lesser compatriots in order to strengthen themselves or to satisfy
consuming passion" (Comaroff and Comaroff 1999: 282). These stories
represent to poor people a certain "sense of alarm" and are thus "told,
remembered, and circulated because they are, fundamentally, existentially true" (Scheper-Hughes 1996: 9). In this connection, one may ask
what the special significance is of blood in the blood-stealing rumors?
In a Guan context, blood (i.e., that of a chicken, goat, sheep, or cow) is
essential as the ritual gift presented to the lesser gods to "pacify" them
and ensure they do *not* feed on human blood; the major fishing rituals
of Senya Beraku are a case in point (Lucht 2003: 55). The use of human
blood for ritual purposes, on the other hand, belongs to the realm of
black magic and is socially unacceptable. Similarly, in an analysis of
blood-stealing rumors among the Luo of Western Kenya, P. W. Geissler
(2005) reports that blood "represents the principle of equality of needs
that underlies human life. Everybody needs an approximately equal
amount of blood to live. Losing blood endangers one's life and well-
being, and the alienation or accumulation of blood is an abomination"
(142). Blood-stealing in Naples, too, may go beyond the bounds of what
can be tolerated, representing a "breaking point," as Jackson puts it,
beyond which existence becomes unbearable (Jackson 2007: 126), an
abomination that throws off the existential balance of give-and-take.
Thus alone on the operating table, losing the struggle for his blood to
vampires siphoning off his life force, the migrant may just feel that "the
always unequal struggle" between where one is taken by the world and

where one aspires to go (Kleinman 2006: 17) is finally slipping out of his control.

Yet, as discussed earlier, there are certain techniques for re-enchanting the world, even in the most challenging circumstances. Thus, mobile phones may be used in a kind of magical play with the constraints of reality (which objectively makes little, if any, difference, but which qualitatively transforms experience), whereby the need to transform one's world is expressed in the absence of real participation in it.

Another technique is the constant migrant attempt to reinvent himself. Indeed, just as an occult economy of negative trade-offs emerged as a corollary of life in the migrants' minatory environment, their social imaginary also produced the figure of the tycoon, a Guan person who could manipulate the frozen circumstances of migrant life in Naples and shift the balance of losses and gains in the migrant's favor. Although possessing little power to change their circumstances, the Guan immigrants would reinvent themselves discursively and create "the live relationship between inner reality and external reality" they so desperately sought in Naples, yet so rarely achieved. In coming to Europe, one obtained the generic status of a burger among other West Africans, meaning a citizen of any given European country, though these burgers were denied the civil rights constituting EU citizenship. Yet a powerless and stigmatized illegal immigrant, or *clandestino*, could eventually (usually after a couple of years in Naples) earn the privilege of being referred to as a tycoon by one's fellow migrants. A tycoon was someone in charge, with powerful connections, capable of making things happen (someone "connected," as they say in gangster movies, without specifying to what or whom), though, from the outside, in reality these qualities appeared largely illusory and things happened to migrants, not the other way round. The figure of the tycoon contrasted with that of the *aba-fresh* (newcomer), the newly arrived migrant struggling to find his footing in an alien, usually hostile environment while making all kinds of "mistakes." Samuel and I interviewed John about tycoons and newcomers shortly after he had received his papers and was on the verge of leaving for Udine in the north, where a better job awaited him. He was in the kitchen frying a fish on the gas stove, wearing a knitted cap and a long winter coat because the power supply had been disconnected again. "I'm on the track to becoming a real tycoon," he exclaimed.

John: We say in our language that a stranger is a person who'll eat a one-eyed fowl, meaning that since you're a stranger, you don't know that the fowl that was killed to welcome you didn't have two eyes; it was sick. In a way you are humiliated because they'll go around the fowls and they'll pick the very one whose eye is no good, while you think you're welcomed the best way and that the fowl is a very perfect one. Since you're a stranger, you don't know anything about what is already going on there. This speaks about so many things: you don't know the language, you don't know the place, whereas the tycoon knows these things. He already knows everything, and the *aba-fresh* has no idea.

To be sure, when real participation is denied, one has recourse to fantasy and play as creative ways of animating the frozen circumstances that have left one with few options for action. As Michael Jackson argues, "Even in the most desperate, humbling, and overwhelming situations, people seek imperatively to wrest back control, to reassert the right to govern their own lives, to be complicit in their own fate." They pursue actions that may make little objective difference in their situation, but that, in permitting them to play with, rewrite, and reverse situations that leave them powerless, transform their experience of the world (Jackson 1998: 30). Therefore, given the gap between these West Africans' aspirations and the realities of the globalized world—a gap they have undertaken a deadly journey to bridge—it should perhaps not surprise us to find the tycoon at the center of the migrant social imaginary, a powerful figure who is master of his circumstances, who has connections to resources the migrants are so desperately seeking.

H.L.: *What is a tycoon?*
John: A person who has been in a particular place for a very long time, who knows certain places and how to reach them, and who has connections to housing. Somebody who knows how life goes on in

that particular place, the language and so on. And more especially, somebody who has a document that shows he's been in a certain place a long time. He also knows the law in Italy. So, for you to be a tycoon, you would have to stay in a place for a long time, and you'll have to be somebody who's connected to places and knows the language.

Benjamin: They give you guidelines, how to live in Italy and Naples especially, how to avoid falling into the hands of the police; they'll tell you not to get fingerprinted, because it'll show up when you apply for papers. They will teach about the buses, what numbers pass by our places, which ones will take one hour, which one will take two hours. And they'll show us the locations where you go and look for a job, how we have to appear to be considered. And when we go to the job sites, they give us one or two Italian words to be able to go about things easily, like how to say "work" and "money." So they'll teach you one or two things, so that when you go, you'll not be in a total mess. Apart from this, they also help in getting houses to rent, they support us with documents because when you don't have documents, you can't rent a place. They are connected as well, for instance, if you come and you happen to know a tycoon—because he knows the system—he can decide to give his job to you, introduce you to his *capo* and say, "This is my brother; work with him," and the tycoon will go out and take another job, because he has got a contact and can speak the language, while you can't say a word in Italian.

Living the life of a tycoon entails certain modes of behavior and appearance that sets one apart from the newcomer.

John: When I first came, I just put on any clothes and went around, but now, since I'm a tycoon, I have to keep myself neat. So, when I go to work, I put on very neat clothes, things I didn't even put on in Ghana. When I came, I just put on anything I could get my hands on. Now, I'm really considering my way of dressing as compared to when I arrived. Though it's working clothes, I still try to keep it neat and clean. I can't bring working attire and change into that, because the people I work for wouldn't like to give me the time to do that. So, I'll have two sets of working attire, one that I use from Monday to Wednesday, and one that I use from Wednesday to Friday, as not to go around in dirty clothes. The newcomer wouldn't mind about that; they'll be going around in dirty clothes; they wouldn't even clean themselves up when they come back from the workplace. Even in their hair, you'll see some kind of cement or pieces of the stuff they work with, and you'll know this is a newcomer.

In a sense, the tycoon, like the trickster, occupies a mediating role between two poles—in this case, between the aspirations and realities of immigrant life in Naples or, in Lévi-Strauss's words, between life and death—and must therefore "retain something of that duality—namely an ambiguous and equivocal character" (Lévi-Strauss 1963: 226). Moreover, in many stories from around the world, the trickster figure is seen not only as a greedy and selfish person (one may, incidentally, find similar qualities in the modern figure of the business tycoon) but also as "a type of culture-hero, specifically as a transformer who makes the world inhabitable for humans by ridding it of monsters or who provides those things (such as fire or various ways of capturing animals) that make human society possible" (Carroll 1981: 305). In the globalized world of late modernity, I have argued, a growing unresponsiveness to one's aspirations is one of the monsters that make life impossible; the tycoon is the imaginary provider of the knowledge and means to overturn this situation or, again, to create a "live relationship between inner realities and external realities."

The figure of the tycoon, however, in inherently possessing the desired powers that the illegal immigrant lacks and thus making life possible, is also imbued with a dubious quality, "an ambiguous and equivocal character." His savoir faire has a dark side to it, reflecting the reciprocal logic according to which powerful interlocutors are always approached at a cost. As Benjamin put it: "Most often they [the tycoons] cheat us, but they're helping us as well. They'll find a place that is supposed to take one person and rent it out to four persons, so they'll exploit the situation because we are new here. But without their help we would fall into problems that we avoid with their help and guidance." There was always a price to pay for a tycoon's help—this was a well-known and accepted fact. And, in the manner of the young Sierra Leonean migrants in London making sense of adversity, the Guan migrants could not avoid completely having to give up certain cherished possessions or being cheated by the tycoons, but had to strike a balance between "the gains one hoped to make for oneself and one's children and the losses one would sustain in doing so" (Jackson 2007: 127).

To some migrants, having "papers" and renting a flat for oneself and one's colleagues were signs of one's status as a tycoon—a real tycoon—as opposed to those, like Sammy and Edward, for instance, who had been in Naples a long time and knew their way around but had no "papers." "Even though you have stayed in a place for fifteen years," Edward explained, "there will be some places you can't go without a document. When you have documents, you can move around without any fears, legally. So the person who has lived here a long time will still have to lay his hands on documents to become a perfect tycoon." As mentioned earlier, however, quite a number of migrants who had documents were still day-laboring. Francis, who was himself considered a real tycoon, having twenty-one people living under his roof at one point, explained that his own unhappy dealings with certain tycoons had made him careful not to abuse his position. As a newcomer, Francis had eventually found his way to Castelvolturno. After walking up and down the Via Domitiana the whole day without seeing a familiar face, not knowing what would befall him, he met a Ghanaian tycoon in the street who took him under his wing. "I was in a different world altogether," Francis recalled. "So many whites, and I don't have any family here—where am I going, what path am I taking?" The tycoon told him of a place he would take him to for 50 Euros, and Francis paid up. It was an abandoned house. There was no heat or water; they had to fetch water from a nearby house and wood from an adjoining field to prepare food on an open fire. There was no glass in the window frames, either. "We had to cover them with cloths and blankets to keep out the wind. And there were so many leaks: when the rain fell, we had to stand up." Francis, the gullible *aba-fresh* in Naples, not knowing any better, paid to stay in that abandoned house for almost six months. "Look at the way of the tycoons! That is one side of the tycoons, the bad side. Normally, they cheat the new ones in some way. I really suffered a lot. So, when I see a new person, I want to help him."

The power of tycoons had to confront the reality check of everyday migrant life in Italy and often fell short. "We use that term [*tycoon*] for those who have been in the system for a long time," Benjamin said; "we believe that they know more, so we call them tycoons. But it's a misuse of words. That term is [correctly] used for successful businessmen who have mastered their field of business." Indeed, measured against the random acts of violence and degradation that migrants faced, the precarious nature of their work situations, and the fact that few were making real headway, the figure of the tycoon was sometimes difficult to believe in, some migrants even maintaining that real tycoons could be found only in the North. (For a discussion of better-established Ghanaian migrants in Emilia Romagna, Italy, see Riccio 2008). Indeed, hope did not necessarily die out completely in Naples, but rather migrated ahead of the migrants, to better places where there would be work and opportunity (Vigh 2009: 105). Billy, the informant mentioned above who took purposeful walks that seemed to take him nowhere, always claimed to be on the way to Norway, where he would surely find a job in the fishing industry. This imaginary project of his appeared to sustain him during increasingly difficult times for him in Naples, and its importance was recognized by his colleagues, who would, much to his liking, refer to him as "Norway"—as if they too understood that this was not who he was. The real Billy had left, and it would be only a matter of time before the rest of him would follow suit.

The disillusion entailed in everyday nullification appeared to influence Norbert's dismissal of his own claim to the status of tycoon despite his having spent several years in Naples working with a regular *capo*. "Here, we don't have any tycoons, because if a person came and met you here, you'd have nothing. Nothing has changed; you're the same." These contradictory influences on migrant life—eventually becoming a tycoon among one's fellow migrants, reinventing oneself, and bolstering one's powers, while remaining constantly on the defensive, at the mercy of external forces beyond one's control—had an objective correlative in the brand-new suitcases piled up against the walls of many Guan migrant homes. They symbolized, of course, the image of the successful migrant returning home, not in a ramshackle boat, bringing nothing but the clothes he wears, but the cosmopolitan traveler, checking in his luggage at the airline departure desk; or else a kind of luxury gift-wrapping around the goods one would eventually collect and ship home to friends and family. At the same time, the suitcases represented the need of the illegal immigrant, tycoon or not, to be ready to liquidate resources at any time—which was the interpretation Benjamin offered. "As illegal immigrants, we're always prepared for whatever might come. If today you're deported and you have the chance, you would come home first and take the luggage, so when you come home, you'll not look all that miserable."

Thus far, this study has dealt with the challenges of the Naples life-world and the many strategies Guan migrants employ to make life possible and to strike a balance between their aspirations and where the world is taking them—between losses and gains—in a situation where they encounter resistance to their plans of acquiring the good life. From a broader perspective, chapters 1–3 discuss the notion of existential reciprocity—defined as the human need to have a relationship of exchange between individual and social needs and the environments capable of sustaining them, thereby drawing external reality into one's own sphere of influence—and the centrality of this form of connectedness to understanding the decisions taken in high-risk emigration. But what circumstances in the village of Senya Beraku produced this need not only to get out of fishing but to leave Ghana by the desperate means available to the less privileged people of the world? This question is explored in ethnographic detail in part 3. First, part 2 looks more closely at the challenges of high-risk emigration by crossing the Sahara and the Mediterranean Sea.

PART TWO The Journey to Europe

FOUR The Mediterranean Passage

In talking about his decision to risk a sea voyage to Europe, Samuel recalled a news report he saw on CNN. One night in a rented room in Accra, when he was about to become a father for the first time and was struggling with the weight of looming responsibilities and with the discouragement of having doors shut in his face, he watched as a boat carrying young African men was intercepted by the Spanish coast guard (apparently a television crew had been allowed on board). Afterward he thought to himself, "If they can do it, so can I." Knowing very well he would be taking his life in his own hands on the desert trail (he had already been to Libya once) and on that boat, he made his decision. A week after the birth of his son, Samuel left for Niger and began the long journey across the Sahara Desert and the Mediterranean.

According to the Italian Ministry of Internal Affairs, 2005 marked a record for the number of African immigrants coming to Italy by sea (the vast majority landing on the tiny island of Lampedusa, just three hundred kilometers north of Libya). That year 22,939 arrived by sea, almost a doubling of the number of people arriving this way in 2004. In the following year, 2006, 22,016 immigrants disembarked in Italy, which, though a slight decrease from the preceding year, maintained the general pattern of increase (Ministero dell'Interno 2007b). This development followed Spain's new security measures—including the erection of razor wire barriers—at the North African enclaves of Ceuta and Melilla. In response, migrants left Morocco for Libya in order to cross the Strait of Sicily to Italy, a development the Italian government has officially complained about to the Moroccan government (BBC 2005). After a drop in 2007, the number of migrant arrivals from Africa by sea rose dramatically in the following year. In 2008, more than 36,000 immigrants arrived in Italy, prompting the Italian parliament to enact new, tougher measures in summer 2009 to fight illegal immigration. These include fines and prison sentences for people who house illegal immigrants, detention of illegal immigrants for up to six months, and establishment of so-called citizen groups to help the police combat street crime. One of these groups, the Italian National Guard, has stirred controversy by proposing to patrol the streets in fascist-style uniforms: khaki shirt, black tie, shoulder strap, black cap bearing a Roman eagle emblem, and armband with black sun wheel. The group is currently under investigation by Milan prosecutors, and Roberto Maroni, the Italian interior minister from the Northern League, who steered the new legislation through parliament, has said the group will not be allowed to patrol, as fascist and Nazi symbols are forbidden in Italy (Owen 2009; BBC 2009a).

The sea route, however, is not the most heavily traveled in terms of undocumented immigration into Italy, even though it attracts a great deal of attention—perhaps because the rickety boats have become such an uncomfortable image of poverty and desperation, mixed with the cynicism of human smugglers. But in comparison to the total number of undocumented immigrants arriving in Italy, the number arriving by sea is not enormous and does not justify the alarmist metaphors sometimes used in the media and in political discourse (see also de Haas 2007: 821–823). In 2006, 124,383 immigrants entered Italy illegally, of which 45,449 were effectively repatriated (Caritas/Migrantes 2007: 2). In fact, the borders most heavily trafficked by human smugglers, as well as by independent migrants, are those in northern Italy, especially the Italian-Slovenian border, which is crossed illegally by immigrants from Central and Southern European countries, the Middle East, the Indian Subcontinent, and elsewhere in Asia.

But in terms of risk, the boat connection is clearly extraordinarily dangerous. How many people have died trying to cross the Mediterranean is unclear, but in May 2006 the UNHCR assistant high commissioner for protection, Erika Feller, said, while visiting the Canary Islands after a sudden wave of open fishing boats arriving crammed with people from central and sub-Saharan Africa, "Rarely a week goes by without some news of an unseaworthy boat that has sunk with its passengers on board, dead bodies being washed ashore on the holiday beaches of southern Europe, and people who have paid huge sums of money to human smugglers whose last concern is the welfare of their clients." Feller continued: "Thousands of lives have been lost over the past decade. But even as illegal migration has become more difficult, African migrants keep trying to reach Europe, taking greater risks" (UNHCR 2006). Although the problem concerns many Mediterranean countries, the focus here is on Italy and Libya.

Regarding the Italian detention centers, for the purposes of this study, I mention only that some years ago the reception center on the small island of Lampedusa was excoriated in the Italian media and by the opposition to the Berlusconi government for failing to maintain adequate standards at a time when large numbers of immigrants were arriving. Moreover, incidents of abuse of immigrants and refugees, including violence, were reported, while the United Nations High Commissioner on Refugees (UNHCR), Amnesty International, and members of the Italian parliament were denied access to inspect the center. Following an article in the Italian magazine *L'espresso* in 2005 by an undercover journalist posing as a Kurdish-Iraqi immigrant, then–minister of internal affairs Giuseppe Pisanu ordered an investigation (Gatti 2005; Davidsen 2005).

I have also recorded humiliations (such as being made to squat naked and jump into the air on the command of the *carabinieri*, shouting "Italy is number one!"), but these incidents predate the investigation and the Romano Prodi administration's (2006–2008) subsequent practice of granting access to humanitarian organizations, and they add little important new information about the conditions. Moreover, most migrants seemed to have a generally pragmatic attitude toward both Lampedusa and the hardships experienced en route to Europe, and in Italy too, for that matter (as expressed in Jonathan's metaphor of the burning plant, mentioned in chapter 3). Interestingly, this attitude has also been registered among sub-Saharan migrants in Morocco. There, Michael Collyer writes, "mistreatment at the hands of the police was fairly widely reported, but it was seen as an understandable response on the part of the police and was generally interpreted as simply another hazard of the journey; like the weather or the physical environment, it was something to be avoided or endured" (Collyer 2006: 138).

Libyan authorities estimated that 1.2 million immigrants resided illegally in the country in 2004 (EC 2005: 4). It is unclear how many of those were in transit and how many were permanent residents, as Libya is both the main transit country in North Africa and the main destination for sub-Saharan migrants looking for work and other opportunities (Simon 2006: 27). From a European perspective, the economies of North Africa may not be thriving, but "in comparison with the majority of African countries even North Africa looks prosperous, and it is moreover closer to Europe and therefore a stepping stone to a better life" (Baldwin-Edwards 2006: 316).

The question of illegal immigration from North Africa remains high on the European political agenda. In general, after the EU summit in Tampere, Finland, in 1999, where the first common asylum and immigration policy was negotiated, the EU has sought to integrate the question of migration into other external relations with third countries. In particular, it has worked to combine foreign-policy issues with readmission agreements, those accords that allow the EU to return rejected asylum seekers and illegal immigrants to either their country of origin or a third country en route. In fact, the threat of reducing development aid has been employed to ensure cooperation on this issue (Gammeltoft-Hansen 2006: 1, 7–8). The issue is rising on the political agenda and becoming an element of security management in a globalized world. Thus, EU justice commissioner Jacques Barrot has argued that the recent influx of illegal immigrants to Greece not only constitutes a humanitarian crisis but is also a threat to the stability of Greek democracy (BBC 2009b). As a consequence, the EU has decided that illegal immigrants may be detained for up to eighteen months and face a five-year reentry ban. And under French EU leadership, a pact to expel more illegal immigrants while promoting legal immigration of high-skilled workers was agreed to by leaders of the twenty-seven European countries. This agreement sparked protests from African and South American countries, among them Libya, whose foreign minister criticized the pact as a product of colonial thinking and for treating Africans as criminals.

In general, African leaders appear reluctant to embrace the EU security agenda on immigration, or rather see it as connected to economic investment and development. Prior to the EU-African summit in Lisbon in December 2007, Organization of African Unity spokesman Mouhamed Mustoofa said, "The most important issue to African countries is to obtain better trade relations with the EU in order to create prosperity and employment in our own countries, but the EU is still not ready to go along with it." Concerning the question of immigration, he added, "Do you really think you can stop them with barbed wire and patrol boats? No, you can't, and neither can we" (cited in Lauritzen 2007; my translation). In the Mediterranean region, the so-called Euro-Mediterranean Program (EMP), also known as the Barcelona Process, aims at establishing, among other things, an open market by 2010 and has integrated into the negotiations the question of immigration. Thus, more than 25 percent of the funds made available to Morocco under the agreement (115 million Euros out of 426 million) is targeted at migration control, begging the question "whether the EU more broadly is refocusing its foreign policy around migration concerns" and, as a result, facilitating "an export of existing migration control measures to third countries" (Gammeltoft-Hansen 2006: 7, 11).

The case of Libya is quite different. The EU lifted the trade and weapons embargoes against Libya in 2004, following a similar UN decision in 2003 in response to Libya's abandoning its program of weapons of mass destruction and taking responsibility and paying compensation for the Lockerbie air disaster, the UTA flight bombing, and the La Belle discotheque bombing. Nonetheless, Libya is not a party to the Barcelona Process, and involving Libya in migration control measures is complicated by the fact that the country has no immigration policy and no asylum procedures or protection programs for refugees. Indeed, Libya has not signed the 1951 United Nations Refugee Convention, which means that although the UNHCR has an office in Tripoli, it has very limited access to detention camps where immigrants are held. Thus, although Libya has in fact ratified the OAU Convention addressing the rights of refugees, protection for refugees, asylum seekers, and migrants does not exist (EC 2005: 6). Yet EU home affairs commissioner Cecilia Malmström signed a border management agreement with Libya in October 2010 worth up to 60 million Euros over three years. Under the agreement, Libya is expected to develop a legal framework in line with "international standards" on the subject of migrants and asylum seekers. Although sizeable, the amount falls short of Colonel Muammar Gaddafi's own estimate of the cost. On a visit to Italy in August 2010 the Libyan leader announced that it would take 5 billion Euros a year to stop African migrants from creating a "black Europe" (BBC 2010).

In 2005, the Warsaw-based EU agency Frontex (formally, the European Agency for the Management of Operational Cooperation at the External Borders) was established. The budget was relatively small—6 million Euros in 2005 and 10 million Euros in 2006—but it rises to 285 million Euros from 2007 to 2013 (ICMPD 2006: 48). In 2007, Frontex was reported to employ only eighty-six people and carried out, in accordance with its mandate, strictly short-term operations (Frontex 2007a). In the Mediterranean region, Frontex, apart from supporting EU member states with expert assistance on the ground, carries out two annual operations that deploy aircraft and vessels in a joint effort by member states at the maritime borders of Southern European countries, especially Italy and Spain. In 2009 the Hera III operation, a response to the increase in the number of people arriving in the Canary Islands directly from West Africa, predominantly Senegal, significantly reduced that number. The agreement between the EU, Senegal, and Mauritania (which adopted the migration measures discussed above) allowed the Frontex operation to patrol along the coast of West Africa, inside third countries' national waters, and turn back would-be migrants before they even departed for Europe, "thus reducing the danger of losses of human lives," as one Frontex news release stated (Frontex 2007b).

Again, the Libya case is more complicated. The so-called Nautilus operation, which seeks to strengthen control of the central Mediterranean maritime border, has no permission to patrol inside Libyan waters, and hence no possibility of turning back migrants before they set out for the journey to Europe. So, even though the EU Commission has repeatedly agreed to expand Frontex's presence in the Mediterranean, such action would do little to stop boats from Africa. In fact, the executive director of Frontex, Ilkka Laitinen, has warned, rather surprisingly, that an increased presence would only attract more boats from Africa because the human smugglers target the Frontex boats, deliberately sinking their own boats, knowing that the passengers will be saved and taken to shore (Camilleri 2008).

Because the EU's efforts to reach agreements with Libya are still in the early stages, Italy, like Spain, has pursued bilateral initiatives on the migration question. During the former Berlusconi government a whole range of initiatives were set in motion. One of the most controversial was the deportation of immigrants directly from Lampedusa to Libya, without allowing the immigrants to apply for asylum. The deportations, which took place between October 2004 and March 2005, were condemned as illegal by both the UNHCR and the European Parliament (Baldwin-Edwards 2006: 320). As a consequence, the Prodi government distanced itself from these deportations. The new Berlusconi administration, however, has resumed the deportations as of May 2009, prompting harsh criticism from, among others, the UN. During summer 2009, Italy is believed to have sent back some nine hundred would-be immigrants and asylum seekers picked up on the high seas, without screening for legitimate refugee claims (UNHCR 2009).

Other dimensions of the bilateral agreement (as described in the report of the European Commission's technical mission to Libya in 2004) included establishing permanent liaisons between Italian security officers based in Tripoli and the Libyan Security General Directorate (EP 2005: 59). In January 2007 the Italian Ministry of Internal Affairs reported that this collaboration yielded results, and not for the first time, when 190 would-be immigrants were stopped from departing for Sicily from the town of Tajura, eighteen kilometers west of Tripoli (Ministero dell'Interno 2007d). The collaboration also included financial support for the repatriation of migrants from Libya to their countries of origin (between 2003 and 2004 forty-seven flights involving a total of 5,688 immigrants either were carried out or were in process) and the establishment of detention camps in Libya. "In 2003 Italy financed the construction of a camp for illegal immigrants, in line with European criteria[,] to be built in the north of the Country" the European Commission reported; "the construction has already been started at the end of November 2004. In the financial exercise 2004–2005 a special allocation is foreseen for the realization of two more camps in the south of the Country, in Kufra and Sebha" (EC 2005: 59). Such cooperation on migration has led to harsh criticism directed at Italy and, by implication, the European Union for exporting "Fortress Europe" (see, for instance, Statewatch Bulletin 2005). The EC report also lists the materials provided by the Italian government in the fight against illegal immigration, including, among other items, jeeps, buses, binoculars, GPS systems, bullet-proof jackets, fingerprinting kits, four anti-explosives dogs, four anti-drugs dogs, and remarkably, one thousand body bags (EC 2005: 60).

The future of EU (and Italian) cooperation with Libya on migration issues appears to hinge, however, largely on the inclinations of Libya's ruler, Colonel Muammar Gaddafi. And although a shift in policy may be on the horizon, some of his most recent remarks on the issue of immigration may be less encouraging to EU immigration hardliners. During a two-day conference on immigration in 2006, Gaddafi, speaking to a group of EU and African ministers in his Tripoli home, stated that resisting migration is "like rowing against the stream." He continued: "The current populations of the world are originally migrants. Political borders, official papers, and identities set for every group of people are new, artificial things not recognized by nature. Land is the property of everyone, and God commands all human beings to migrate on Earth to seek a living, which is their right" (BBC 2006a).

The Italian desire to reach an agreement with Libya on immigration in the absence of EU progress on the issue is evident in the latest political development surrounding the phenomenon: the new pact of "friendship, partnership, and cooperation" between Libya and Italy, signed in Benghazi in late August 2008. The friendship pact followed months of heated exchanges between Rome and Tripoli. When Silvio Berlusconi returned to power in April 2008 and appointed as a minis- ter Roberto Calderoli, from the anti-immigrant Lega Nord (the Northern League), relations between Libya and Italy hit a new low. Calderoli, who in 2006 appeared on Italian television wearing a T-shirt depicting the Danish Mohammed cartoons, is a despised figure in Libya. In fact, ten people were reported to have died in 2006 when crowds, allegedly angered by Calderoli's television appearance, tried to storm the Italian consulate in Benghazi (BBC 2006b). Gaddafi's influ- ential son, Saif al-Islam, warned that Calderoli's appointment as min- ister would have catastrophic implications for the relationship between Libya and Italy. On the very night Prime Minister Berlusconi appointed his new cabinet, including Calderoli, Libya backed out of an agreement to handle illegal immigration, saying it would no longer "protect the Italian coasts." Moreover, Colonel Gaddafi threatened to annul lucra- tive oil agreements between the two countries, ventures in which Italy has invested billons of dollars (Nigro 2008a).

It was during the summer of 2008 that, as a sign of the indisputable importance of Libya's cooperation in dealing with migration issues, the aforementioned rise in the influx of African immigrants to Lampedusa occurred. Politically, this posed a serious problem for Berlusconi, who during the 2008 election campaign, had promised to crack down on illegal immigration. In a surprising turn of events, Berlusconi then trav- eled to Benghazi and met with Gaddafi. The parties signed a deal worth $5 billion, and Berlusconi symbolically handed over the famous Roman marble statue *Venus of Cyrene*, captured by the Italians in 1913. The money is compensation for the damage inflicted on the Libyan people during Italy's colonial rule and is to be used for the construction of a coastal highway from Tunisia to Egypt. Indeed, investment in infrastructure along Libya's vast Mediterranean coastline may have future strategic importance for the control of immigration routes. Along with delivering this compensation, Berlusconi apologized on behalf of the Italian people and declared the book closed on forty years of misunderstanding. There is no reason to believe that the Berlusconi administration or Italians in general have no genuine regrets about the colonial era; Italy certainly committed crimes in Libya, killing thousands of people. But to the Italian media, Berlusconi was quick to point out the other benefits of this agreement: fewer illegal immigrants, more oil (Nigro 2008b). Concerning immigration, Italy hopes that joint maritime patrols inside Libyan territorial waters, to be carried out by six Italian patrol boats handed over to Libya, will prove effective. The success of Frontex, Mauritania, and Senegal in preventing immigrants from reaching the Canary Islands strongly indicates that the agreement between Italy and Libya will reduce the numbers arriving in Italy.

What would happen to migrants turned back to Libya is another question. Initial reports, which confirm the trend in my own data, indicate that African migrants, refugees, and asylum seekers turned back to Libya, apart from being denied their right to seek asylum, are subject to abuse, beatings, and other ill-treatment (see, for instance, Human Rights Watch 2009).

THE CAPTAINS AND THE SMUGGLERS

According to the International Centre for Migration Policy Development (ICMPD), about 100,000 people cross the Mediterranean each year. An estimated 30,000 are sub-Saharan Africans. The main arrival points for maritime immigration into Europe are the Canary Islands, the southern Spanish coast between Malaga and Almeria, Sicily, and the connected islands of Malta, Cyprus, and those of the Aegean Sea. The main point of transit is Libya. Two out of the three main migration routes on the African continent as defined by ICMPD, the northern and eastern routes, are orientated toward Libya (and, to a lesser degree, Tunisia), encompassing West African migrants as well as those emigrating from Sudan and the Horn of Africa, whereas the western route is orientated toward Western Sahara, Morocco, and the Spanish enclaves (Simon 2006: 42, 44, 48). But outside the media, little information exists on the experience of crossing the Mediterranean from Libya, and even less, for obvious reasons, is available from within the smuggling operation. One exception is Sara Hamood's report on the experience of migrants from Egypt, Sudan, and the Horn of Africa who travel via Libya to Europe (Hamood 2006).

To begin with, in light of the empirical data presented in the following, the assertion that the "boat pilots are primarily Libyans and Tunisians" (Ammendola 2005: 14) must be revised. The Libyan human smugglers involved in West African transit migration and the organization of the boat trip, the data suggest, do not themselves take part in the actual crossing. In fact, most passengers have no connections with the Libyan smugglers at all. Moreover, the captains are often reported to be migrants with no seafaring experience who report as captains only so they can get a free ride. Obviously, this phenomenon creates even more danger at sea. As a case in point, one informant, Alex, whom Samuel and I met on the street in Naples where he was day-laboring, had no previous experience with seafaring before agreeing to take a boat across, but the offer of a free journey to Europe was too tempting. Being from Koforidua in the southeast, where Ghana's gold and diamond industries are located, Alex had never sailed on the sea before, but, as he argued, he had owned a motorcycle and knew how to repair an engine, and sometimes went to the coast. Other than that, he was a boxing champion who had won seven cups, and he had no fear of anything or anyone. As he put it himself, "I can throw blows from every angle. Any fight I go into, I make sure I am going to win. That gave me the courage to go ahead, though the sea is not my work." But on the sea he was made to regret his daring. Posing as a captain together with a friend to obtain a free ride, he was given a small rubber boat with nineteen West African passengers. Soon after their departure, they ran into bad weather. They quickly lost their way, and the journey they had been told would take about twenty hours lasted four days. They had brought food and water for one day, and most of that was ruined by seawater. Though visibly a strong man, Alex found his arm grew numb as he held the tiller of the relentlessly vibrating outboard motor, making it extra painful to keep to a steady course. On the high sea, they met a Tunisian fishing boat that offered them bread and water, directions, and seven fresh fish. The migrants ate the fishcraw from head to tail, taking one bite each and passing it on to the next person. The journey continued, apparently without approaching Europe.

Alex: The sea was empty, water here and there, no end, sometimes a bird, otherwise nothing, nothing. The passengers were crying, all of them, even myself, I cried. On the last day, three people collapsed. I could not move myself—I was feeling so weak. It also seems our skin got rotten from the seawater and our faces got very swollen. Then a helicopter came, and after that a big boat. We were taken into the boat. We were suffering very badly. They had to cut off our clothes with scissors not to spoil the skin. Then they gave us hot water to drink and some injections. The rescuers said that we had lost our way because we kept entering Italy and then going back again to Africa [in circles].

There are many examples of migrant boats getting lost and drifting about for days and even weeks—in one case up to twenty-three days—while the passengers go through stages of panic, suffering, and eventually death. In this connection, research on the dangers of Libyan transit migration emphasizes the role of inexperienced captains, or people posing as captains though they have no real seafaring experience (Hamood 2006: 52–53; Coluccello & Massey 2007: 81). On the other hand, the impression that the captain in these transits is "essentially just another passenger" (Hamood 2006: 52) should not be accepted too readily. Although the passengers may have this impression, in many cases the smugglers organize the operation together with a connection man, who again leaves it up to selected migrants with seafaring experience to handle the boat. The Guan fishermen are sought after precisely for this reason.

Guan migrants with seafaring experience thus occupy the role of intermediaries, neither smugglers nor passengers. For this effort they are paid in the form of a ride for themselves as well as seats they can sell to friends or relatives at a reduced price. The appeal of this deal, however, is not financial. Most are themselves migrants en route and view the captaincy primarily as a means to reach Europe. Moreover, whereas the Libyan smugglers are paid up front and thus, on the face of it, have no financial incentive to care for the lives of the passengers (Hamood 2006: 52), the connection men, who are often but not always of the same nationality as the migrants, do appear moderately concerned with their passengers' safety—from a financial point of view, if nothing else. The connection men, who often personally handle several groups of passengers waiting to go, many of whom are their acquaintances or relatives, ideally want the boat to arrive in Italy so the passengers will let their friends and families know that the connection is safe. As Samuel put it, "If we go safely, the connection man will be having more passengers. People will be calling back, telling others how this man's connection is better, how everything has been put in place to see to it that the boat reaches its destination. So go and give your money to him; he has good plans." In short, it is bad business to lose too many boats, as migrants keep tabs.

Samuel came to Libya for the second time with the aim of reaching Europe. He had been in Libya before as a temporary migrant worker, but was deported following the riots between Libyans and West Africans, predominantly Nigerians, in Tripoli in October 2000. As it happened, rumors that a Nigerian had raped a Libyan girl sparked the riots, leading to the killing or wounding of thousands of African migrants, the burning of the Nigerian embassy, and the lynching of a Chadian diplomat. All over Tripoli, the police carried out mass roundups followed by deportations (Onishi 2001). As Samuel recalled, "Our place was set on fire—the police rescued us and brought us to a military barracks. Some of our guys were killed in their workplace." Most migrant informants considered the living conditions in Libya in terms of violence and abuse much worse than in Naples. The brutality, migrants repeatedly stated in interviews, was frequent, organized, and life threatening. (For an introduction

Naples is not great, but Libya sucked

to migrant living conditions in Libya, see, for example, Hamood 2006). It seems safe to say that migrant life in Libya, though economically better than in Ghana, was generally unattractive to the West African migrants. Samuel quickly learned to look after himself in Libya. One day as he was working with his master, who happened to be his brother-in-law, he unexpectedly got into trouble.

Samuel: In the morning, you have to prepare some tea and fry some eggs for yourself and for the master. When you're a helper, you have to do those things. So I was just going to buy some bread when I saw some guys on the other side of the road; they were talking to me, and before I realized it, these guys threw a stone and hit this place [*points to a scar on the back of his head*], and then I was bleeding. They kept teasing me, so I shouted, "Fuck you!" at them. Though the Libyans don't understand English, they'll know from movies that I was using some kind of insult, and they came for me. I managed to escape and reach my house. They would have killed me. This is how they are. My brother-in-law told me, "This is your first welcome to Libya, so be careful."

Testimonies of this kind, and some worse, abound in migrants' stories from Libya. Based on them, one could argue that Libya does not invite long-term stays, though it should be noted that most migrants who plan to use Libya as a transit point fail for one reason or another to reach Europe and "remain in very poor conditions in North Africa" (Baldwin-Edwards 2006: 316; see also Collyer 2005 for a discussion of sub-Saharan migrants stranded in makeshift encampments in Morocco with nowhere to go and nothing to live on). "You can only stay in Libya if you have real determination," Sonny explained—"like when a goat is hungry it won't respond to any kind of beatings; you can beat it all you like, but it won't stop until the stomach is full. Only when it's satisfied will the goat run away. You need determination in Libya, and as soon as you've finished with what you want, you leave."

Indeed, having been thrown out in 2000, Samuel had no intention of returning: "I promised myself never to go back to Libya." But back at home in Ghana, he soon realized that the little money he had managed to put aside for himself in Libya would not last him long and there would be nothing between himself and a harsh situation.

Samuel: I was just holding on, waiting, thinking of the next thing to do. One of our friends, who remained in Libya [during the riots in Tripoli], managed to get a connection to Europe. That really challenged us guys, because he used to call us from Italy and tell us that if we stayed behind we were not going to be able to move ahead; we would just rot down there. So I decided to go back instead of staying in that mess [in the village]. I was thinking that I would not be able to survive. Then I started planning a journey, but this time I didn't come to stay in Libya — I was looking for a connection to Europe.

When Samuel returned in 2002, he stayed eight to nine months in Tripoli, plastering a house together with some friends from the village. He was informed that a connection in Zuwarrah, a small Libyan town on the border with Tunisia, was operative and that the smugglers were looking for captains. While finishing the house, he began to prepare himself for the journey.

Samuel: One of our guys, Edward, had a landlord who was a navy officer. He brought us some charts and pointed out the features on the sea and how many kilometers and how many hours we should expect. So I began studying how to use a compass and how to read a chart, because I knew as soon as I came to Zuwarrah and met up with a middleman, they would interview me about that. So every night after work, I tried to learn something before going to sleep. We speeded up everything because of the connection and finished within a couple of weeks. Normally, plastering an apartment with three to four rooms, one big hall, and a kitchen would take roughly two months. Even in the evening when we were about to close, we kept working with a very big flashlight. People were even tracing us; they heard of us and were coming from Tripoli and wanted to grab us for their own boats. One guy came for me. He said he had a boat ready right there in Tripoli. "So let's go."

But Samuel declined the offer. Rumors had it that setting off from Tripoli was even more dangerous. Instead, he wrapped up the plastering job and, together with a group of young men from his village in Ghana, headed for Zuwarrah. Here, they divided themselves into three groups of three captains each. They split up so that each group would contain some people with several years' fishing experience and some who could read and write and thus handle charts and compasses. At the time, Zuwarrah was the main point of departure for boats going to Europe (it may still be [Simon 2006: 55]), but according to my data, Libyan authorities had put so much pressure on the connection by late 2005 that immigrants were hidden away up until the very time they were about to leave, whereas earlier this small town was "like an African town," to quote Samuel. The streets were filled with sub-Saharan migrants running up and down, preparing for the journey, and making inquiries. Little information exists to explain why Zuwarrah became the main Mediterranean transit point. Apart from its favorable geographical position (about three hundred kilometers south of Lampedusa), one report emphasizes that the Berber town once dealt in contraband, including alcohol, petrol, and cigarettes. Moreover, the local police are invariably low paid and "open to corruption" (Coluccello & Massey 2007: 88).

Samuel: As soon as we get there, we meet these connection men who have lived in Libya for a very long time and who speak the language so fluently. They move around with the Libyans. So we were invited to see one of these men, a Ghana man. He asked us about fishing, if we knew how to swim, and whether we would be able to get the passengers ashore if there was a problem. He gave us a compass, and I studied it very well. I was always playing with that compass.

As is customary in this kind of operation, the captains were installed in a separate house and given special treatment not usually shown to West African migrants in Libya. "He was giving us food and money to move around," Samuel said. "If we said we needed some girls, he could even get us girls. He would always try to make us feel all right." The three captains in Samuel's crew all knew each other from Senya Beraku. One of them, Eric, had a lot of fishing experience and at one point had been involved in petrol smuggling in West Africa; Samuel and Justin were former schoolmates. It was agreed that Eric and Justin should take the tiller, while Samuel would take charge of the compass and navigation.

During their wait, the smugglers were completing the operation. It appears that a boat leaves Libya when three basic conditions are met: when enough passengers have been gathered, when a seaworthy boat has been acquired, and when the weather is suitable (Hamood 2006: 50). To avoid winter and summer storms, the crossing should take place between March and July or in September or October. Among the three conditions, smugglers seem to consider the first—gathering passengers and collecting thousands of dollars in payment—as the most important, whereas the other two, pertaining to passenger safety, are not fastidiously pursued. However, compromising these latter two factors even slightly can turn a safe journey into one that ends in death. The condition of the boats and equipment supplied, especially with regard to the motor, varies significantly. Some captains report having been cheated by the smugglers, who have been known to present them with a new boat for inspection but replace it with a ramshackle one by the time the migrants arrive at the beach in the dark. Owing to the pressure and the fear of getting caught, most decide to take their chances anyway; the same form of deception is reported by East African immigrants in Libya (Hamood 2006: 62). Many also report having been pushed out to sea in dubious weather conditions, clearly putting the lives of the passengers at even greater risk.

During their wait, the captains prepare for the journey not only by studying the map and compass but also spiritually, by praying and fasting. During their final mass, Roger, another Guan captain, who was a strong believer and well versed in the Bible, acted as priest and urged everybody in the group to come forward and confess his sins. Nothing should stand between them and a safe journey. Among those who came forward, Eric confessed to having sold a plot of land that didn't belong to him and to having used the money to travel to Libya. The buyer had been furious with Eric and had threatened to take his name to a juju priest. Eric now begged both the buyer's and God's forgiveness. Edward, known among them as a stand-up guy but not too elegant with words, also came forward and confessed to having visited a prostitute in Tripoli, adding, much to the amusement of his colleagues, that it was only out of curiosity and he had meant no insult to anyone.

Eric: The Bible says that even if you are annoyed, you shouldn't let the sun go down on your anger. You should try to forget and forgive; if not, it means you have sinned. And we believe that the sea is also God's creation and he is the only one who can control it; so if you have sinned or offended someone at home, you should pray to God, because he is the only one who can direct you safely to Italy.

As these rites of purification that preceded the sea voyage may attest, something final about the journey seemed to set it apart from other, less dramatic journeys that involved a return or a cyclical motion. It was not a journey people considered doing twice—unless they had for some reason failed to reach Europe on the first try. This is not to say that the emigrants had no intention of returning. As discussed earlier, that was generally the idea, but they would expect to return as a new person, a transformed person. In this sense, to paraphrase Samuel, the journey is a strategy not only for moving physically and geographically but also for moving ahead in life, socially and existentially. This dimension of the crossing had an intriguing discursive and symbolic expression associated with it: migrants unable to make it across—because, for example, bad weather prevented their leaving Libya—would be classified as "ghosts," persons involuntarily fixed not only between the points of departure and arrival but seemingly between contrasting points of being, or even between life and death, like a ghost proper. As shown later, many informants invoked such terminology when talking about their journey. It was a turning point, a situation one willingly entered into, that would decide whether one should live or die. (For similar statements of definiteness recorded among East African undocumented immigrants, see Hamood 2006: 57–59.)

Regarding the notion of ghosts, one is inescapably reminded of the work of Arnold van Gennep and Victor Turner, in which the subjects of rites of passage are, during the liminal period, structurally if not physically invisible. Furthermore, subjects in transition from one state to another—the *no longer* classified—are often associated with images of death; neophytes undergoing initiation rites, for instance, may indeed be treated as dead, as by being made to lie motionless, stained black, ritually buried, or forced to live in the company of interlocutors representing dead people. That said, in transitional rituals, the no longer classified are at the same time the *not yet* classified, often associated with infancy or immaturity (Turner 1967: 95–96). This latter dimension also seemed to pertain to the ghosts. More than being feared, their fellow migrants regarded them as inconvenient and somewhat witless or childlike in the way they would helplessly roam about looking for new information or new boats, and gullibly stampede a boat and its captains should news of a crossing reach them. Viewing the unfortunate migrants waiting for a new chance—neither dead nor living—from this liminal perspective would not appear too unreasonable, given the ontological change associated with crossing the Mediterranean. Moreover, migrants who failed to make the crossing—even if they made it home to the village in one piece—seemed for years to come to have trouble finding a way back into their former lives and selves, as if they were neither here nor there. Finally, from the smugglers' practical point of view, the ghosts represented only expense—a kind of dead weight—once they had paid their fees. Usually, they would be mixed in with new passengers, who brought new funds for the operation; thus, little by little, the ghosts moved out of Libya toward Europe.

Another aspect of the captains' religious rituals prior to crossing the Mediterranean may be seen through the notion of existential reciprocity, discussed in previous chapters. Unlike the private and often unarticulated exchange with the secular extrahuman world of day-to-day life, religious life facilitates the anthropomorphizing of circumstances that one seeks to influence. Thus, to secure a safe passage across the sea, God is reciprocally approached. Stewart Guthrie suggests that the understandable reluctance of theologians to accept anthropomorphism as an inherent part of religion may be a hesitancy to view religion as *nothing but* anthropomorphism [Guthrie 1995: 179]. Clearly, no religious adherent would accept categorizing anthropomorphism, as

Guthrie does, as cognitive failure. Although my argument adds no positive, let alone normative, support to religious claims, either, anthropomorphism, I have suggested, should not be understood as a mistaken or false mode of perceiving the world; rather, I view anthropomorphism as a strictly human, and therefore authentic, aspect of being-in-the-world that entails certain modes of action and thinking.) That existential reciprocity may have this religious dimension does not mean, however, that it is essentially a secular expression of religion. On the contrary, following Pierre Bourdieu's thesis in the *Logic of Practice* (1990), I would argue that religion is better viewed as a sacred and collective expression of the fundamentally mundane nature of existential reciprocity. Thus, in an adaptation of Max Weber's analysis of religion, Bourdieu argues that "magical and religious actions are fundamentally 'this-worldly' . . . orientated towards the most dramatically practical, vital, and urgent ends." He continues: "It is as if ritual practices were wishes or supplications of collective distress, expressed in a language that is (by definition) collective (in which respect they are closely related to music)—forlorn attempts to act on the natural world as one acts on the social world, to apply strategies to the natural world as one acts on other men, in certain conditions, that is, strategies of authority and reciprocity, to signify intentions, wishes, desires, or orders to it, through performative words or deeds" (Bourdieu 1990: 95). Calling these attempts to control one's circumstances "forlorn attempts" might come across as a bit normative (such a position also goes against my previous argument, which stresses the real importance of having a sense of connectedness in both the social and the nonsocial world in order to maintain a sense of ontological security). Yet the religious rituals performed by the Guan captains may readily be understood in this way, as collective attempts to act on an anthropomorphic natural world, to apply collective strategies imported from the social world to an anthropomorphic natural world. Moreover, the "sins" brought forward certainly appear to be of a "this-worldly," if not social, nature. One can find comic relief in Edward's confession, which does not appear to have the serious social ramifications of Eric's confessed deed. Although sleeping with a prostitute is formally considered a sin, it does not strike one as a grave trespass in this context, and Edward was, as usual, ridiculed for not realizing that.

But what reciprocal strategies can be identified in these predeparture rituals? Witnessing the prayers of Christian believers in a fishing village in Ghana's Central Region sometimes leaves one in doubt as to whether the congregation is pleading or indiscreetly demanding, or both at the same time; and this ambiguity may further testify to the solidity of the moral dimension of human relations with the extrahuman world. If, to follow Zygmunt Bauman again, we regard sacrifice as abstinence in the form of compromising one's body by denying oneself food and drink, the very necessities of life, for an unnatural period of time, however short, this act could be viewed as a strategy for invoking the natural human impulse, supposedly shared by God, to mind the well-being of unfortunate others (Bauman 1998: 77–78). That is to say, through one's vulnerability, intensified by begging forgiveness for violations of certain moral rules and by displays of reverence, as in pleading and praying, the very normativeness so positively missing is magically instilled in the natural world. Through prayers and sacrifice (abstinence) to God (for giving up is also a form of giving that, morally speaking, should be reciprocated), the Guan captains thus seek to bring into their sphere of influence those external conditions, namely the sea, that are objectively beyond their control.

To return to Eric's quotation from the Bible (which reads in full: "Be angry, yet do not sin; do not let the sun go down on your anger, and do not give the devil an opportunity" [Ephesians 4:26–27; New American Standard]), another aspect of existential reciprocity is at play here that bears emphasizing. As discussed earlier, in this form of existential exchange relations, the profits procured by one's activities sometimes appear of less concern than maintaining the activities themselves. It is perhaps not surprising, therefore, that one can detect a concern with keeping open the channels, so to speak, as a kind of ongoing maintenance or rejuvenation of existential reciprocity. Consider, for instance, what mobile phones meant to the Guan migrants and the case of Samuel's golden key (see chapter 3). Conceivably, at stake here is the desire to keep things flowing in a favorable direction, in uninterrupted succession, an ideal condition constantly at odds with the positive unresponsiveness of the essential constituents of the life-world and, in the case of the less privileged, with the power discrepancies inherent in the social field. In fact, as Mihaly Csikszentmihalyi argues, achieving this quite mundane, but to some extent socially and economically stratified, experience of "flow" in the life-world might be the closest that human beings come to happiness (Csikszentmihalyi 1991, 2005). This optimal experience, which in subsequent contemplation might be classified as happiness, consists of immersion in the task at hand, a task that consumes all one's energy and capacities—neither too much nor too little—in an ideal moment when effects received correspond to actions put forward and the temporal dimension of the life-world is radically altered. This experience of "flow" is not a passive or reflexive encounter, but a form of action upon the world that, at the time of engagement, may not be particular joyful, but quite strenuous and difficult. Eventually, however, if the action succeeds, the experience provides a sense of mastery of one's circumstances, which again implies leverage in terms of having a say in choosing the direction of one's life (Csikszentmihalyi 1991: 12). Yet, as Bourdieu (2000) argues rather somberly, being caught up with a center of interest, or *illusio*, in which seconds, minutes, and days pass unnoticed is not necessarily an experience reserved for the well-heeled, for aspirations tend to be roughly adjusted to objective chances, whereas below a certain threshold of power to influence the game, aspirations become detached from reality (216).

In his understanding of the verse from Ephesians, Eric imagined the sinful nursing of ill feeling toward another person (not anger itself, incidentally, which is an emotion belonging to the practical and direct engagement with the world) as standing between himself and a smooth journey to Italy, thereby possibly denying him the chance to act on the world and take his life in a desired direction. From this perspective, the Mediterranean crossing is a strategy of moving ahead in life—but moving ahead in life is not only about the actual crossing. The captains' rite of purification may thus be seen as magically facilitating the desired *quasi-perfect coincidences* between subjective desires and where one is taken by the world, coincidences that pertain to a plethora of incidents, the deadly sea voyage being the most immediate and urgent one.

THE KILLING SEAS

The week after the migrants made their confessions, the connection man came to their house and told Samuel and the other captains that that evening was the time to leave.

Samuel: Our guys in Tripoli, some young police boys, worked out everything very fast for us guys to get a boat down to Zuwarrah. Very often the boat is stolen from Tunisia, so as soon as the boat is there, you have to leave right at this point, because if the police see the boat hanging about on the sea, they come straight for it. As soon as they bring the boat, you go. That day of departure, the connection man took us to meet the passengers; he advised us and we prayed together. All the passengers were West Africans. There were about two hundred passengers there, but he chose about a hundred to leave with us. The man told us that if we got there and the Libyans loaded more than ninety, we shouldn't get on the boat. It was too many. The man had gathered that this was one of the reasons why former boats of his had gotten sunk. But he didn't make it known to the passengers; he only told us. The two boats following our boat went down.

The Libyan guys are always busy pushing more people on the boat, because the more people, the more money they get. They pay between 800 and 1,000 dollars—it's a lot of money; a hundred people, that's 100,000 dollars. The connection man will get about one-third of that, and the rest will go to the Libyans and to the boat.

In Samuel's case, as with other migrants, the Libyan human smugglers were young policemen. Other testimonies confirm that it is not unusual in Libya to find the authorities involved, though the extent of this co-operation is unknown (Hamood 2006: 51). Some reports have found "clear evidence that smugglers operate in highly organized networks, exploiting the lack of adequate national criminal law and the lack of co-ordination between the police and immigration authorities" (Simon 2006: 43). Indeed, the Harig police operations in Italy, concluded in April 2007, exposed one such transnational human smuggling and trafficking network, with a surprisingly high level of organization. Charged with smuggling, kidnapping, and trafficking 2,500 individuals from Libya to Lampedusa and later enslaving and exploiting them, the network had members in Italy and in Libya and Egypt who were "interactive and complementary and acted as small networks within an overarching network" (Coluccello & Massey 2007: 85). The data I have collected add no new information to this dimension of human smuggling from Libya to Italy. In particular, there is no evidence that migrants are led from their countries of origin to the shores of the Mediterranean by an organized network, or then kept inside the network in Europe. Rather, as the case of the Guan captains shows, the smugglers at each stage the migrants go through do not appear interconnected, though, as we shall see, in the desert, migrants are often led from one smuggler to another in order—most cynically and effectively—to empty their pockets. But the desert smugglers do not drive them into Libya. Likewise, the Libyan smugglers do not deliver the migrants to Italy, and there is no evidence that smugglers and migrants remain in contact after arriving in Italy. So, rather than being the victims of a transnational criminal organization, Guan migrants seeking to go to Europe depend on a loose and complex "network of recruiters, middlemen, actual smugglers, local and foreign financiers, and government officials and police on the take" (Kyle & Koslowski 2001: 13).

The Libyan policemen came at 8 in the evening. They began to move the passengers to the beach and transport them to the boat in small, inflatable rubber boats (the captains call this type of boat a Zodiac, after the U.S. brand), carrying about twenty people at a time. At 12 P.M. they were fully loaded and ready to go.

Samuel: They came with a freezer truck, the one's that you keep fish inside. When it was dark, they started to load the freezer truck. They drove it up to the gate of the house, and people's names were called and they ran straight into the truck. They didn't want the police, the real police—the responsible ones—to come and disorganize the whole thing. They made three trips, and we, the captains, joined the last trip. I almost collapsed in there. There wasn't any air; this truck is totally sealed off and we were heaped up in there. We were a lot of people and we couldn't breathe. We just moved from the house to the beach side, but it seems it was a bit far. Some people started hitting the car to stop because they were dying. Just then, we arrived at the beach and they opened up. If not, they would have whipped or beaten those guys because, if the police find out, they can disorganize the whole thing and their thousands of dollars will go away. So we got there and they started loading us. They would count ten to twenty people: "You, move ahead." Like a batch of soldiers being distributed on the battlefield: "You this way, you that way." They took one group at a time, making them run down onto the beach and drop down on the sand, like soldiers, while waiting their turn. The waves were very loud, boom-boom, and I was sweating so much because I was nervous. They loaded all the passengers on board before they called for us. . . . You know, they played a trick on us—the man [the connection man] told us that if we could see they were bringing too many, we should just leave—but they loaded all the passengers first. So when we came, the boat was already full—what could we do? We had to leave. We were afraid if daybreak came something bad would happen to us. But there were too many passengers. Myself, I was at the beach looking to see if I could see a real boat, because I was thinking of a boat a bit bigger than this one. My God, I couldn't see anything—only a very thin white line, not knowing they had already loaded this thing and it was so heavy already. I couldn't even see the boat, only the people.

In Samuel's case, the smugglers provided a wooden fishing boat, reportedly stolen from Tunisia. This type of vessel is frequently used in human smuggling, as it is relatively large and will take between one hundred and two hundred passengers. Samuel estimates their particular boat to have been twelve meters long. Other captains, however, were given a Zodiac, which takes considerably fewer passengers, only about thirty.

Samuel: Then we took out the boat. The Libyans escorted us a bit further in their Zodiacs and told us to follow the course straight to

Lampedusa, ten–twelve, ten–twelve [ten to twelve degrees north-northeast]. Eric handled the tiller and we began making it slowly, making it, making it. He asked me, "Samuel, how do you assess the movement of the boat? Is everything in order?" At the same time, Justin was in the far end of the boat keeping an eye on the passengers, making sure they didn't move around. There were people all over the place, we couldn't even move from one end to the other. We started this way and everything was moving okay.

At one point Justin came to take over Eric's position, and sometimes I would also take the tiller. We kept changing places like that. Everything went okay, except the boat should have moved faster. It was very slow, but we showed patience not to force the engine. Our passengers cheered us with gospel songs.

I'd be sharing a joke with the other captains, and the passengers would be sitting down panicking, but perhaps feeling a bit more courageous. I had to gather my courage, because if I regretted this, what about those people whose lives were in my hands?

Myself, when I was getting on that boat, I said, "Oh my God, what have I done?" But I didn't want them to know exactly what I was thinking, so I didn't show them a face of someone who's discouraged. I always tried to cheer them up. I would say, "I am going to make you a burger this year." We knew in our souls that we were afraid, but we should not make them afraid too.

Given that the boat was overloaded, one of the Guan captains' main concerns was how to keep the passengers calm during the voyage. If they should suddenly panic and begin moving around, the boat could capsize and throw everybody in the water. The captains therefore divided the passengers equally, about fifty people on each side of the boat. But as they entered the open seas and the waves became bigger, the passengers began to cluster on one side, where the waves could not reach them, causing the boat to tilt.

Samuel: I told them, "You guys, if this boat sinks, we are going to die. I myself, I will be able to swim for a time and maybe, if a boat comes, I will be alive by then. But you guys, as soon as the boat sinks, you're going straight under. So you have to be very careful and follow any instructions that you have been given. If you move, this thing is going to flip, and if it flips, you're all going to die."

Eric grabbed a piece of rope and told the passengers to behave or he would "whip" them, adding that if that wouldn't help, he would throw them into the sea.

Samuel: We had to be very hard on them because some of them came from the bush and could easily panic. They would keep asking us, "When are we there?" and, "Are you sure you know what you're doing?" Even though we were also afraid inside, we had to remain calm. So I talked to one old man among them and made him talk them into coming back to their normal places—if not something bad would happen to us. That made the boat more stable, and we were able to proceed. One guy said he would take some pills and lie down and sleep, so that if he should die, he would die without suffering.

Christopher, a Guan captain from Winneba who was hired to command a rubber boat carrying twenty-three passengers, encountered another risk involved in managing the passengers on overcrowded boats. When the voyage was prolonged, the worried passengers turned against the captains, accusing them of not being in control of the operation, though Christopher estimated them to be only two hours within sight of Lampedusa. Refusing to listen to the captains, the passengers threatened them with knives. "The passengers told us that if they were going to die, they would make sure that we, the captains, were killed first. So we turned the boat around and went back to Libya. Being the only ones who could swim, we discussed whether to capsize the boat and let them drown, but were afraid it wouldn't work." Arriving back on the shores of Libya, Christopher was caught by the Libyan police. He was thrown in jail for three months and "beaten every day" before being deported. It did not take him long, however, to gather enough money to travel back to Libya for a second attempt. This time, he had eighteen passengers in a small rubber boat. They encountered bad weather only two hours after their departure, but nevertheless continued. Eighteen hours later, Christopher finally reached Lampedusa. Summing up his dogged pursuit of the opportunity to go to Europe, Christopher said: "Any good thing doesn't come easy. It was a challenge, and I had to forget what had happened and try again."

To return to Samuel's journey: Eric was the most experienced of the three captains in terms of seafaring. Like other Guan captains, he emphasized the challenges of West African canoe fishing in the Gulf of Guinea as important in preparing him for the crossing—practically, physically, and mentally—as he explained in an interview at Sammy's house in Castelvolturno.

Eric: Before, I was very weak; people could easily cheat me and beat me. But when I entered the fishing business, it made me strong in whatever I set my mind to. If you go fishing and you are able to say to the rest of the crew, "Let's go to that fishing ground; I have seen fish over there and want to go for them!" and if you land a big catch, that will gain you the authority to decide other matters also, and no one will say "no" to you. They will see you as an older person, as one of the captains. Even if someone is misbehaving, you can just shut that person up. This way, the fishing experience made me very strong. In the course of the work, pulling the rope [of the purse seine], you are built up physically, and also the mind is growing because you learn to use the brain, to see what is going on and to make decisions. Fishing makes you mature and strong.

H.L.: *Were you afraid to take a boat across to Italy?*
Eric: I was not shaking. I think you know what I mean. I was not afraid about anything about the trip. I was not afraid of any sea at all, be it the Mediterranean or any other sea. . . . I am afraid of a river. If you fall in a river, it can just pull you away like that. But for this sea, if I fall in, I am just going to swim. I have been working with the sea for years and find it almost like a home. The only thing that could be a problem is that I am not too clever reading a compass. The practical side of being on the sea never scares me. The only thing that might get me down, or disappoint me, or affect my performance is cold weather, and I worried about that, or if a big fish would come over us and eat

us all up. These are the only things that I am afraid of. But about the sea, I felt I could do a perfect job and that I had the courage to take a boat across to Italy.

The fact that the Mediterranean Sea is a quite different body of water than the Gulf of Guinea did not worry Eric. He had studied the map before coming to Libya and found out that the Mediterranean, "unlike the sea in Ghana, was a sea between two countries, and it would by all means have an end. So, as long as we have taken off and the water is without bad weather, we would surely reach the other side." Apart from the reservations mentioned, Eric, like most other Guan captains, felt the biggest challenge lay in controlling the passengers. Although he had made lengthy sea voyages before (among other things, illegally smuggling oil from Nigeria), the prospect of sailing human beings worried him.

Eric: Any work that has to do with human beings is very, very difficult. Sailing human beings from one point to the other, I had never done anything like that before, so I prayed to God that there shouldn't be a problem. I was praying that all the passengers should be obedient, because the boat was so heavily loaded that any mistakes might mess up the balance and throw us all in the water. The boat should hold about thirty-five passengers, but it was loaded with about a hundred. It was too many.

The trip took more than three days because of the weak engine and trouble with the battery. Finally, Samuel, Eric, and Justin entered Italian territorial waters and were picked up by the Italian navy. As the navy vessel approached, the Guan captains threw the compass overboard and blended in with the other passengers. This kind of entry, called an "open landing," is the most common form of illegal immigration to Lampedusa (Coluccello & Massey 2007: 80). In many cases, however, deadly accidents take place before the migrants reach their destination. From Senya Beraku, at least twelve captains commanding four boats have died in the crossing, taking with them to their probable deaths three hundred to four hundred passengers never accounted for. From Winneba, at least six Guan captains have died in the crossing, taking an undisclosed number of passengers with them. Because these operations are clandestine, authorities are rarely notified of accidents or boats gone missing, and estimates of death tolls are rather uncertain. One report states that, once one is lost at sea, the probability of one's corpse being found "is one out of three," leading to the conclusion that about ten thousand people lost their lives on the Mediterranean from 1997 to 2002 (cited in Simon 2006: 41).

As discussed above, the three leading, often concurrent causes of death are bad weather, faulty equipment, and overcrowding of the boats, combined with the inability of inexperienced crews to respond to sudden problems. To the Guan captains, though, encountering trouble with boat equipment was not necessarily a cause for panic. The Senya dugout canoe (the *pole* or *canoe-canoe*), used for lengthy sea voyages, is typically quite battered and cracked due to the extreme weather conditions and the lack of harbor facilities, and sea water has to be scooped out of the hull regularly. The outboard motor often needs ad hoc maintenance while on the high seas. Fishing in the Gulf of Guinea, the captains learn to keep their cool during the tropical storms that appear out of nowhere and force crews to ride them out while seeking the nearest shelter. That is not to say that the challenges of the Mediterranean crossing were trivial to the Guan captains—the tally of dead captains and passengers speaks for itself. However, the West African fishermen's abilities to respond to meteorological and technical setbacks appear to have been crucial in dealing with many incidents. Practical seafaring skills apart, other factors may explain why Guan fishermen have become involved in Libyan transit migration. Chapter 6 discusses how the regional decline in West African fishing has intensified an already well-established tradition of emigration among the canoe fishermen from Ghana's Central Region.

Most of the Guan captains exhibited the same confidence in their seafaring abilities, with Jonathan, as always, being the most assertive. Asked whether he was nervous about the prospect of taking a boat across from Libya, which he did five days after Samuel, he replied, "If you were a driver in Denmark, would you be afraid to drive a car in another country?" As it happened, however, Jonathan and his crew (including Roger and the late Richard) encountered life-threatening difficulties on the sea, which they and the passengers might have survived only because of the Guan captains' fishing experience and their readiness to respond to sudden technical problems. The Guan crew had been told to be wary of Tunisian trawlers, because their boat had been stolen from Tunisia. As Jonathan recalled, "If the Tunisians see us, they will try to get us one way or the other, force us or fool us to go to Tunisia." In fact, they did meet a Tunisian trawler on the high seas. With Jonathan at the helm, the captains decided to try to escape, but the trawler was much bigger and faster.

Jonathan: They wanted to stop us, and I refused to stop. But they got ahead of us and blocked the way, and their boat was a very big one and fast too, so I had to swerve [away from] them and forget about the compass and the course we were taking, and just keep going. But our boat collided with theirs. And the front part of the boat got damaged. It did not break apart—but it opened up. The collision was very heavy and three people fell in the water. But we were able to go in after them.

Roger: That's what they'll do when the boat is from Tunisia. They'll take you there and deport you to Libya. So, when they started directing us to Tunisia, we refused. But we ran into the side of their boat and had to fill the cracks with pieces of clothes.

Jonathan: They also threw some ropes at our boat to try and drag us closer, but the rope fell in the water and got tied up in the propeller and broke the engine too. When those people saw they had broken the boat that way, they just went away. They didn't like it because they knew something was going to happen.

The captains dived under the boat to untangle the propeller, but the engine was ruined. So the three captains tied the same rope around their waists, jumped in the water, and began pulling the boat, little by little, in the direction of Italian territorial waters.

Roger: We call it "pulling the goat" [harbour aponchi] in our own language. We had to tie the rope to the waist, pulling the boat, like you put the rope around the neck of the goat.

So much commitment and determination!

Jonathan: You swim until the rope holds you back and you turn and pull. This is what we do in the village if the engine breaks down. One of the captains takes the left side—he swims and he pulls—and another takes the middle and he swims and pulls, and one takes the right side. Sometimes we got tired, dropped the anchor, rested a while, and got in the water again and began pulling. This continued all day, from early morning, about six o'clock, until late in the evening, about four o'clock in the night [when the Italian navy came to pick them up]. It was very scary. But we were at a point where we were either going to be dead or going to be alive, so we had to do whatever possible to help ourselves.

We even saw dead people in the water. It was the bodies of other people, who tried to cross but couldn't make it. We didn't want the passengers to see the dead people, because they don't know how people look when they die in the water. They get very white and the fishes eat up their skin. When a boat gets into problems, everybody dies.

Other collisions have been reported, some with disastrous conse-quences, most notably the death of 283 migrants—mostly Indians, Tamils from Sri Lanka, and Pakistanis—following a collision off the Sicilian coast in June 2001. As one local fishermen was quoted in *La Repubblica*, on retrieving bodies from the sea: "We found dozens of them. They ended up in the nets, and we took them up on board with the fish. At the beginning it was whole corpses, then pieces, [and] finally, white clean bones" (cited in Albahari 2006: 14). Collisions, however fatal, do not appear among the most typical mishaps at sea. In fact, captains report that other vessels usually pull away if migrant boats come close to ask for help or directions. Even in the case of shipwreck, victims can expect no help, as one widely reported incident in May 2007 demonstrated. For three days, twenty-seven African migrants clung to a tuna net thrown out by a Maltese tug that refused to take them on board, while Malta and Libya argued over whose responsibility they were. Eventually, the migrants were picked up by an Italian navy vessel searching the area for fifty-three Eritreans who had made telephone calls to relatives in England,

Italy, and Malta before disappearing at sea. Initially, the migrants cling-ing to the tuna net were believed to be the survivors of the Eritrean shipwreck, but they were not. The fifty-three disappeared.

Under pressure from the owners of the trawler, the captain of the Maltese tug did not want to take the migrants to Malta and risk being refused entry, which had recently happened to a Spanish trawler that had rescued fifty-one migrants from another shipwreck. The *Francisco Catalina* had stood off Malta for a week because authorities in Valetta refused it permission to enter the harbor. In the end, Malta received three of them, while Spain, Italy, and Andorra accepted the rest. Such a delay, the captain of the tug later explained, would have ruined the expensive catch of tuna in the pen. In the wake of the incident off Malta, a UNHCR spokesperson criticized EU countries for not encouraging their fishermen to think of human lives first and for violating international maritime law, which calls for the speedy disembarkation of people who have been rescued at sea (Popham 2007; Bompard 2007). Indeed, in the case of Italy, the state has done little to encourage private rescue missions. Instead it has prosecuted fishermen who have aided people in distress for compli-city in human smuggling, confiscating their boats and searching their homes, thus institutionally discouraging "the solidarity any sailor is ready to extend to *any* fellow seafarer." At the same time, it enables the state to claim a monopoly on "humanitarianism and rescue operations involving migrants" (Albahari 2006: 16; emphasis in original). The UN's criticism goes to the heart of the moral and political dilemmas at stake: humanitarianism versus border enforcement.

STATE OF EXCEPTION

These deadly incidents shed light on a particular aspect of the political economy of the globalized world, that is, the simultaneous restriction and acceleration of the movement of people. As Zygmunt Bauman sar-castically frames the phenomenon: "The challenge is truly awesome: one needs to deny the others the self-same right to freedom of movement which one eulogizes as the topmost achievement of the globalizing world and the warrant of its growing prosperity" (Bauman 1998: 76). As it happens, Bauman finds precisely this hierarchy of mobility at the heart of new forms of social stratification in the so-called global world (Bauman 1998, 2004). According to this hierarchy, inhabitants of "the first world" travel "by their heart's desire and choose destinations according to the joys they offer," whereas inhabitants of "the second world," even if they don't move, feel they are on the move anyway, as the places under their feet are pulled away. But, "if they take to the roads, then their destination, more often than not, is seldom enjoyable, and its enjoyability is not what it has been chosen for" (Bauman 1998: 86–87). Needless to say, these migrants from the second world are not welcomed on arrival; they are "vagabonds," emissaries of misery, and wherever they turn up, "walls built of immigration controls, of residence laws, and of 'cleans streets' and 'zero tolerance' policies grow taller" (Bauman 1998: 89). Indeed, it would be better, from the first-world point of view, if the migrants stayed put; it would be better "to keep the locals local," because, as media representations of their chaotic homes attest, "attempts to save that world from the worst consequences of its own brutality may bring only momentary effects and are bound in the long run to fail; all the lifelines thrown may be easily retwisted into more nooses" (Bauman 1998: 75–76).

As a consequence of the growing legal and political concern with reducing freedom of movement—even at the cost of human lives—death appears to have become commonplace, the maintenance of external EU borders being a case in point. Maurizio Albahari (2006), in a critique of Roger Rouse's notion of the postmodern space of transnationalism (Rouse 1991), argues that migration may indeed challenge the spatial domains within which it unfolds, may even highlight the social nature of space and the collective human agency that creates space. But the discourses on migration, Albahari continues, also *revitalize* certain spatial imaginaries pertaining to the nation-state and its borders. In these spatial imaginaries (and practices), to which even human lives must ultimately yield (or, conversely, become subjects of romantic salvation missions), borders, as he points out, "become (or remain) substantial icons of surveillance, sovereignty, control, low-intensity conflict, and even warfare" (Albahari 2006: 6). From this perspective, migrant deaths are unfortunate—though a certain air of routine surrounding them can sometimes be detected—but do not call into question the sovereign right of nation-states, or of the EU, to enforce border control, even if this entails, indirectly at least, creating a graveyard of migrants trying to enter Europe by the desperate means available, and even if these deaths clash with European moral standards normally applied to human beings in distress. "Death . . . is essentially part of the machinery by which liberal-democratic society is supposedly defended," argues Albahari, "and its life and common good fostered." At the same time, those states and the EU "must abide by their own universalistic proclamations and allegedly shared values of humanitarianism" (Albahari 2006: 30). Indeed, how to keep some people moving while denying others that very right, even at the cost of human lives, is one of the dilemmas of globalization, a moral ambivalence perhaps echoed in political statements on the issue. For instance, former French president Jacques Chirac, referring to illegal immigration at the 2006 EU-African immigration summit in Rabat, Morocco, called for a response "with respect for human dignity but with firmness."

Modern nations-states are perhaps better equipped to display firmness than to show respect for human dignity, as Zygmunt Bauman has repeatedly argued. Rather than creating a structure of morality, modernity—and late modernity, but in different guise—neutralizes moral responsibility (which is based on proximity) and the "animal pity" we feel toward other human beings. Indeed, Bauman (1989) asserts, "the significance—and danger—of moral indifference becomes particularly acute in our modern, rationalized industrial, technologically proficient society because in such a society human action can be effective at a distance, and at a distance constantly growing with progress of science, technology, and bureaucracy. In such a society, *the effects of human action reach far beyond the 'vanishing point' of moral visibility*" (185, 193; emphasis in the original; see also Arendt 2006 on Eichmann and the banality of evil and Arendt's argument that, at the end of the Holocaust command chain, there was not a monster but an obedient bureaucrat). Bauman's point is that morality is not something any given society creates, but something that society manipulates, the Nazi concentration camps being the *mene tekel* of modern state building, not its contradiction (Theodor Mommsen, cited in Bauman 1989: 184). The structure of morality belongs to primary intersubjectivity and is almost impossible to replace with abstract ideas of Otherness. Himmler himself, when the Holocaust was in full train, complained to colleagues that even devoted Nazis who had never harbored any reservations regarding the destruction of the Jewish people had their own individual Jewish friends, who were, they argued, different from other Jews and thus should be spared extinction (Bauman 1989: 183–187).

Indeed, a kind of blindness forms, not to what goes on as such, but to the individual trajectories of those who have been marginalized, objectified, and mythologized—and even left to die. To illustrate, this process may be viewed as a social correlate of prosopagnosia, the medical condition in which, following acute brain damage, one's ability to recognize faces is impaired, though normal vision is otherwise retained. Accordingly, migrant bodies washed ashore on the southern coasts of Europe do not go unrecognized. But instead of giving rise to ethical protests, Bauman suggests, the migrant bodies serve to reinforce the walls of distinction between those on the inside and those on the outside, a process that has become especially significant of late as nations-states in the era of globalization have become more and more porous and threatened by outside violation. Existentially, Bauman argues, dead migrants washed ashore or caught in fishing nets remind Europeans of their own painful disposability in a world where risk has become the predominant theme and where "all places and positions feel shaky and are deemed no longer reliable." This anxiety, which is of our own making, is ritually transposed onto the dead migrant bodies washed up by the sea. "One is tempted to say," Bauman continues, "that were there no immigrants knocking at the doors, they would have to be invented" (Bauman 2004: 56–59).

Following Bauman's line of thought, we should not be too surprised that nation-states, in the declared effort to protect most efficiently the liberal-democratic interests of their citizens, are capable of creating such contradictory exceptions—gray zones at the doorstep of Europe where lives are silently lost—while embracing universal ideals of humanitarianism, though in a depoliticized and dehistorized context. For example, just prior to Italy's unlawful deportation of migrants directly to Libya, Prime Minister Berlusconi declared before the European Parliament, "Our Christian tradition compels us to look to these immigrants with a spirit of reception worthy of our level of civilization" (cited in Albahari 2006: 4). The very nature of modern nation-states consists of order-building, Bauman argues, and this entails disposing of human beings who do not fit into the inclusive categories, those "flawed beings, from whose absence or obliteration the designed form could only gain, becoming more uniform, more harmonious, more secure, and altogether more at peace with itself" (Bauman 2004: 30). Keeping the second world from moving—through technologies of border surveillance (including de facto border extension beyond EU territory into, for instance, Senegalese territorial waters), control, and subsequent detention in isolated centers, even centers in North Africa—has thus become a central order-building project of late modernity, to be managed with firmness. Enigmatically, the nation-state sees this project to be in the interest of the migrants themselves, "thus reducing the danger of losses of human lives," as one report states (Frontex 2007b). The key to understanding this moral paradox, Albahari argues, is to view the nation-states' efforts to keep people from moving, even at the cost of human lives, while also conducting rescue missions as not contradictory but as complementary features of the political economy of the globalized world. The discourse on humanitarianism—rescuing migrant lives at sea—serves as legitimation for further increases of border control measures, and vice versa (Albahari 2006: 16).

In connection with the issues discussed above, the Italian philosopher Giorgio Agamben (1998) argues that since ancient times, a ruling body has been considered to have sovereign power if the juridical order grants it the means to proclaim a *state of exception*, thereby "suspending the order's own validity." That is to say, the legal order is made to withdraw from the exception and abandon it, whereas the exception remains in a relationship with sovereign power, which asserts itself most forcefully precisely by maintaining this relationship to an exterior being excluded from the law (Agamben 1998: 15, 18). To the human beings who are excluded from the law, but not from the power of the sovereign rule—quite the contrary, in fact—Agamben gives the name *homini sacri*. The *homo sacer* (sacred man) is a figure of ancient Roman law whose existence Agamben characterizes as "bare life," as having value in neither a legal nor a religious sense. Thus, the *homo sacer* is the person who may be killed but not sacrificed—that is, killed without the killer committing a legal offence, and not as an offering to the gods (Agamben 1998: 8). The paradigmatic space of the modern state of exception is, Giorgio Agamben argues, the camp—"an apparently innocuous space . . . in which the normal order is de facto suspended and in which whether or not atrocities are committed depends not on law but on the civility and the ethical sense of the police who temporarily act as sovereign" (Agamben 1998: 174). Inhabitants of the camp, having been stripped of their moral and political rights, are reduced to "bare life" in confrontation with sovereign power, and anything can happen to them, as Agamben argues, echoing Hannah Arendt. In other words, juridical procedures and the deployment of power merge to deprive human beings of their rights and prerogatives so completely "that no acts committed against them could appear any longer as a crime" (Agamben 1998: 170–171). Although Agamben reserves a place in modern history for the Nazi death camps as "the most absolute biopolitical space ever to have been realized" (Agamben 1998: 171), he insists that an investigation of this paradigmatic state of exception and the transformation of the inhabitants into *homini sacri* offer insight into current situations in which state power withdraws legal protections and political recognition only to assert itself even more forcefully.

Agamben develops the notion of the camp as being independent of whatever "crimes" take place and of its "denomination and specific topography," to include all spaces where a state of exception has been invoked. The stadium in Bari into which the Italian authorities provisionally kept Albanian immigrants in 1991 before sending them back to their country of origin, for instance, denoted such a camp or space where the normal order had been de facto suspended and the fate of the migrants depended not on the law but on the inclinations of the police officers

(Agamben 1998: 174). In the case of the migrant deaths on the Mediterranean and the secular context of modern nation-states, it could be argued that such a state of exception is in effect as a gray zone, or camp, where political rule operates outside the law, where the law has been made to abandon certain human beings deemed exterior, though these exterior beings remain in relation to sovereign power. These human beings, caught in the state of exception, are reduced to "bare life" (recall the twenty-seven migrants clinging to the tuna net for three days). They either perish at sea, their deaths having no legal or political consequences, or become the subjects of erratic rescue missions aimed not at protecting their rights or restoring them as sociopolitical subjects, but at handling them as "bare lives," as biological beings only. Accordingly, it is doctors (not lawyers) who give them food, water, and injections and who receive them in the camps before they are deported or slip into the Italian underground economy.

The belief that anything can happen to them may be found in the statements of the migrants crossing the Mediterranean. They have in a sense been reduced to "bare life" and abandoned, in the absence of legal protections and political recognition, to the whims of sovereign power. As Jonathan explained, "We were at a point where we were either going to be dead or to be alive, so we had to do whatever possible to help ourselves," while dead bodies floated by in the water. The intolerable regime of arbitrariness that characterizes the camp could also be identified in migrants' statements regarding the challenges of illegal immigrant life. As cited earlier, Francis, talking about day-laboring, said, "Our life is shaking in the hands of these people." On the same topic, Jonathan said, "We don't know who'll pick us up. Maybe they'll kill us. We don't know."

Two points from the Italian context should be added to this analysis. First, in the moral and religious dimension of life, the Catholic Church holds a historically strong position in Italy (by contrast, the nation-state has a relatively weak position in this realm [see, for instance, Harder 2006: 190–219]), and the Italian nation-state, though having a monopoly on rescue missions, for instance, is almost constantly being challenged by the Church on social and moral issues. Thus, the Catholic Church is not indifferent to the fate of migrants, and so it is not surprising that migrant protest demonstrations for better living conditions or amnesties look for moral support from the Vatican. In this respect, Pope Benedict XVI appeared to walk a fine line between respecting the autonomy of political rule and pressuring Italian politicians to act according to Catholic precepts when he commented, "Even if the specific expressions of the ecclesial charity can never be confused with the activity of the State, it still remains true that charity must animate the entire lives of the lay faithful and therefore also their political activity, lived as 'social charity'" (cited in Caritas Europa 2006: 8). In practice, this means, as one Caritas report on migration and poverty states, that the Catholic Church works in "dialogue" with policy makers with the aim of "bringing migrants, especially those that are 'undocumented' out of the shadows and ensuring their access to the same rights as those enjoyed by their fellow European citizens with regard to employment, housing, health, education, and participation in public life" (Caritas Europa 2006: 8). Thus, the Catholic Church claims that those deemed "exterior" human beings by the Italian nation-state belong to Italian society and have value in a social and religious sense. Apart from running shelters and providing moral and political support, the Catholic Church, as reported in Mikkel Hansen's fieldwork in Sicily, in some cases even openly helps illegal immigrants find work, all without the police interfering. In fact, the police in Catania apparently drop off illegal immigrants at the church gates, where the local Polish priest, who is known to walk around with a dossier filled with the telephone numbers of potential employers, finds food, living quarters, and work for them. Asked about the paradox of aiding the illegal immigrants, the priest answered, "They have their rules to be followed. We, in the Church, have other rules, if I may put it that way. The national authorities cannot touch the solidarity the Church has with the illegal immigrants" (cited in Hansen 2007: 79; my translation).

A second point my research in Italy suggests is that from an analytical point of view, the *homo sacer* might work to grasp the dynamics of the production of indifference and the conditions it entails for those living on the fringes. But from the migrants' point of view, from below, though they have no legal or political power, they do have means of action on a smaller scale by which at least something qualitatively new may appear. In other words, Giorgio Agamben, and to a lesser extent Zygmunt Bauman, gives little attention to human experience or to how the "state of exception" is actually lived. In the absence of legal and political pro-tections on the sea, for example, migrants undergo purification rituals to deal with the regime of arbitrariness characteristic of the state of excep-tion. And in Naples, the Guan migrants reinvent themselves as burgers and tycoons, as people with power and connections, when confronted with the harsh realities and nullification of illegal immigrant life. More-over, lives may be silently lost on the Mediterranean, but in the village of Senya Beraku, dead captains are not routine statistics; they are sons, brothers, and fathers. And what is lost in a far-off place is reclaimed and circumscribed in local magico-religious rituals, as chapter 7 further explores. But before turning to Senya Beraku, I discuss the organization of trans-Saharan migration.

FIVE

The Maghreb Connection

LIBYA AND A DESERT TO CROSS

Francis was sitting on his bed in a small shared room in a six-story high-rise on the outskirts of Naples, the ever-present noise of the expressway to Rome coming through the open door, the walls lined with suitcases piled on top of each other as if in readiness for an instant departure, when he surprised me by asking if I would like to see a picture of the place where he almost died in the Libyan desert. He opened a suitcase and showed me five pages torn out of an Italian travel magazine. Under the headline "Adventure Tourism" ("Turismo Avventura"), an Italian journalist reports driving a jeep through the Libyan desert with his wife, passing various natural and architectural sites well known for their beauty. Although many consider ancient ruins, sand dunes, and desert solitude beautiful, immigrants from West Africa passing on their way to the north fear them as godforsaken places where one would not want to get lost. One photograph shows the journalist's wife sitting on the sand (presumably drinking tea) alongside the desert guides. The guides pose like postcard Bedouins, wrapped in bluish garments in the manner of the Tuareg, with long, crooked knives in their belts and turbans covering their heads and much of their faces, allowing only their serious eyes to be seen. "This is where we passed in the deep night," said Francis, and Sammy nodded his head in surprise at seeing the very place where he himself came close to losing his life. "And these are the people that beat us and robbed us," Francis added, pointing to the guides. The article says that, although obtaining a tourist visa for Libya requires long and tedious work, seeing the "New Horizons" ("Nouvi Orizzonti") of "adventure tourism" is worth the effort.

Although the perilous way to Lampedusa may take more lives, as when a boat with one hundred passengers suddenly capsizes, the risky trip from Agadez in Niger, across the Sahara Desert to the border towns of Libya, is equally feared among most migrants. Indeed some Guan fishermen dread the desert journey even more than the voyage across the Mediterranean. Many captains say they have experience in handling the sea, whereas in the desert they are at the mercy of human smugglers whose lack of regard for human life is well established, not to mention the gangs of armed robbers that prey on the defenseless caravans of migrants (sometimes in cahoots with the drivers), who often travel with their life savings. As Samuel put it, "I don't usually shed tears—you know that, Hans. But in the desert I cried. Tears rolled down my cheeks. I knew we were going to die."

For Guan migrants, the first part of the voyage goes from Accra, Ghana, via Ouagadougou in Burkina Faso to Niamey, the capital of Niger, and from there to the truck station in Agadez in Central Niger— here the trucks bound for the Sahara depart. Legally, the Economic Community of West African States (ECOWAS) guarantees free movement of people in the region, making this part of the journey unproblematic— though bribes are reported, especially since many travel without relevant documents—and it is therefore not dealt with further here. The ICMPD estimates that sixty thousand to eighty thousand migrants use the route from Agadez to Algeria and Libya every year, making it "the most important migration channel from sub-Saharan African countries to Maghreb countries" (Simon 2006: 54). Agadez is a market town at a crossroads in the desert, on the southern edge of the Aïr Massif, and was once the seat of the Tuareg Sultanate. Tuareg and Fulani nomads trade their livestock and hides, as well grains and vegetables, in the marketplace; mining has also become important, especially of tin, coal, and uranium. But now another type of business prevails. Long a transit point on the trans-Saharan migration and trade route, over the past twenty years Agadez has also become the nucleus of the migration flows toward North Africa (Simon 2006: 49). Thus, at the Agadez station, trucks leave on the two main routes to Libya. The northern route—through Algeria, passing Djanet and then crossing the border and entering the Libyan town of Ghat—entails walking through the Ahaggar Mountains, which rise from Algeria's southern desert. The northeastern route goes via Dirkou through the Ténéré Desert, eventually toward the Libyan town of Al Qatrun.

The worn-out trucks each take hundreds of people crammed in the back, "looking like mobile cathedrals in the desert," the prices varying between 25 and 80 Euros (Zarro 2007: 123–124). A couple of trucks leave every day, carrying mostly cigarettes and, on top of them, young West African men looking for short-term work in Libya or a connection to Europe. Sometimes passengers have to wait in the bus station in Agadez for weeks until the smugglers are satisfied with the number of people moving out. As with overloading the boats that smuggle people across the Mediterranean, the overcrowding of trucks makes a risky journey in a rickety vehicle in extreme weather conditions even more dangerous. Little is known about the crossing of the Sahara Desert, however, because no systematic research has been conducted (Collyer 2006: 134; Hamood 2006: 47). This part of the journey "doubles the risk" of suffering and death; in fact, this land route to Libya "is considered the most dangerous and deadly . . . that migrants can take" (Simon 2006: 54, 62). Consequently, the testimonies of migrants crossing the Sahara are, like those of the sea voyages described earlier, full of death and suffering (the same applies to East African migration via Sudan into Libya [Hamood 2006: 47]). I explore four cases (two for each route) that reveal the organization and challenges of the first leg of the long voyage to Europe via Libya.

Prior to leaving the village in Ghana, Samuel had convinced a friend, Martin (Madame Hope's boyfriend, mentioned earlier), to forget about his aunt in America, who had promised to help him travel abroad, and come with Samuel to Libya. But the journey got off to an unfortunate start. In Agadez, Samuel and Martin were delayed in the truck station for two weeks while the drivers and the connection men kept collecting money and gathering more people, though most of the passengers felt that there were already more than enough. In an interview with the *New York Times*, Dodo Aboube, one of the main organizers at the Agadez truck station, commented on an overloaded truck crammed with more than a hundred people getting ready to leave: "Our trucks don't even meet the conditions for safe travel, but we manage somehow. If they break down, the desert is the desert. People can die after a couple of days in the desert" (Onishi 2001). In the end, out of desperation the passengers staged a demonstration and vandalized the drivers' office. The police arrived on the scene, and the passengers explained that the smugglers were being greedy and were trying to overload the truck, making it likely that they would "suffocate and suffer."

Early the following morning, the organizers began shouting out passengers' names and getting ready to move out. They were also selling water by the gallon; water is kept in a rubber container wrapped in a sack, which is then tied to the outside of the truck. Samuel and Martin bought some, along with a piece of tube to sip the water out of its container when, during breaks, they would have a chance to drink. All the while, Sammy was listening carefully to the names being called out. He had been on the desert track to Libya before, and he knew it was important to get good places to stand, as close to the edge of the load as possible, in order not to suffocate. On board the trucks there is little solidarity among the migrants, and nobody wanted to be packed in the middle under the harsh desert sun with no possibility of resting. Migrants have reported people falling down from exhaustion and being trampled underfoot by their fellow passengers, their bodies eventually thrown off the truck and left in the desert. "As soon as we heard our names," Samuel said, "we jumped on the truck and found the place that would be most comfortable for us. Sometimes the Niger people will occupy those good places, and they'll use a knife to keep you away. If you try to talk to them, they'll come in numbers and jump on you; so we were very careful."

Once the trucks entered Libyan territory, considered a no-man's-land by the West African immigrants, scores were sometimes settled between the different nationalities. "In Libya, the Niger people weren't as strong as in their own country, and we guys from the West Coast would want to go for any Niger person who had misbehaved along the way." The migrants also had to be careful not to get on the wrong side of the drivers, who apparently killed people at will. "These drivers behave in any way they like; if you fall off the car, they may come and use the knife on you."

The truck moved slowly through the desert, taking almost three days to reach Dirkou, the small oasis town five hundred kilometers northeast of Agadez. Originally constructed as an army base during the Tuareg uprising, over the last ten years, this small point in the desert has become a main transit point for people and goods moving into Libya, even expanding to include "makeshift markets, prostitution, and ghettos." Stranded migrants thrown out of Libya without sufficient means to go home or make a new attempt also end up here, where they arrange "junk markets or improvise as carpenters and the like," the atmosphere generally being one of "disenchantment and frustration" (Zarro 2007: 126).

In Dirkou, Samuel and Martin got off the truck and joined a caravan of four smaller jeeps rigged to carry thirty to thirty-five people each. During the next two days they drove toward Al Qatrun in southern Libya, stopping only to rest during the night. One night, however, as they lay sleeping on the ground, the driver suddenly took off with all their food and water. Terrified at the prospect of being dumped in the Sahara, they rushed to hijack the only jeep that had not yet moved out. But the driver convinced them to get off, since the jeep would surely break down if the number of passengers were doubled. He told them that he would move ahead two or three kilometers, drop off his own passengers, and then come back for Samuel and Martin and the rest, thus moving them slowly ahead. "You don't have to stop walking," the driver told them. "You should keep walking, so as not to waste any fuel." The first time, the driver did just as he had promised, taking his own passengers ahead and coming back to pick up the rest; and the second time also. But the third time, he did not return. Soon, they realized they were on their own, and they did not know where they were going.

Samuel: Since we were in the desert, we would follow the car tracks in the sand. That would take a very long time, but it would be better to start walking in order not to die. We were about thirty people walking, but because people were not strong enough, they started falling behind. The rest of us were moving faster and faster, because in a short while we would be without water and food, and we wouldn't be able to walk anymore. We walked in the day and in the night, and when we were tired, we lay down on the ground to relax. We had no food, no water, so we drank our own urine. Martin had some glucose in his pocket, and we mixed that into the urine and kept moving forward. A lot of people dropped off, and soon we were left with about eight people. The remaining ones kept telling us to wait, but I was forcing them to move on. It would be better to get as close to the town as possible, so that even if we were lying down dying, a car could come and find us. Since they [the weaker passengers] couldn't do that, I don't know what happened to them. We could only think of ourselves. The old men soon started falling behind, so we were left with the youngsters. I was keeping an eye on this guy [Martin] to make sure he was okay. One guy who was traveling with us suddenly said, "Sammy, I know there's a town straight ahead," and he got up and walked from here to the kitchen [a couple of paces] and fell down and died. It seems he was ready to die and left with the last power in him; he wanted to do something. It was dark and the rest of us just kept walking until daybreak. At six o'clock in the morning, we met a car, and they treated us very well and gave us water and food. We were left with five people, but one collapsed after we had met the car, and I am not sure what happened to him. So we were only four people who made it: Martin, two others, and myself. When we came to Tripoli—very black from the sun, our skin peeling off—and our friends said, "Oh God, what happened to you?" We said that we had died, but that we came back to life.

Samuel is not the only migrant to have been abandoned in the desert on the way to Al Qatrun, as the story of Michael illustrates. Michael was traveling in a caravan of four jeeps with his brother and about one hundred people, "packed like sardines," when the driver seemingly lost his way. Earlier, the driver had taken all the passengers to a "rebel camp for soldiers from Chad," where they were forced to pay to be allowed passage farther into Libya. Leaving the camp, the driver had brought a jerrican filled with twenty-five liters of water, but it was too little, "because we got lost, and soon we were going up and down. There were no roads, only desert, extreme desert. It was very hot, like fire, I tell you, my brother. But when the night fell, it became so cool, very, very cool." Most of the passengers were ready to drop, when the drivers suddenly announced that "they wanted to manage the water, so we could reach Libya safely." Since the water was nearly gone, they would not allow anyone to drink for the next three days. Those who died would be buried, and the survivors would share the remaining water.

Michael: They were wicked people; they wanted to rob and kill us. One brother tried to get to the water by force, but they stabbed him, and he died. The brother was so thirsty—he told the man that three days was too long, so they should give out water. Those people are wicked, always with a knife. They didn't even bury him; they just threw him in the desert. During that time people started dying, fifteen to twenty people, dead in the desert, sometimes we couldn't bury them—there was not strength for you to dig and bury a person. So we had to leave them and continue. Sometimes the jeep got stuck in the sand, and we had to get down and push it; but if you don't manage to get back in the car very fast, they would leave you. My brother was very weak at the time; he was sleeping in the car, so I told the ladies—

we had six ladies in the car—to take care of him. But when the people jumped back on the car, they stepped on him. Everybody was fighting to get inside the car. When the car was moving, I tried to separate the people [from the brother], but I could not. They were all weak; I could not. When we came to that last place to share the water, I called on him but no response. I saw the eyes opening like this [*half open*]. He faced Ghana; we were going to Libya, but he was looking at Ghana—eyes opened.

Unfortunately, Michael's elder brother died only shortly before the drivers again allowed the passengers water. They received only a very little, though. "One tablespoon each. I put it in my mouth, and a little bit here [*in the nostrils*]." Those who were still alive were now severely affected by exhaustion and dehydration. "When we stood up, we walked like drunkards [*shows how people wobbled on their feet*], you see? People were dying." One of the cars broke down, and all the passengers were offloaded while the drivers left, claiming to be looking for water in a nearby village. But they never returned. Paralyzed, Michael sat in the sand next to his dead brother, while some of the passengers decided to walk in the direction of the jeeps.

Michael: They told me to wake up because they were leaving. But because of all the deaths, something fell upon me; it was very difficult to even lift up my head. Me, that time, I behaved like a crazy person; I don't know what was going on. I lay on the desert like this [*on his side, staring*], thinking about what happened. I saw people moving toward those cars, and I asked myself, How could I manage to reach that place? I lifted up my head; it was getting dark. I would reach that place too, to survive, because I was among the dead people now. I called him, called him [*clapping his hands*], "Wake up, my brother, Charlie, let's go, Charlie, wake up, wake up, wake up, wake up. Eh, Charlie, you're dead!" He was our leader from Senya to that place. Eh! I tried to bury him there, so I dug a small hole in the sand, and I pushed him and he fell into it. I took my coat off—I still had my coat—and I put the coat upon my brother and covered him. I was grieving, but I knew that if I didn't leave that place, I would die there.

I called my older brother [*clapping his hands again*], but he had died. Really, I am among the dead people now. If I don't fight to leave this place, I will die here. So, I tried, I was trying. I walked small, then I fell down and woke up; I walked small, small, then fell down and woke up again.

Somehow, Michael managed to get on his feet each time he fell and reached the place, only to find out there was nothing there and the jeeps had long since left. The remaining passengers—about half of the group that had set out from Dirkou—discussed what to do. They decided to collect all the jerricans and the petrol from the abandoned jeep and build a big fire in the desert night to signal for help. Although a fire would also attract the attention of the Libyan army, which most migrants feared, they thought it better than inevitable death.

Michael: We get all the rubber we can. Some people brought a petrol tank, but we are looking for fire, a lighter, there's no lighter. We call to everybody. One Nigerian man is a smoker—we thought that man would die in the desert, but he's still alive, and plenty others have died, so, you see, God's ways worry us.

The Libyan army saw the signal; soldiers came and gave the migrants water and instructed them how to drink carefully, both hot and cold water, and eat small pieces of biscuit. Since Michael was a mason, he was taken to a nearby army base to work on the construction of an airstrip. The military commander was so pleased with Michael and his colleagues' work that after eight days they were allowed to move on toward Al Qatrun. From there, they headed to Tripoli to look for a connection.

The other route frequently traveled by West Africans on their way to Libya heads north from Agadez through Algeria and the Ahaggar Mountains, reaching the town of Ghat in Libya. Eric traveled this route, which skirts the dreaded Ténéré Desert but is plagued with robbers. He had heard stories of this route beforehand and had planned for the trip, dividing his money into three parts. The first part he wrapped and put into his bag of millet that he would live off of in the desert and in the mountains; the second he stuffed down his underwear; and the third he wrapped in cellophane and inserted into his rectum. "So, if the robbers were able to find one package they could take that, and I would still have something to go with, whereas if they found everything, it would be very bad." Driving in an "old soldiers jeep" covered with a sunshade, Eric's group soon ran into the first band of armed robbers in the desert; in total, they met three such groups at different points along the route. The first group wanted money for directions to Libya. They paid them five hundred CFA francs each, and the robbers led them to another point in the desert, where they were forced to buy water at five thousand CFA a gallon from a second group of armed robbers. Finally, the third group approached them prior to entering Libya and charged the migrants to enter the country.

Eric: This journey is very deadly. Instead of showing us the short route, they took us to see armed robbers, so that they could have their share. If I am a driver, and my brother is a robber, I am going to pass by his place, so that he can get his share, and at the end of the day we split the money. But because of the hard situation in Ghana, people will try to go, even though the little money they have can't really take them anywhere.[And even though you really don't have money, the robbers will think, when you go on such a journey, you surely bring money and you're just being troublesome, and [so] they will shoot you. On our trip they shot about seven people and took the rest of the money they had on them. If you insist on not buying their water, they will force you—they have guns, and if you mess up, they will blow your head off, just kill you like that, and take your money. They dress like the Arabs, the ones that ride on camels. Their faces are covered; you can only see their noses and their eyes. They are white Arabs from the northern part; they carry long knives and AK-47s on their backs. On that road they have a lot of robbers, who can kill you easily.

Many died of thirst and exhaustion on the way, too, so many that Eric lost count. Especially crossing the Ahaggar Mountains, "a lot of people died, some just fell down and couldn't get up again. I walked and walked. I never walked this long before, and even the soles of my shoes got ruined." The long walk also affected Eric's knees very badly, and they now hurt whenever he lifts heavy things at work.

Eric: Our forefathers made long trips by walking because they had no cars, so we know how to walk on very long journeys, but that was not the case here. They made us suffer throughout the journey by letting the armed robbers take advantage of us, and that was the very terrible thing that made the trip so difficult.

Apart from robbery, which is so common that most talk of it matter-of-factly, migrants who have trekked along this route to Libya mention the Ahaggar Mountains as an especially difficult obstacle to overcome. Louis, for instance, lost a friend along the route and almost perished himself. Since he had been to Libya once before (though he was deported after the Tripoli riots of 2000), he led a group of three young men from Senya. Originally they wanted to go through Dirkou and the Ténéré Desert, but they were told in Agadez that the route had been shut down because the Libyan military was then active in the southern borderlands. So they took the mountain trail into Algeria instead. Setting out from Agadez, they drove north in a truck until they reached the mountains and began the long climb.

Louis: There's nothing there, no living things. You have your food and water in your bag, and if you run short, it's a problem. The sun too, it's very hot; you have to drink all the time, and soon your water is finished. The journey is three to four days, walking, so it's very dangerous. People used to die on that route.

They were about 250 people, but as soon as they started the climb, people began dropping out of the group. As they walked farther up, they began passing dead bodies strewn along the path.

Louis: I went with my two colleagues—one of them died; it was very, very painful. He fell down, and he could not walk again. So we had to sit down and wait for him, while all the people left us. The following day, still he cannot walk, so we have to leave him, because at that time, there was no food and no water. It was a difficult decision, but it was the only solution or we would all die. So we decided that the two of us should go, and when we reached that country [Libya], we could come back and get him. We were supposed to go and get water, but the country was very far; that was the problem—it was too far for us.

They soon realized that they were not approaching Libya, and without the guides, they were lost.

Louis: We think the country is close, but it is not close, because we don't know the road. We walked a long time, from morning to evening, but we don't get close; it means we have lost our way. Rather, we have returned, going back to Algeria.

The next day, there was no strength left in me; I also fell down. So we were left with only one colleague who had the strength to continue. I drank my urine and that saved me before my colleague came back to get me. Luckily he met an old woman in the desert who was bringing some goats. He told the woman that he would like to get water for his brothers, but the woman said he had lost his way, and from that place to Libya was very far, three days. So she took him to her village, a small village in the desert. She gave him some water, and he came back and looked for me. But the place we had left our brother was very far; you cannot go back there. That time there was no strength left; I had to use everything in me just to reach the village of that woman. Even if we get to a bigger village, and get a car to come back and look for our friend, we cannot say where we passed; we cannot identify the road because of how the desert is. Three years now, I haven't seen him, and I am thinking he's dead by now; that is the dangerous side of the Ahaggar Mountains.

In the absence of much statistical or comparative material, I summarize the recurring themes in the four case stories above. Most important, the first leg of the journey across the Sahara to Europe is extremely perilous, and migrant accounts of desert journeys completed without mishap are quite rare, though they do exist. Indeed, the dangers awaiting the migrants traveling from Niger to Libya take a heavy toll on migrant numbers even before the migrants even board ramshackle boats for Lampedusa, with possibly as many lives lost as on the sea voyage to Europe. Whether traveling via the northeastern route through the Ténéré or the northern route across the Ahaggar Mountains, there are major obstacles to surmount. (Although the Niger routes into Libya may be unique in brutality, other trans-Saharan routes—for instance, to Mauritania and Morocco via Tamanrasset in Algeria, or from the Horn of Africa and East Africa into Libya via Sudan—may also entail a significant loss of life.) As Michael Collyer (2006) argues, "The dangers of crossing the Mediterranean are now widely appreciated, in part due to the frequency of reports of migrants who have drowned attempting it, but the dangers of becoming lost on the desert leg of the journey are at least as extreme and much less widely understood" (134). The most imminent threat to trans-Saharan migrants, apart from being brutally murdered, appears to be getting lost, whether one is abandoned by the smugglers or is too exhausted to follow one's group; when the water is finished and one is unable to urinate, there is not much hope left. Indeed, the stories of Samuel, Michael, and Louis show how they only narrowly escaped the fate that many migrants before and after them have suffered.

One can only guess at the reason for abandoning migrants in the desert, as documented especially in the Ténéré. It might be that drivers do get lost and calculate their own chances of survival as better if they offload the migrants; it could also be that the fear of meeting the Libyan army or the paramilitary groups that move about the borderlands makes the human smugglers anxious and quick to take abrupt measures if they are alerted to any problems. And perhaps, as Michael suggests, some human smugglers are in fact "wicked people," in the sense that they do not value the lives of the migrants, but take their money and dump them in the desert—not a crime likely to have any consequences for the perpetrators. But as Louis's case also shows, in which suddenly an old woman with a herd of goats appeared out of the blue, some people do live in the (to the West African migrants) deserted place that is the Sahara, and getting lost might be more a question of straying just slightly off course and not knowing how to navigate in such an extremely harsh landscape than of the Sahara being unpopulated or uninhabitable. Moreover, though the migrants have good reason to be skeptical about the people they encounter in the desert, their experiences also show that some are willing to help and some, like the old goat herder, even save the lives of migrants they come across. The Libyan army, as described by Michael, also appeared to come to the aid of migrants who otherwise would have perished.

In addition to the danger of getting lost, robbers prey on migrants, especially in the Ahaggar Mountains, and many report erratic killings when disputes arise or migrants cannot afford to pay bribes. Most migrants deal with this situation in a practical manner, preparing their money—dividing it into parts and wrapping it, as Eric did—so they are ready to pay at all the robber checkpoints.

In general, the Guan migrants seem well informed beforehand about the dangers of trans-Saharan migration and the risky sea voyage to Europe; they are aware of the risk of drowning at sea, of dying of thirst and exhaustion in the desert, and of getting killed by armed robbers (the picture is much the same in East African migration into Libya [Hamood 2006: 57–59]). In fact, once the decision to emigrate has been made, some migrants appear almost eager to force the issue of whether they'll live or die, leaving, as they say, the decision up to God, as if death would be a kind of liberation from the slow but inevitable "death" of modern African village life. To be sure, this all-or-nothing attitude is quite typical of migrant interviews concerning the risk of illegal immigration (and should also be kept in mind in connection with the disillusionment that many face in Naples, when the transformation they risked their life for fails to materialize). However, the cases also show that migrants pursue particular strategies so that not everything is left unresolved. Samuel's case, for instance, documents that the migrants first mounted a demonstration in Agadez to pressure the human smugglers to refrain from overloading the trucks; then they equipped themselves for the journey and fought for good places on the trucks in order not to collapse; and, finally, when Samuel and Martin had to walk across the desert, they set a fast pace, condemning others to oblivion while stretching their own resources to the limit. The fatalistic statements most migrants made were thus accompanied by action, however insufficient, directed at keeping the endless risks and uncertainties at bay and, concurrently, the need for divine intervention to a minimum.

Although migrants are aware of the risks involved in trans-Saharan migration, they are, as documented above, unprepared for the *horror* of the actual incidents. Most manage to deal with the experience and move on, whereas some give up and travel back to Ghana. For instance, Samuel and Eric made it all the way to Italy, whereas Michael and Louis went back to Senya Beraku—Louis after staying three years in Libya and Michael in the wake of a police crackdown in Zuwarrah in 2003. To Louis, sitting at the small plastic bag–making machine he bought with money he saved up in Libya, his near-death experience in the Ahaggar Mountains convinced him to turn down all offers to take a boat across to Italy. "I tasted death. My intention going to Libya was to go on to Europe, but because of the troubles I met in the desert, I don't want to try that again." Michael, sitting in the shade of his father's house in Senya, a grubby white duck shrieking endlessly from the corner of the house, lapses into a thousand-yard stare as he recounts the terrible things that befell him and his brother in the desert. He never wants to take that route again; but then he added, "I am thirty-three years old; I will try again. I have that in my mind, that I want to go again, to fight for my future. We cannot stay in our homeland; we have to go forward to survive."

This chapter has dealt with the dangerous intermezzo that precedes illegal-immigrant life in Naples and that underscores the choices later made in Naples. That is, one is perhaps more likely to dig in one's heels, however discouraging the situation may appear, having made it across the Sahara and the Mediterranean into Italy. Moreover, the point of this discussion is to show that the movement of people in the globalized world takes place on very different terms and that, following Bauman, freedom of movement is heralded as the paradigmatic characteristic of globalization, even while enormous efforts are made to stop particular people from moving. Yet, though measures of control are expanding, migration does not seem to be disappearing. As Hansen and Stepputat (2005) argue, "Although immigration and accelerated movement of people around the world undoubtedly have brought the illiberal, exclusive, and sometimes openly racist dimensions of democracy and nation states to the fore, it is equally clear that even the richest nations in the world are unable to contain and control these movements" (18). But the tightening of immigration controls does affect the conditions under which the "outcasts of modernity" (Bauman 2004) eventually find their way to Europe. Rather than refraining from emigrating in the face of growing border enforcement and political pressure, migrants take greater and greater risks.

In this connection, an ethnographic account is needed to show how sensitive trans-Saharan migration routes are to efforts to control migration in North Africa, as well as EU border enforcement and, just as important, to show what these new measures mean for people on the move (see also Simon 2006: 48). Analytically, one could then ask whether the EU is pushing a *state of exception* deep into the African continent and, in the absence of legal and political protections for migrants, actually facilitating the criminal activities, dangers, and deaths that it purports to combat. In the case of Morocco, for instance, the enforced systems of surveillance along the Spanish coasts have led human smugglers to take fewer risks, in that they no longer accompany migrants but send them off on their own (Simon 2006: 48), which of course leaves it up to the ethical judgment of the human smugglers whether they choose to provide migrants with seaworthy equipment or not.

Another question is whether the globalized world's political economy is promoting a version of *necropolitics* by which *death-worlds* are created, as Achille Mbembe calls them: "new and unique forms of social existence in which vast populations are subjected to conditions of life conferring upon them the status of *living dead*" (Mbembe 2003: 40; emphasis in the original). The special position of West African fishermen in illegal immigration into Europe is presented here as a case through which one might not only glimpse life in the shadows of the global political economy but also see how the less privileged struggle in surprising ways to regain a sense of direction in their lives, through a string of critical events in which the dynamics of what is given and where one aspires to go come together—often with disappointing results. But, as argued above, a more comprehensive understanding of the factors that push and pull West African migrants to Europe has to take into consideration regional differences and local economic and social transformations. Part 3 addresses the Guan fishermen's reasons for leaving the village of Senya Beraku, the many deaths this decision entails, and how lives lost at sea or in the desert are reclaimed and encompassed.

PART THREE

In the Village of the Lost Captains

- Reasons for leaving
- Deaths due to this decision
- How lives lost at sea are reclaimed

SIX The Guan of Senya Beraku

Senya Beraku, a fishing village of five thousand to ten thousand people, is about forty-five kilometers west of Accra in Ghana's Central Region. It is reached by leaving the Cape Coast highway, following a narrow dirt road for about five kilometers, through low bushes and reddish anthills, until the road suddenly drops steeply and the Gulf of Guinea comes into view. Senya sits on this slope that leads down to fishing places—two sandy beaches separated by steep rock faces reaching into the sea. Having spent five months among the Guan fishermen in 2002, I returned here in 2006 to do fieldwork for this book.

Everywhere one goes in this fishing community, there is an old man sitting in the shade of a tree mending a net. On the street corner, fishing crews hang around in the cool of the afternoon, having returned from the sea, cleaned themselves up, and changed into nice clothes, and are now maybe playing cards or having a drink. Behind most houses one can find a couple of clay smoke ovens operated by the women fishmongers. When the fishermen have catches, the whole village lies under a drowsy blanket of oily smoke, as the women preserve and store the fish before they are shipped north. But as catches have failed drastically for the fifth year in succession, the village is struggling. From a nutritional point of view, fish is the village's most important source of protein and is not easily replaced. Indeed, the importance of fish is stressed discursively; thus, in the Guan language the same word, *inu*, is used for fish and meat, and if one desires a special kind of meat apart from fish, one has to specify, adding the kind of animal one is requesting—for instance, *kyidinu*, "fowl meat"; *owotunu*, "bush meat"; or *nentwinu*, "beef."

[When the main industry of the village is in decline, a loss of economic and social agency appears to follow, prompting the Guan of Senya Beraku to wonder what the future has in store for them. Economically and socially, the fishing industry has established and maintained lives and livelihoods, the sea providing fish in turn for hard work, magical action, and ritual sacrifice. Now, existentially, the necessary balance between where one would like to go and where one is taken by the world is, one could argue, tipping in an undesirable direction, making it increasingly difficult to preserve "what really matters" (Kleinman 2006: 6). Although the situation is serious on many levels, the fishing community is not passively waiting for a collapse. As this chapter demonstrates, the fishermen are using new technologies. One example is the nationally banned "mechanical system," which consists of a power generator and a thousand-watt light bulb that is lowered into the water in the hope the fish will come from afar, attracted by the light. So far, however, these innovations have yielded disappointing results. The strategy that the overwhelming majority of young men therefore pursue, or express their intention to pursue, is illegal immigration to Europe, even though they are aware of the dangers awaiting them, perhaps having attended the funeral of a friend or relative who did not make it. At the same time, they see former colleagues, now living in Europe, putting up houses on the outskirts of town.

Ethnically, Senya Beraku is a Guan-speaking fishing village. The people are also known as the Effutu, literally meaning "all together," the name given to them by their Akan neighbors—the Fante—who believed the Guan dialect to be an amalgam of all languages (Ephirim-Donkor 2000: 25). Unlike the predominantly Muslim Guan of northern Ghana (the Gonja, for instance, with whom the people of Senya Beraku have little or no relation), the Guan-speaking people on the coast are predominantly Christians and largely follow matrilineal decent, like the Akan; in some cases, patrilineal descent, in the tradition of the Northern Guan, is traced. For example, the son of the chief fisherman will eventually take his father's stool in the same way that sons become members of their father's *asafo*, one of the two paramilitary groups protecting the Senya Beraku king (see also Wyllie 1967: 84). In fact, this dual descent system is the cause of much tension and conflict and plays a role in the chieftaincy dispute currently dividing Senya Beraku. In total, the Guan district on the coast consists of Senya Beraku; Winneba, the largest Guan community; and a few remote inland villages. Regrettably, many accounts of people living on the coast ignore the Guan or assume them to have been absorbed by their Fante neighbors (Christensen 1997: 72; Buah 1998: 14; Walker 2002: 392), when in fact the Guan consider themselves to be "the first people" to settle on the coast of Ghana's Central Region. According to tradition, they came down from Timbuktu and are therefore the rightful owners of lands now occupied by the Fante. As the chief fisherman explained, "We came from the North in the olden days to settle here; we were here first."

Thus, the Guan-speaking people of Senya Beraku now live in a small pocket of land surrounded by Fante who occupy territory the Guan believe was once theirs but was generously given to the Fante. The Fante, especially in the neighboring town of Fetteh, much to the Guan's dismay, have never compensated them for this gift of land, and there is the feeling that Senya Beraku has been "robbed." The feeling is so strong that in the 1990s the Guan almost went to war with Fetteh over the issue because of the latter's refusal to acknowledge this alleged debt. Moreover, Fetteh has become a tourist attraction now that several luxury hotels have been constructed on the beach where Europeans go to swim and relax over the weekend, bringing jobs and business to Fetteh—both of which Senya Beraku also desperately needs. And to make things even worse, Senya Beraku is reported to "encapsulate much of what is disturbing about modern Africa," as travel writer Philip Briggs reports in his influential *Guide to Ghana* (1998). "Senya Beraku is, in a word, depressing," Briggs declares, "and visitors may want to take a break to visit the nearby town of Fetteh" (115). In the end, the land dispute with Fetteh was taken to court and the Guan claims were dismissed. This preoccupation with borders and demarcations and with infringement from outside exemplifies the Guan concern with both extrusion and intrusion. This concern can also be found in the spiritual map of the village, which situates powerful guardians to the east, north, and west, whereas to the south intruders are cut off by the sea and the divine powers dwelling there, ready to slay any that come to do harm to the people of Senya Beraku.

The main tourist attraction of the village is Fort Good Hope, a former Dutch slave trader's castle—rusted eighteenth-century cannon still on display along the walls—dramatically located on the top of a cliff at the end of the main road, overlooking the most important beach, where fish are traded directly off the canoes. However, since the former Gold Coast has numerous colonial castles that are bigger and more impressive than this one, business is relatively slow. Thus, Fort Good Hope, which has been turned into a government hostel, was my residence during both periods of fieldwork in Senya Beraku. One might ask whether a structure with such a brutal past is a dubious place for an anthropological fieldworker to be quartered. However, the cruel legacy of the slave trade has not made the fort a place of mourning (except, perhaps, to accidental European and American visitors); on the contrary, the community (the better-off families mostly) uses the fort to celebrate important social functions, especially elaborate Ghanaian funerals. As a consequence, it was not unusual for the quiet of a Sunday morning to be suddenly disturbed by the horns of an ambulance (followed by a film crew documenting the event) carrying a dead person from the mortuary in nearby Winneba to Senya Beraku for burial. (This was, incidentally, one of the rare appearances of an ambulance in Ghana.) Usually, the family keeps the body stored in a "fridge" until sufficient funds are in place and people based abroad can be summoned to participate (for a discussion of how the business of modern mortuaries has changed Ghanaian funeral rites, see Van der Geest 2006).

But Fort Good Hope offered many practical advantages for me. From the walls one has the best view of the beach where fishermen were busiest, making it a crucial point of observation. Moreover, due to the chronic lack of business, the cool but somewhat scruffy lobby on the fort's first floor worked well as a location for interviewing informants undisturbed; as a consequence, more than half of the 101 taped interviews I conducted in the village took place here. Because of the relatively short duration of my stay in Senya Beraku, it appeared imperative at the time to reach as many people and record as many testimonies as possible, whereas in hindsight, there is perhaps too much redundancy in the many interviews, and my time could have been used more wisely. In this connection, one is reminded of George Devereux's work on "countertransference": the researcher should collect not only data on the subject or subject matter of the study, otherwise masking or ignoring the disturbances caused by the observer, but also include these disturbances and the behavior of the observer in the field—the anxieties, defensive maneuvers, and research strategies that affect his or her work. As William F. Whyte (1964) observed about methodology, the lived circumstances of fieldwork and the choices made in the field are as much a part of the findings as the findings themselves (3–4). The methodological challenge of anthropology is thus to deploy "the subjectivity inherent in all observation as the royal road to an authentic, rather than fictitious, objectivity" (Devereux 1967: xxvii). A large number of taped interviews conducted within a relatively tight time frame might indeed be viewed, concurrently, both as a disturbance created by the fieldworker—involving his or her anxieties and defensive maneuvers—and as scientific necessity.

In practice, the interviews were organized in order to reach as many groups of informants as possible and were usually conducted in the morning; after the midday break we would go around the village to visit other people and places. The informants include fishermen, women fishmongers, officials (i.e., village elders and leaders), spiritual authorities, and relatives of young men who had been lost on their way to Europe. The 2006 fieldwork in Senya Beraku differs in important ways from that done in 2002: the earlier fieldwork was concerned with understanding the actual experience of fishing as a bodily practice unfolding in a marine environment, which experientially, I argued, had a moral and authentically anthropomorphic dimension. I therefore went on numerous fishing expeditions and interviewed fishermen—all young men—working the big canoes. In part, that focus was a response to previous research on Ghanaian fishing, which focused predominantly on gender relations and found that women are the ones in control of the business of small-scale canoe fishing, whereas the men do the actual fishing (see, for instance, Vercruijsse 1983; Christensen 1984; Odotei 1992; Overå 1992; and Walker 2002).

In 2006 I was concerned with the impact of the decline in fishing, as well as the darker effects of the globalized world's political economy, and so went on significantly fewer fishing expeditions; instead, I expanded the range of subjects and the spectrum of informants. I conducted the interviews in collaboration with Ebenezer, a friend of Samuel's who had a large network of contacts in the age group that considered traveling to Europe, and also among migrants' wives. Samuel's schoolmate at the Senya Senior Secondary School, Ebenezer prided himself on never having to go fishing because of his allegedly prestigious family background. Unlike many of his colleagues, he had not attempted to travel to Europe; though he gave rather flimsy reasons for this—he didn't fancy sitting down in a bus for more than four hours, for instance—his decision not to travel via Niger to Libya and from there to Europe, considering the hardships as depicted above, was perhaps a sound one. Yet the fact that he was going nowhere while some of his former schoolmates were putting up houses in the village made him bitter toward his friends now in Italy. "They are greedy and ungrateful," he would often say. "We used to do everything together, but now they don't know you when you ask for a little help. They just like to come home, flash their mobile phones, and drive fancy cars—how is that helping anybody?" Ebenezer's work in arranging and interpreting interviews of people from his large network of friends and colleagues was vital to the success of the fieldwork, as was his self-assured style, though his reluctance to undertake fishing expeditions may have curtailed this aspect of the research. "That's not an experience I am longing to have," he would object. "It's not in my heart. I can't do what's not in my heart." Later, he would change his mind. "I have decided to go with you. The work could benefit from it." But when the day arrived, he'd announce, "It's too sudden—I need time to prepare for something like that." Thus, fishing expeditions were either carried out without an interpreter or in the company of the chief fisherman, who normally never went fishing but did so as a courtesy to me.

DELICATE INFORMATION

The core of my informants in 2006 still consisted of fishermen. They are the primary actors in two of the book's main themes: fishing, or rather its decline, and what it meant to the fishermen's conception of the marine environment and their chances of obtaining a desirable future; and the strategies deployed to deal with this decline, including illegal immigration to Libya and Europe. Other informants included women fishmongers, whose businesses were highly sensitive to the outcome of the fishing and who, as sisters, mothers, and wives had social, emotional, and existential stakes in the trajectories of the young fishermen heading to Europe in search of brighter opportunities. The chief fisherman and his elders played vital roles not only as gatekeepers to the social field but also as providers of information about village fishing's past and present and its general state and development. The chief fisherman (or *aponipa*) himself, Chief Kwamena Mortey VI, was an especially important person in the field; he would frequently take time to explain the details of life in the village, as in the evening over a Guinness in the fort's courtyard bar. At other times I would join him at his house, located very close to Fort Good Hope, where he would sit on the porch under the shade of a tree talking to his people, or where, in the hall, he would be settling a legal case pertaining to the fishing business. In the absence of a paramount chief (because of the chieftaincy dispute in Senya Beraku), the chief fisherman—a relatively young man (still in his fifties) and otherwise classified as subchief, would handle a wide range of issues normally decided by the paramount chief and would also lead ritual processions. Therefore, sitting in the main room of the chief fisherman's house, the strong smell of fresh onions emanating from two sacks stored under the tin roof, one would occasionally glimpse some of the important themes of village life.

The chief fisherman's "linguist" (spokesperson, ambassador, and councilor), Papa Kweku Tawaih, a tall, bald fisherman, "born before they kept records," and a father of ten living and eight deceased children, was also a central figure in the fieldwork. He was the most senior person among the chief fisherman's elders and the most knowledgeable on the issue of the lesser gods and the Senya Beraku spiritual world. Pressed on the issue, he guessed his age to be eighty-something; he was at least old enough to remember British colonial rule and that "they sometimes came in buses and handed out goods for free." He added, to the amusement of most, "Some of them were so fascinated by our women that they paid them to take their blouses off." Although the *aponipa* and Papa Kweku in some sense represented the continuity of Senya Beraku fishing, they did not live in the past. Papa Kweku, for instance, enjoyed watching karate movies. Once when I was looking for the *aponipa*, I found him and Papa Kweku relaxing in the darkness of his television room, watching a Chinese Jet Li movie with English subtitles. Papa Kweku had not learned to read and write and obviously did not understand Chinese, but he "especially enjoyed the part where they fight." Thus, as I argue in part 1, the immaterial forms of globalization may reach all corners of the world map, while the economic and material resources of the globalized world show no such propensity for diffusion.

The ubiquitous town crier and village joker, the so-called gong-gong beater, also provided me with important information and points of view. An elder to the *aponipa*, the gong-gong beater announced important messages on behalf of the chief fisherman and was thus well informed about village affairs. One day, for instance, he came down the street alerting people to his presence with the strange, toneless sound of his gong-gong, a longish bell he struck with a short wooden cane. A young woman and a young child accompanied him. The gong-gong beater announced that from today, no one should take advantage of the young woman's retarded son, whom people, unbeknownst to the mother, had sent all over town to collect things and dump waste, when in fact those chores were not his responsibility.

Yet another important group of informants included spiritual authorities, both the semipublic caretakers or guardians (*nsow*, pl. of *osow*) of the eight major shrines of Senya Beraku, and the independent traditional or fetish priests (*nbrew*, pl. of *obrew*), who were consulted, for instance, when relatives had disappeared on their way to Europe (unless the family was devout Christian, and even these families typically drew on traditional spiritual resources). Most of the *nbrew* communicated through the *mmoetia*, mysterious, capricious little people who lived in the bush and who could be encouraged to travel far and wide to seek information as to the whereabouts, for example, of lost Senya captains. On the subject of migrants' disappearing en route, I also interviewed knowledgeable Christian religious leaders.

Part 3 of the book also focuses on relatives of people who tried to reach Europe but could not make it. This group of informants posed the greatest ethical challenge. Practically speaking, it was difficult to arrange interviews on this subject because many had not given up hope that their husbands, sons, or brothers would return home, though they had been missing for up to three years. When there is no one to verify the actual death, as when a boat disappears on the Mediterranean, the family finds it difficult to accept that the person is gone and so awaits further "evidence." However, the migrants who do make it to Italy are not eager to provide their families at home with information; to avoid conflict with or emotional distress for their families, migrants tend to keep their worst fears to themselves and to ask their families to be patient, though the latter might have every reason to believe that the migrant in question has perished en route. Thus, Jonathan's brother-in-law died trying to reach Europe. Jonathan is almost certain of it because his brother-in-law's boat left a couple of days before his own and, due to horrible weather shortly after the boats' departure, neither reached Italy nor made it back to Libya. However, when Jonathan's sister called him to ask for news of her husband, he hesitated to tell her what he knew, and eventually asked her to stop calling altogether. "I told her that when I received news of the husband, I'd call her and let her know. I went about it this way because another sister of mine died very suddenly and I am afraid that if the news of her husband is directly broken to her, something of that sort might happen again."

In other cases, if a migrant in Italy or Libya had not actually seen the bodies of his colleagues when, say, their boat capsized on the sea, he could not make a conclusive response to the question of whether the persons were dead or alive. This was the case with Louis, who, after his return to Senya Beraku, was unable to give the family of his lost friend information of his whereabouts, because when Louis left him in the Ahaggar Mountains, he was still alive. "But they didn't accept it very well," Louis said. "They say they are waiting for me to say if he's dead, but I cannot say that, because he was alive when we left. All I know is, if you spent the whole day in the desert without water, then by all means you'll die. So now they are making their own decision, whether to consider him dead or alive."

Louis's cautiousness reflects the fact that a messenger of bad news who is not an eyewitness or has no other "proof" can be brought before the *aponipa*—if, for instance, a woman has a miscarriage following the emotional distress caused by the bad news—accused of causing the mishap, and be made to pay compensation. For these reasons, migrants in Italy or Libya are usually reluctant to share information, and families are often left guessing as to the whereabouts of their relatives. In practice, therefore, we mainly approached those families that had acknowledged the death of a son or were in the process of doing so; that is, the burial rites may not have been concluded but had been put in motion.

Ethically, these interviews were difficult. They were intrusions into intimate family affairs, and sometimes the strong emotions stirred by the incidents we asked about were still unresolved, leading informants to break down and cry. Especially vivid is my memory of interviewing

Michael, who had lost his brother in the desert. Staring into the distance, his face shaking with emotion, he said, almost as an apology, "I feel pain when I am telling the story. I feel the pain now." After such an interview, I sometimes wondered whether the purpose of asking these questions was legitimate, and I still have ambivalent feelings about the issue. As a consequence, I granted anonymity to those for whom reliving their experiences by reading about them in print (though very unlikely to happen) might inflict on them more pain or embarrassment, even though they agreed to share their stories. I have not masked the identities of those who were not friends or relatives of the lost migrants, such as the chief fishermen and his elders. In fact, they might be disappointed were I to do so.

In his advocacy of multi-sited ethnography, George E. Marcus leaves unexplored certain practical issues (Marcus 1995). Aside from the financial and temporal challenges, multi-sited ethnography has one strange implication: while engaged in present fieldwork, one is constantly contemplating the findings of one's previous fieldwork, which have yet to be explored and organized, when one should perhaps be more alert to the empirical world of the present. In Senya Beraku in 2006, it was as if the richness of the Naples fieldwork was still appearing and developing in puzzling ways in the midst of participant observation or interviews in a different world altogether, one I was trying to grasp. Although these interferences were mostly fruitful (and, of course, interferences take place whether one does multi-sited fieldwork or not), concern regarding the depth of my commitment to ethnographic detail was unavoidable. However, the fact that I was returning for the second fieldwork phase to a site I had visited previously was clearly advantageous; traveling between two unfamiliar field sites within the space of three months might otherwise have produced the kind of sketchy knowledge that in-depth ethnographic investigations are supposed to prevent. The fact that I was already integrated into Senya village life meant that the collection of data could commence without delay.

Methodologically, my position in the village was even strengthened when, during my stay, I was appointed chief fisherman of Denmark and given the name Nenyi Kow Ekuffo I (King Kow [Thursday Born] Old

One I), an honor shared with "dozens or maybe even hundreds of foreigners from the West" who have been installed as chiefs or queen mothers in Ghana since the early 1990s (Steegstra 2006: 603). This newfound status, however, was characterized less by the acquisition of any real political power and privileges than by the fact that I was now formally placed under the authority of the chief (Steegstra 2006: 615). I was thus domesticated and even made to swear allegiance with a sword held to my neck in front of two hundred people and the chief fishermen of the neighboring towns. Returning to Senya Beraku, I experienced that confusing mix of emotions that many ethnographers going back to a previously studied field site have experienced: "anxiety about how one will be received, anticipatory pleasure at seeing old and new friends, and hope for whatever project one has in mind" (Ridler 1996: 241).

This final section of the book considers the dwindling marine resources in West Africa and how the effects of this decline are prompting young Guan fishermen to adopt new strategies to protect their lives and livelihoods. These strategies include, among others, the use of illegal fishing methods, the sale of children to other fishing communities, and emigration through the dangerous channels available to the Guan fishermen.

Michael: Most of the guys here are fishermen, or hustling on the beach, but because of the decline they are rushing to go to Libya. It's because of poverty, because you can't sit down idle like that. It will be a very terrible and hectic time for us if it keeps going down like this. We have reached an age where we should be making some kind of investment, but rather we are sitting down, getting frustrated, thinking so much. If you think too much, you'll die from all the pressure you put on yourself. So, even though it's risky, we have to try to make ends meet.

In discussing the many deaths connected with high-risk emigration from the viewpoint of the bereaved, I focus on the hardships they undergo and the difficulties families face making sense of their loss, while also exploring how those who do make it to Europe bring hope and resources to the village.

THE EU AND THE STATE
OF WEST AFRICAN FISHING

Like the West African region in general, Ghanaian fisheries are struggling with a dramatic decline in catches. The contributing factors are many, but several fisheries researchers point to the long-standing overexploitation of fish stocks and overcapacity in the fishing fleet. This situation is made worse by growing pressure on fish stocks by foreign vessels from especially the EU, China, Korea, and Japan. In fact, the United Nations estimates that the pressure on West African fishing from foreign fishing fleets increased sixfold from the 1960s into the 1990s. The marine habitat is thus undergoing negative changes, as many species are severely depleted or have vanished altogether, not to mention the effects of illegal, unregulated, and unreported fishing (so-called IUU fishing), which, in some reports, have also been linked to the EU fishing fleet. Because there is little or no effective monitoring, control, or surveillance, European vessels allegedly enter West African Exclusive Economic Zones (EEZs), often using banned or environmentally destructive gear, and trawl the already overexploited stocks (Alder and Sumalia 2004; Atta-Mills et al. 2004; Kaczynski & Fluharty 2002; UNDP 2005).

Illegal fishing aside, the regular EU-African fisheries agreements have been widely criticized for putting West Africans at an economic and social disadvantage. Thus, as Kaczynski and Fluharty (2006) point out, the demand for seafood in Europe and the capacity of the industrial fishing fleets to extract living marine resources from European fishing waters far outpaces marine reproductive capacities. In particular, some fisheries technologies used by European fleets threaten marine habitats and thereby reduce the ability of overexploited stocks to recover. "In order to address these constraints," Kaczynski and Fluharty (2006) reveal,

the EU is spending millions of Euros to re-deploy fishing fleets of the member-states into other nations' waters mainly through international fisheries cooperation agreements with developing countries. . . . Yet, for millions of people in developing countries, especially in West African coastal nations, fishery resources currently provide and have significant potential to be the primary source of animal protein and livelihood. The policy which accords high priority to agreements for extraction of marine living resources from the waters of developing countries, with little contribution by the EU to the development of coastal state capabilities to use and process their resources with indigenous labour and land infrastructure, undermines the social and economic development goals of these nations. (76)

In short, the EU exports harmful methods and industrial overcapacity to developing countries, while on a global scale, according to a Food and Agriculture Organization estimate, about 70 percent of conventional species of fish are in danger of depletion or are already depleted (FAO 1995). The EU heavily subsidizes this export; in fact, during the 1990s the European fishing industry paid only one-third or less of the price of the EU license to fish off West Africa, suggesting that an unprofitable and unsustainable business would otherwise not be feasible (Alder & Sumalia 2004: 170). This export of overcapacity and harmful methods may reflect changing conditions for the European fishing industry as an increasing portion of the European public considers environmental issues more important than the jobs, wealth, and "progress" generated by European industries (Beck 1997: 13). This trend makes access to foreign fishery resources all the more important for securing European jobs and satisfying domestic demand for fish, whereas the EU sees any real commitment to the economies or industries of West African coastal states "as a burden and a cost factor that should be minimized" (Kaczynski & Fluharty 2002: 91).

Today the EU has standing fishing agreements with eleven African countries, most of them in West Africa. The agreements initially involved only the payment of financial compensation for access to maritime resources; however, following strong criticism from conservationists and humanitarian organizations, they have evolved from a cash-for-access model to a "partnership agreement" that also addresses the "developmental and environmental needs" of the Third World countries involved. But fisheries researchers are still skeptical about the ability of the EU's fisheries partnership agreements (FPAs) to secure a sustainable harvesting of West African surplus marine resources. Thus, an Institute for

European Environmental Policy (IEEP) report commissioned by the World Wildlife Fund in November 2002 to review the new FPAs concludes: "It is widely accepted that many fish stocks in West Africa are overfished and that people in these countries are dependent on fish as a food resource. Since access under several of the agreements [between African costal countries and the EU] has in fact increased from the previous period, without sufficient knowledge of the available resources, few limitations on catches, and as yet apparently inadequate monitoring and control provisions, it seems questionable whether these new agreements are indeed moving towards sustainability" (IEEP 2002). In an analysis of the latest fishing agreements with Senegal (which expired in 2006), the United Nations Development Programme (UNDP) criticized the EU for "policy incoherence." Rather than integrating developmental and environmental concerns into the new agreements, the UNDP reported, "the Senegalese agreement is very much 'business as usual' for the EU— the old story of 'cash for access'" (UNDP 2005: 8). Considering the EU's reluctance to receive African immigrants, described in part 2, one could add that undermining West African food security and local socioeconomic structures not only runs counter to development objectives but is inconsistent with the growing EU desire to keep the less privileged of the world from moving to Europe.

To return to the question of connectedness and globalization, one may reasonably ask whether these fisheries agreements represent West African integration into the world economy. Certainly, the agreements meet African nation-states' needs for hard currency, but whether they bring wealth into those countries' societies or into the local fishing communities that depend on declining marine resources is another question. James Ferguson argues that recently established outside businesses in Africa are "socially thin"; that is, like the gold-mining industry of Ghana, they lack "wider societal investments" and are often "walled off with bricks, razor wire, and security guards." Consequently, Ferguson argues, "the movement of capital does not cover the globe; it connects discrete points on it. Capital is *globe-hopping, not globe-covering*" (2006: 36–38; emphasis in the original). The EU fisheries agreements could be viewed as an example of how rich countries do business with poor countries without actually having to engage with anybody locally—without making a commitment on the ground or transferring technology, jobs, or expertise to West African countries. Although colonialism involved atrocities, earlier investments in Africa entailed a social investment and, in the mining industry in the Zambian Copperbelt, for example, 100,000 local jobs (Ferguson 2006: 35). The EU, in contrast, seeks continuous access to African resources while incurring little or no obligation to Africans—everything is centralized and above ground level.

THE DECLINE IN GHANAIAN FISHING: THE CASE OF SENYA BERAKU

Unlike many of its West African neighbors, Ghana has no fishing agreement with the EU (bearing in mind that regional pressure on marine resources is not necessarily confined by maritime borders), yet both industrial and canoe fishing are on the decline. Fish are the major source of animal protein, with Ghanaians consuming twenty-two kilos per capita per annum, thus falling short of the government's ideal of between forty and fifty kilos per capita. Until recently, Ghana was considered a major fishing power in the region, having a large international fleet of its own; now, however, it relies on imports to satisfy market demand for fish, prompting many to look for protein substitutes (Atta-Mills et al. 2004: 13; DFMFA 2003: 8). As a consequence, biologists and zoologists have noted that, to replace fish when marine resources are dwindling, the hunting of bush meat in Ghanaian wildlife reserves, including protected and endangered species, has increased, adding to West Africa's already "catastrophic wild life decline" (Brashares et al. 2004: 1182).

Ghanaian fisheries, especially in the semi-industrial commercial vessels that flourished from the nineteenth century until the early 1960s, began declining in the mid-twentieth century when many newly independent West African countries denied access to Ghanaian fishermen. Political instability and the exhaustion of Ghana's own inshore marine resources worsened the situation. But even though Ghana no longer has an international fishing fleet (and has no financial wherewithal to compete with the EU for access to foreign waters), Ghanaian fisherman can still be found throughout West Africa sailing under other flags. As representatives of a former regional fishing power, Ghanaian fishermen have a strong reputation in West African fisheries and range widely, from Mauritania in the north to Congo in the south, to follow the migratory patterns of fish and seek fishing opportunities, in the process transferring innovative methods and technology and knowledge of food supplies to areas where coastal fishing was formerly less developed (Marquette et al. 2002: 330). In the 1970s and 1980s, Ghana began investing in off- shore tuna fishing as joint ventures with foreign capital, and catches grew during the 1990s; but lately, the tuna industry has also been showing decreased landings. Small-scale canoe operators proved more stable than Ghana's international fleet and kept yielding positive results up until the 1990s. The abundant landings of sardinella, anchovies, and mackerel, which are the main targets of Guan fishermen too, were attributable to the biannual upwelling in the Gulf of Guinea that brings cooler water, nutrients, and higher concentrations of fish near the coast. Then even canoe fishing began showing decline due to overexploitation or, possibly, natural fluctuations in the pelagic, or midwater, fish stocks (Atta-Mills et al. 2004: 14–15; Walker 2002: 391; Marquette et al. 2002: 328). In Senya, the scarcity of fish and the negative socioeconomic consequences have led many fishermen to either give up fishing or adopt new strategies and technologies.

Fishing in Senya Beraku is generally carried out in dugout canoes. The hull is made out of the soft *wawa* tree, while the upper part is reinforced with the much harder *odun*. In a sample of ten canoes, the Senya Beraku *pole* or *canoe-canoe* was approximately 18 meters long and 2.35 meters wide (Lucht 2003: 20). The larger canoes are typically equipped with a forty-horsepower Yamaha motor and a purse seine; they can accommodate more than twenty people and are used for longer sea voyages to other fishing communities or to neighboring countries. Although men conduct the fishing, except for beach seines, in which women also participate, both men and women own fishing gear. In Senya Beraku, as among the Fante, women fishmongers are often the owners and financiers of the fishing operations.

The other type of canoe in Senya Beraku is the *ohonsoebi,* literally "those who go to the deep side." Much smaller than the *pole,* this vessel carries only two or three people; older fishermen who no longer have the strength to fish with the *pole* typically use the *ohonsoebi.* Fishing in small canoes is conducted by hook-and-line or by setting up trap nets for shellfish, and it generally targets a wide variety of demersal, or deep-water, species of fish. With its small but regular yields, this is essentially subsistence fishing. It often provides only "chop-fish," for consumption within the extended family, whereas fishing with a purse seine is a business that ideally yields both income and chop-fish. Although hook-and-line fishing is traditionally reserved for the elderly, the scarcity of fish and the discontinuity of the bigger fishing operations have prompted many, even young fishermen, though ridiculed for it, to the smaller canoes. Senya Beraku has no harbor facilities, which means that the large canoes are pulled directly up on to the beach by the use of manpower after an expedition, typically tied to a coconut tree, and in the morning pulled out again.

The work situations allow the large group of unemployed young men, so-called hustlers, to take part in the effort, though they are not formally part of any crew; usually, if there's a catch, their work entitles them to a small part. Otherwise, the catch is split proportionally among the crew, the captains, and the gear owners after the cost of petrol has been deducted. Usually, the fish are then handed over to the appropriate fishmonger (often the owner of the canoe), who processes the fish and sells it in the market. However, crews sometimes decide to take the catch to another beach to obtain better prices and avoid the women, especially their wives or sisters, who upon discovering the amount of money thus obtained, make demands that the fishermen can hardly refuse, such as paying the children's school fees or medical bills. Typically, fish are salted, dried, or smoked and kept in a storage facility until outside buyers arrive to collect what can amount to a full truckload of processed fish that are distributed all over the country, thus supplying Ghanaians in rural areas with animal protein, essential minerals, and vitamins A, D, and E (DFMFA 2003: 9). Needless to say, the dwindling fish stocks are causing major problems for owners of fishing gear as well as for women fishmongers. The latter are the ones paying for the petrol, but when fishing crews keep coming back empty-handed, they risk accumulating major debts; in fact, they risk becoming insolvent, and in the end they might choose to cut their losses or have the canoe beached while waiting for better times. In a number of fishing communities, women and girls migrate to the urban centers to engage in petty trading (see DFMFA 2003: 37).

Moreover, Senya Beraku canoe fishing takes place against the backdrop of a relationship of exchange with the gods of the sea, the *bosompo*. Fishing is prohibited on Tuesdays to allow the lesser gods a day of rest. This relationship with the sea and with the gods dwelling there has a collective expression every five years when a major fishing ritual, headed by the chief fisherman, is carried out. This ceremony, involving animal sacrifices to all eight major shrines in Senya Beraku, culminates in the decapitation of a bull in the main square. The blood is subsequently mixed with magical herbs and collected in bowls that are paddled to the east, south, and west, where it is poured into the water for the gods to consume, thus inaugurating a new five-year period of access to fish (see Lucht 2003: 53–66). The whole village contributes to this ritual: not only the direct stakeholders in the fishing industry—the fishermen, gear owners, and women fishmongers—but also the indirect stakeholders, such as drivers, mechanics, masons, and carpenters.

This public ritual can be viewed as a ritual and collective expression of the all-important reciprocal connectedness with the constituents of a given human life-world, as discussed earlier, entities that sustain indi- viduals, bringing them into existence. Reduced responsiveness on the part of the sea and the powers dwelling in it is, therefore, an immediate source not only of social and economic uncertainty but also of existential unrest, in the sense that an insufficient response to one's efforts brings on disorientation and uncertainty concerning one's future plans. As one fisherman expressed it, "The sea is our source of everything; we depend on it, like a parent. That's the sea; it's our father and mother, everything, the parent of the fishermen. So, when things are not going the right way, we get very disturbed; we get disappointed that the sea is not favoring us. Surely we feel rejected. And we don't understand why it is happening this way." Indeed, the accelerating deterioration of the existential reciprocity between the fishermen and the marine environment that sustains their existence, upon which their sense of ontological security is ultimately based, is causing great distress. Reflecting the obvious loss of leverage in striking a balance between one's aspirations and where one is taken by the world, a recurrent focus of this distress is the sea's growing erraticism.

In Senya Beraku, fishing depends on one's practical experience and ability to gather information through the senses. A fisherman known to have "good eyes" can see where, for instance, a school of fish is moving or how the weather is developing, or "knows" the behavior of sea birds and how they follow the fish. A fisherman can also have a "hunch," "dream," or "feeling" that is then collectively acted on. So whereas, formerly, the fishermen who had worked in the canoes for many years and undergone an education of bodily engagement and attention had a practical and sentient knowledge of the sea (see Ingold 2000: 22–25), they now complained that the sea had become unpredictable, if not capricious. Having no success with fishing was experienced as rejection, for the effort made represented not only a practical but also a moral engagement with the sea. Mostly, however, the fishermen turned the failure of response inward. As one expressed it, "We think it is the will of God; we have sinned too much; that's what creates this problem." Interestingly, when the connectedness with the marine environment is challenged by an insufficient response, even the physical attributes of the marine environment appear to change, as if suddenly seen in a new light, or rather as if what was once there, under the surface, has undergone a change of unwanted transparency and lightness. Thus, some fishermen said that the current had become "too swift," others that the color of the water had changed to a "lighter shade," and still others that the seawater had become "thin." To many, these changes announced the coming end of the world. "The end of the world will begin in Senya Beraku," one fisherman explained, "and spread from here to the rest of the world." The sense of connectedness with the constituents of a given human life-world not only sustains individuals and brings them into existence but also creates a sense of external reality as a coherent and continuous whole, permanent, reliable, and substantial (Laing 1973: 39), a sense produced and reproduced in action; whereas an insufficient response tampers with the perception of reality. Thus, the once rich and inexhaustible sea has become fragmented and "light."

Due to the biannual upwelling system, the high season for pelagic species is roughly from June to October, with a smaller upwelling in December and January. Guan fishermen use the lean season, from February to June, mostly for mending nets, farming (if they have access to land), and preparing for July when the sardinella returns. But usually in April or May the *opoku*, or chub mackerel, runs for three weeks or less, breaking up the lull. Then, in the hour before sunrise, the village again awakes to the sound of outboard motors being tested on the beach, sometimes demonstratively so, before the canoes are taken out into the surf toward the fishing grounds in the gulf. The beach is once more busy with women selling food and water, elders giving advice, children helping out or hustling for handouts, and goats and chickens alerted by the general commotion. Everybody is maneuvering in and out among the canoes, which the crews pull out by the use of rope and long iron rods tucked in under the hull, fiercely competing with one another to be the first to reach the fishing places. However, this year (2006) even the chub mackerel was a disappointment. On the way home to Senya Beraku from one of these fishing expeditions, which caught nothing at all but wasted a whole barrel of petrol, I talked to the chief fisherman about the decline.

We had left before dawn. As usual, having cleared the surf, the crew members stood and prayed to God for a good catch, arms raised to the sky. But when we came to the fishing grounds, there were too many canoes there already, with forty or fifty other canoes from nearby fishing villages already circling the area and even a couple of small trawlers. Nevertheless, the engine was switched off and the canoe glided quietly across the water as the crew looked for signs of fish in the morning sun. We circled around for hours in silence while the fishermen watched the sea, the sky, the currents, the surface of the water, and the small black-capped seabirds that follow the mackerel. The fish were there, sometimes coming up to the surface as a stream of silver, flashing briefly and disappearing again. On two occasions our net was almost in the water; it was even dipped in the sea once before being pulled back again. One has to be very sure before casting the net, because retrieving it takes fifteen to twenty people forty-five minutes of heavy work. In the end, the fishermen concluded that "the fish had dived to the deep side."

Heading home while most of the fishermen lay sleeping in the canoe, caps and hoods covering their faces from the sun, the chief fisherman explained that he found it increasingly difficult to believe that the fish were coming back or that the future of Senya Beraku fishing was bright. "The researchers are saying," he told me, "that the fishing is going down, but by two, three years' time it will rise again; according to them it is rotating, so it will come back. But we have waited long and it is not coming. We are still waiting, and this is the third year we have no catch. In the olden days there were plenty; the women couldn't even smoke them all before they became wasted." I asked the chief fisherman whether he believed the fish would eventually return. "They are the research-ers . . ." he responded. "We believe that when we perform the ritual [the major fishing ritual], we will have a catch. I have told the net owners to ask their people to give a small, small contribution, so that we can buy the goat and sheep, and a bull, when the time comes." Concerning the long-term decline in Ghanaian canoe fishing, some researchers attach little importance to the effect of human activities (Marquette et al. 2002: 334), whereas others are concerned about the overcapacity of the fishing fleet; population growth; environmental degradation, including the dis-appearance of certain species; destructive means of fishing; outside pres-sure on West African fish stocks; and inequitable access agreements to resources (Alder & Sumalia 2004: 157; Atta-Mills et al. 2004: 18–19; Bannerman & Quartey 2004: 7; Kaczynski & Fluharty 2002: 91). Concern-ing outside pressure, illegal intrusion by foreign vessels is a growing problem, though measuring its scope is difficult because of the weak enforcement of Ghana's EEZ; some researchers report it to be consider-able (Atta-Mills et al. 2004: 16; Marquette et al. 2002: 328). In Senya Beraku, too, illegal fishing from outside appears to be a large problem, especially during the high season in August, when the pirate trawlers "come like thieves in the night," as the chief fisherman put it. The illegal trawlers carry few or no lights and are reported to have collided with Senya Beraku canoes conducting night fishing, leading to loss of both fishing gear and, in some cases, human life. I witnessed one such episode myself during the first fieldwork period, when suddenly a giant trawler, making the Senya canoes look like little sticks on the water, appeared out of the darkness and much too close to the coast. From the walls of the fort, one could see older fishermen in the smaller, inshore canoes quickly respond by putting up their small kerosene lights to avoid collision, lighting up the whole Senya Beraku coastline (Lucht 2003: 75).

In addition to the overall pressure on marine resources in the West African region and the fact that too many fishermen are chasing too few fish (Atta-Mills et al. 2004: 19), the fish stocks pursued by the canoe fishermen are negatively influenced by the use of illegal means of fishing to boost failing catches. In Senya Beraku, for instance, local crews use nets with mesh sizes that are too small, and the chief fisherman has had the gong-gong beaten to announce that this practice is against the law, but so far without effect. In the same way, the authorities have banned the "mechanical system" described earlier. This method has only just been introduced into Senya Beraku fishing but is reportedly in use all along the gulf coast. In this case as well, the chief fisherman has had the gong-gong beaten. Formerly, the use of dynamite was also widespread in Senya Beraku, but the chief fisherman reports that it has now practically ceased. But when it comes to fighting illegal fishing, the chief fisherman is caught between his responsibilities toward the fishermen and those toward the authorities in Accra, and he does not appear to possess the authority to enforce government regulations, nor perhaps does he always have a clear interest in doing so. To the chief fisherman, the ideal solution would be to have the police head an effort to collect and burn illegal nets and seize the mechanical systems, but this has not yet happened.

One afternoon we met with two seasoned fishermen, each of whom had about twenty-five years of fishing experience and was the captain of his canoe, to discuss the mechanical system, or light fishing operation (LFO). At first, Isaac and Michael were reluctant to talk. Only after we had come to know one another better and had exchanged the names of common acquaintances did they apologize for the hesitant reception; they had been worried that "we had come to take the system away." Eventually, they agreed to show the mechanical device to us. Disappearing through a half-open door in the small compound, they came back out carrying the power generator that is connected to the thousand-watt light bulb lowered into the sea. They had adopted the system only a few months before, having seen it in use along the coast, especially by the small inshore trawlers; thinking it might work for them also and perhaps turn their situation around, they had decided to invest the necessary 1,200 Euros.

Incidentally, Ghana's Marine Fisheries Research Division, with assistance from the FAO-UNDP Technical Assistance Programme, originally introduced the LFO in 1962 on an experimental basis aimed at increasing commercial operators' catches, especially during the lean season, when pelagic species are normally in a resting phase. Although the practice is now banned because it "naturally obstructs or impedes the biological cycle of the fish species" and could thus have "serious repercussions on the spawning stock biomass" (Bannerman & Quartey 2004: 2, 6), it has been adopted by the canoe fishermen along the coast for use in the off-season. The use of the mechanical system has long been a point of dispute between the small inshore trawlers and the canoe fishermen, who accuse the trawlers of "chasing the fish to the deep side" by using these lights. Thus, although ambivalence surrounds its use, Isaac and Michael estimated that about fourteen crews in Senya Beraku were currently working with the mechanical system. "What prompted us to use the system was the fact that all the small trawlers were using them; some even use four pieces [bulbs] at a time. So we wanted to try it also to see if it could work for us, and that is what we're using now. But it's a kind of artificial way of getting the fish," Isaac explained. In fact, though LFO was producing results, the two captains were not at all happy about using it. "The mechanical system is the most useless kind of fishing," Isaac said; "it's a very bad thing. If we don't put an end to it, the fishing industry will go down completely. The fish we catch this way don't look normal; they look half-baked or something—because of the heat. They look unconscious before they are even dragged aboard." Apparently, the fish are "spoiled" in the process of being attracted to the bulb's light and heat. Fishermen report that fish caught this way have bloody eyes, generally do not taste "sweet," and thus bring a lower price in the market.

Whatever is behind the decline, there is considerably less access to fish in the fishing communities, and the decline is putting pressure on an industry already struggling. Moreover, according to Atta-Mills and his colleagues, the Ghanaian canoe fishermen have few opportunities for work outside of fishing since they are generally uneducated and often do not own land. The dwindling of fish stocks also affects the fishermen's families and communities, creating serious social and economic problems, eroding local lives and livelihoods, and leading to "a freeze on development in fishing villages, and in some cases the gradual deterioration of existing facilities and traditional social support systems" (Atta-Mills et al. 2004: 18). As one recent report on poverty in the Awutu Effutu Senya District, to which Senya Beraku and Winneba belong, points out, the widespread unemployment and associated decline in incomes put access to basic health care and educational services beyond families' reach; children are consequently being taken out of school and put to work. At the same time, the cost of living, especially food prices, is increasing, making it difficult to acquire the basic essentials of life. The decline also entails a forced change of diet in that, when fish are scarce or too expensive, they are replaced with beans, vegetables, shellfish, or species of fish people are not used to eating—or else they simply eat less. The scarcity of fish means that the fishermen are forced to travel farther to compete for fewer fish, while the costs of petrol are on the increase; in many cases the solution is simply to stay in the house in order not to incur too many losses or, alternatively, to invest in new technology such as the mechanical system or other destructive fishing gear. These disruptive factors are likely to increase in the future because "whilst coping strategies exist, not all of these are sustainable and some such as eating less or changing diets and the use of destructive means of fishing gears may in the long term exacerbate what appears to be a worsening situation" (Ward et al. 2004: 59).

I spoke with Papa Kweku, the chief fisherman's linguist, about the decline in the fishing industry. "I feel saddened that one day things are going to get out of hand," he said.

Papa Kweku: I have played my part, and sooner or later I'll go away, but I cry for the little ones, who have made fishing their profession. If things keep going from bad to worse, I don't know what will befall the younger ones, and it worries me a lot. Even my own children are fishermen, and they find it very difficult to get fish, even fish to eat. Some of the fishermen are sensible; they'll have a good catch and use the money to buy cement and put down some blocks, whereas others have this rowdy lifestyle and will spend all the money, thinking tomorrow there'll be another catch.

CHILDREN'S AMERICA

The decline in fishing reaches all corners of Senya Beraku life. For instance, prior to the planting of maize in May, I had on several occasions tried to see the chief fisherman, but had been told repeatedly that he had gone to Accra. Later, he told me that this was only an excuse he had instructed his people to give out so that he would not lose face. He had in fact been going to his plot of land in the bush to work, though it was not proper for a chief fisherman to do farmwork. Because of the slump, however, he had no other option. The decline affected everybody, from the chief fisherman to the children of the poor sent away to other fishing communities where they work in slavelike conditions.

We walked up the main road to the ridge above the village, then across the school playground to the last rows of houses, Eugenia, the chief fisherman's daughter, led the way down a narrow path into the village hinterland, where Senya Beraku people have their farms. This stretch of bushy low hills and valleys reaches all the way to Winneba in the west; in fact, one can see in the distance the highest building in that town. Here, mainly during the lean season, the fishing community grows peppers, onions, tomatoes, maize, and other crops. On this occasion, the chief fisherman and some of his entourage, among them another of his four daughters, were already there, getting the ground ready to plant maize. It was a calm, hot day and the air was filled with hovering dragonflies; from the bush came a strange electronic chirp that the chief fisherman—showing a typical lack of interest in things pertaining to the bush—attributed to "a certain bush fowl." The rocky field, covered in tough bush, had been cleared with a cutlass, using a slash-and-burn technique. It was located on a slope descending toward the south, where the valley met the Gulf of Guinea. On the other side of the gorge, the little figures of people could be seen moving around in another field. "That's Papa Kweku and his people," said the chief fisherman, pointing to the tall figure of his interpreter. "They are also farming. So, you see, the old man is still very strong."

The chief fisherman led the work and ordered everybody about in his pleasant, jovial style, instructing the daughters to work more and gossip less. We began planting the maize, eighty-five rows in total; a couple of hours later, the work was finished. While the rest of the party rested under the shade of low bushes, the chief fisherman himself raised scarecrows so "grasscutters" (cane rats) wouldn't come and eat the seeds. This event was significant on many levels. Maize is planted in May so that the harvest coincides with the fishing high season, culminating in the village food festival in the third week of August. But the planting was also a significant break with tradition in that the chief himself was in the field, revealing how the effects of the decline had moved upward.

Aponipa: When my grandfather was alive, this is was what he would do. On Tuesday [when fishing is taboo], he would get a canoe crew together, send for about twenty to forty people, and then send them out to the farm to do the weeding. When they came back, he would give them food and drinks, and that was it. Later he would send them to plant the maize. Why should I, the chief fisherman, go farming? As a chief I have to be in the house, and when there's a problem, I have to solve it. So I don't want people to know that I am farming; I tell them that I go to Accra or Winneba.

That evening it rained heavily, lightning flashing violently above the fort. The next morning the chief fisherman came by early to make sure

I was up and getting ready for church; during the service he was unusually cheerful, humming softly to the psalms. "I had to go today," he said, "to thank God for the rain last night."

Indeed, the decline is affecting all strata of Senya Beraku life; but the harshest consequences fall, perhaps not surprisingly, on the poorest families, whose capacity to adapt to change is limited. Thus, as the village's economic struggle has worsened since the mid-1990s, the sending of children to other fishing communities for a fee has grown in proportion (see also DFMFA 2003: 37; Ward et al. 2004: 26). The practice of "giving" a child to relatives or townspeople from Senya Beraku currently living in another fishing village for a sum of money, however, is not unusual in a Guan context. Rather than "trafficking" or the deliberate selling of children for exploitation, the families involved consider this practice economically meaningful and part of the child's education. (The practice is also customary among the Gonja, the Guan society in Northern Ghana [Nukunya 2001: 36].) That said, rising numbers of impoverished fishermen may very well have intensified a well-established practice and forced some struggling families into pushing their children off under more dubious conditions than normally accepted. Most of the children are sent to Yeji, a town on the Volta River where Guan fishermen have traditionally migrated looking for work. Here, the boys help out in the fishing, and the girls assist the women with the smoking and selling of fish. However, the conditions are rough, and the children, sometimes as young as four years of age, are not treated well. Very young boys work long hours on the lake without sufficient protection, and fatal accidents have been reported, whereas the girls mind the smoke ovens; they receive no schooling and are generally undernourished. The issue attracted national attention when pictures of the children working in Yeji under these slavelike conditions were shown on television. Now, Senya Beraku leaders, together with regional authorities, have been called upon to halt the practice, especially after the Ghanaian government passed the Human Trafficking Act of 2005. The chief fisherman has formed a committee to patrol the beach and make certain children are in school and not hustling for food. "But they are playing hide-and-seek with us," the chief fisherman explained. "Some children say they are on the afternoon shift. Some say they went in the morning—and the parents, too, they're dodging us. They say they're going to Accra, but before you realize it, they have sent a child to Yeji. It's all due to poverty. Since the fishing is going down, they have to find an antidote."

Inspired by a program on television describing the work of Mother Teresa of Calcutta, Mr. Kumsen, a successful local business entrepreneur known as KEK, decided he would do something for the children living in these harsh conditions in his childhood community. He established a school for girls in Senya Beraku with the purpose of retrieving Guan children from their Yeji masters, freeing them from their ordeals, and giving them free education. Today, the Mother Teresa School for Girls, run by the Catholic Church, has nearly six hundred children, of which about one hundred have been brought back from Yeji, either when their masters no longer had any use for them or through the work of NGOs, that combat child trafficking. One of the teachers at the school, Ebenezer Kingsley, knows the problem very well. As a child of eleven he was himself almost sent to Yeji because his mother was in Liberia working and the family was too poor to take care of him. In fact, he was eager to go, as the village is known among Guan children as "children's America." But in the end his grandmother intervened and his older brother was sent in his place.

Kingsley: When he came home, they had cut his hair very roughly and he was wearing only one piece of cloth tied around him. You couldn't look at him; you don't feel happy that he's your son or brother. My senior brother! We look very much alike; we have the same height and everything. He was there for more than six years and he didn't like it; in the end he ran away. Because of that he never had the chance to go to school. I am not happy about the situation he went through because he was sent instead of me. On my part, I was saved from the things he passed through. But though he was better than me in a lot of things, people see me as better than him because he's not been educated.

The people there don't have any love for the children; they treat them anyway they like. They'll send the boys to work in the night and only allow them a few hours of sleep, and early in the morning they'll send them back fishing on the river. When they make the least mistake, the guardians use the paddle to beat them. Sometimes, too, when the net is entangled underwater, the children have to dive into the river to bring it up—some of them die in the process. They don't get any good food, and they're always working. They are punished severely and don't get proper clothes to wear; they don't even get sandals to wear.

It's due to this same poverty. Because we don't have any money, we don't feel content over here. Some people don't eat for days; some can't even give their old ones money to buy food. There are children who need help, but they have nothing to give them. So the rate of poverty is running high in every family.

My brother has been back for almost three years now. He has gone to learn a trade; he's a photographer, and when you see him in the street, he looks like a gentleman.

Although sending children to Yeji is still one of the strategies the poorest families employ to deal with the hard times, the general perception of the phenomenon may be changing, as Kingsley explained: "When you come back, you're teased because you can't speak English, and you're considered low in the society. The children are even shy to talk about it, because they are ashamed of what happened."

GREAT EXPECTATIONS

The decline in Ghanaian canoe fishing has created widespread unemployment among the fishermen. Atta-Mills and colleagues (2004) suggest that in the period 1992–1996, 100,000 canoe fishermen lost their jobs. This trend is confirmed in Senya Beraku, and has quite possibly worsened of late. Eventually, the bleak prospects create in the fishermen "frustration and loss of hope in the future" (18). The general economic situation in Ghana offers little hope for employment elsewhere. After the economic crisis of the 1970s, Ghana, like many other African countries, embarked in 1982 on structural adjustment programs (SAPs) under the direction of the International Monetary Fund and the World Bank; yet poverty rates and unemployment levels have continued to grow. The SAP, of course, has at its core the neoliberal ideology of rolling back the state and vigorously promoting private enterprise, an approach also advocated by the government led by then-president John Koffour under the banner "The Golden Age of Business." But today, "the general consensus is that after more than two decades of SAPs, much of Africa is still characterized by precipitous economic decline, lack of access to social services, environmental degradation, high levels of external debt, and increasing rates of poverty" (Arthur 2006: 36). In fact, Ghana, which once had one of the highest living standards in sub-Saharan Africa, now has "more than half of its population living in absolute poverty, very high levels of unemployment, and levels of health and literacy not much higher than those in other African nations" (Takyi & Addai 2003: 224). According to Takyi and Addai, many Ghanaians' real income has stagnated or declined, and the cost of health care and education is slipping out of the reach of ordinary people; at the same time, the population continues to grow, and the imbalance between national income and population further reduces the standard of living. As in the rest of Africa, the growing population is changing the demographic face of Ghana; thus by the year 2000 people under the age of fifteen accounted for almost half the population. This has been accompanied by a high degree of urbanization, though the influx of people to the cities does not match investment in housing and community amenities, as exemplified by the emergence of squatter settlements in urban wastelands (Takyi & Addai 2003: 232–233). In sum, the general economic pattern of rising unemployment and increased social and economical inequality, combined with rapid population growth and a changing demography, does not offer bright opportunities to fishermen forced out of canoe fishing by the depletion of marine resources.

One of the consequences of the economic decline and the large number of unemployed young people is that Ghana has become a major exporter of labor, both skilled and unskilled. Concerning the latter, because of emigration to the West, the health care system in Ghana in particular is struggling to attract the necessary nurses and doctors (Takyi & Addai

2003: 234). Many Ghanaians see emigration as the best way of improving their living standards. In a recent survey, almost 50 percent of male respondents and 37 percent of female respondents stated that they intended to emigrate. Hendrik P. van Dalen and his colleagues (2005) have found that the main reason for wanting to emigrate to the West is economic. This reasoning makes financial sense, as the gap between the developed world and Africa was wide already fifty years ago but today has widened even more. Per capita income is now more than twenty times higher in the United States than in Ghana, whereas it was "only" eight times higher half a century ago (Van Dalen et al. 2005: 753). Although economic constraints are a driving force behind the desire to emigrate (keeping in mind that, though poverty may well be a reason for emigrating, it can equally be a barrier to moving if one cannot afford the costs of traveling), so is the growing awareness of the globalized world and the possibilities of growth that lie out there, beyond one's reach. As Wisdom J. Tettey (2006) argues, "In the midst of the deprivation . . . and the disparities that define the global political economy, globalization and information technology are teasing Ghanaian youth with images of the consumer life that characterizes the industrialized world. Unfortunately, however, most of them cannot replicate that lifestyle" (43). Perhaps even more than being pushed out by poverty, the desire, against whatever odds, to participate in the fields of social and economical power appears to be the main theme of emigration, as Van Dalen and colleagues (2005) conclude from their survey: "If we had to sum up what dominated the pressure to emigrate out of Africa, it would be just two words: great expectations" (775).

In Senya Beraku, too, the vast majority of the young men expressed a desire to emigrate. It is perhaps more precise to say that most young men were already in the process of emigrating, in that they had made up their minds to go but were at different stages, depending on their access to financing. Some were about to leave, whereas others had little or no real chance of obtaining the necessary funds (about 500 Euros to reach Libya) in the near future. The lack of opportunity in Senya Beraku, and in Ghana generally, and the dream of making enough money to establish oneself in the future, to acquire a business or a house, were cited as the main reasons for leaving. Talking about Senya Beraku's place in the world, many stated that the village had no place at all. "We're not even on the world map," one fisherman claimed. "Rather, Senya Beraku is in a cave underground."

Francis sometimes helped out in the off-season in a small tavern (called the After Church Drinking Spot) on the main road. Like so many others, he stated that he was "really anxious" to go and would leave for Libya tomorrow if he had the necessary means. "But since I have no money, I have to be hustling to get small money for myself, until I am ready to make an attempt. I have fishing experience and I have learned how to use a compass, so if a crew's getting ready, I'll go with them." Risking one's life in the process was accepted as a loss one would have to reckon with. As one fishermen said, "All of us know about the people who got drowned, because their funerals have been observed. But [just] because it's dangerous, people shouldn't stop going—that's the path that people can take and make it, and where there's life, there's also death." To Francis, the problem for the present was rather that, as for many others in the same situation, "just getting food enough is a challenge, and you can't save up money. I am living from hand to mouth." Francis continued: "We don't have any work; we only hang out with friends all day. So people even see you as a lazy person." Concerning the dangers of high-risk migration, he was ready to take his chances. "Going to Europe is a quite dangerous adventure, but since the whole thing is embarrassing here, this is what we have to do. I don't have any other alternatives; there are no other means. I can't stay here and be going hungry." Francis's aspirations are typical for the fishermen—to establish oneself in the community and become respected. "I would like to have my own business up and running, and two or three bedrooms for my family and myself. I wouldn't think of traveling if I had those things in place; I would be safe here. I wish I could stay and make it here, but since that is not possible, my main aspiration is to travel to Europe, or America, or one of the Asian countries." The fact that life in Europe was reported to be hard did not discourage him. "Even though the living conditions are not good over there, and it's difficult to be an immigrant, it's still better than here. I have so many friends in Europe; they complain that life is not good; but if you compare what they are making to what we are earning over here, it's far better. You can do something good with that money when you come down to settle."

In the evening, hours after the interview had ended, when night had fallen and covered the village in complete darkness, Francis came careening by Fort Good Hope on a small bicycle, having been drinking heavily since we first met. He had some trouble getting off the bicycle in a dignified manner, and in the end he just left it on the ground and walked over it. He greeted me with a wave, walked straight into the courtyard bar and ordered two measures of local Ghanaian bitters "Here, I don't grow," he said, as if the interview had never been terminated. "I am twenty-eight and I'll be thirty soon—but I have nothing."

The future of West African, including Ghanaian, fishing does not look bright in terms of creating jobs and generating incomes, in part because of local overcapacity of fishing fleets, destructive means of fishing, and outside, especially EU, pressure on resources. Moreover, the general economy of Ghana offers little support to unemployed fishermen and does not encourage a belief that one can find employment in other lines of business. To be sure, there's a world of opportunity out there, but it does not recognize the people of Senya Beraku. What one fisherman said bears repeating: "We're not even on the world map. Rather, Senya is in a cave underground." It appears that whatever effort they make to emerge form this world of shrinking opportunities and disappointment, it remains unreciprocated; wherever they turn, the world is determined not to accommodate their wishes and expectations, condemning them to an existence as the playthings of external constraints. As a consequence, emigration stands out as the most promising opportunity to reconnect with the fields of social and economic power, and perhaps to retrieve one's life from the arbitrariness entailed in dispossession. Indeed, high-risk emigration is viewed as the only way of acquiring the kind of western lifestyle that globalization promotes and celebrates, even though it does not provide the means of acquiring it (Tettey 2006: 43). Guan fishermen, however, are perhaps a step ahead of their countrymen: fishermen from the Central Region are known to have traveled far and wide for centuries, as Marquette and colleagues (2002) have documented.

They are reported to have fished in present-day Benin in the nineteenth century; Ghanaian fishing expertise in Côte d'Ivoire is recorded from 1906, a little later in Nigeria, and then in Liberia, Sierra Leone, Guinea, and Senegal. In the 1940s Ghanaians extended their activities as far south as the Republic of Congo (Marquette et al. 2002: 330; see also Ward et al. 2004: 59).

This Senya tradition of emigration—as when a crew takes a canoe to Côte d'Ivoire for several months and comes back wearing new watches and clothes, celebrating through town with bottles of beer and smeared in white powder—is reflected in the Guan fishermen's image of themselves as travelers, wise in many matters that "primitive" people from the bush have no knowledge of (Lucht 2003: 9). Indeed, in Libya, the Guan migrants seized the opportunity made available by their reputation as seasoned fishermen—an image of themselves as experienced travelers, rooted in the emigration tradition, that should be kept in mind when considering the (sometimes bold) statements concerning the crossing of the Mediterranean. Ghanaian canoe fishermen today are increasingly restricted from traveling in West African waters, partly because of the pressure placed on resources by the international industrial fleet, and partly because of political turmoil in the region, as well as growing tensions between Ghanaian fishermen and local fishing communities in, for instance, Côte d'Ivoire. Nevertheless, the fishermen from the Central Region consider emigration part of the process of "becoming a professional fisherman," for it provides "an opportunity for self-realization through access to natural, economic, and social resources beyond one's local community, which—if accumulated—can be reinvested at home" (Marquette et al. 2002: 333).

Thus, it could be argued that the Guan fishermen's role in Mediterranean transit migration conforms to an already established pattern of fishing-related behavior, though clearly the destination is new and the risks taken are considerably higher than in the tradition of West African migration. Moreover, the route to Libya was well established long before the sea voyages to Europe even began, and many West African migrant workers, as discussed in chapter 5, have seen Libya as a destination country, whereas Libya only recently became a transit country to Europe.

Since the late 1980s many people from Senya Beraku have traveled through the desert to Libya in search of work.

An example of this pre–sea voyage labor migration is provided by Godfather, a huge man with sunglasses and a gold medallion around his neck. A six-time veteran of the deadly Sahara Desert route, Godfather earned his sobriquet because, "in Libya, I am the one that people come to if they have problems." When I met Godfather in the spring of 2006, he was preparing to depart for the desert again that fall. He followed a regular procedure: In Libya he worked with a Syrian man, whom he would call upon arriving in the country. The Syrian would then set up a work situation and help him out with a flat. Thus, having settled in Tripoli, Godfather would begin taking in other migrants under his roof— but only people from Senya Beraku. "I know them," he said, "whereas somebody from Accra . . . I wouldn't know that person's mindset." Spending time with Godfather, one inevitably had the impression that it was precisely this kind of alertness that had seen him through the desert six times. Yet the sea voyage to Europe did not appeal to him. "The boys from this town are very strong; they are good swimmers. But if something happens on the deep sea, there's nothing you can do. That's why I'm not going." His position in Libya, however, allowed him to follow closely the trajectories of those Senya Beraku migrants who tried to cross the Mediterranean. "I kept a list of boys lost at sea," Godfather said, "and I think it came to twenty-seven. Only six of those have been confirmed. The families come to ask me of their whereabouts, but I can only tell them what their intentions were; where they are now, I cannot say." Concerning the desert journey, Godfather's preferred route was into southern Algeria and across the Ahaggar Mountains. Usually, he would head a small group of people embarking on that trip; they came to him in advance, and he would tell them what they needed to know— where to stand on the truck, how to divide and conceal one's money, how much water to bring, and when to drink it.

Indeed, the special role of Guan canoe fishermen in illegal immigration to Europe did not appear out of the blue. Certain developments have taken place under the radar of the global political economy that facilitates this surprising turn of events. The long tradition of West

African fishing emigration and the already established pattern of Guan labor migration to Libya, combined with a radical decline in catches and a rise in aspirations not easily accommodated, appear to have interlocked with the concurrent need for cheap labor in Italy and the EU's stepping up of external border control and putting pressure on Libya to enforce its borders, thereby creating a sudden window of opportunity for captains of smuggling boats ready to risk everything to go to Europe. Certainly one can appreciate how these chains of interdependence, or figurations (Elias 1970: 132), carve out a special role for the West African canoe fishermen in Libyan transit migration, a role the Guan migrant captains readily take.

Such high-risk emigration, however, creates much tension in the village when some get lost on the way and their families are kept in the dark for years, whereas others make it to Europe and begin sending money home.

SEVEN The Body Stays, but the Soul Returns

In talking to John, one could glimpse the challenging process of obtaining information as to the whereabouts of relatives lost en route to Europe. John lost his older brother, Simon, while the latter was on the way to Italy three years ago. Even today, it is difficult for him to talk about the dramatic events that so severely dented the family's future plans. "The pain is so deep, I don't even like to recollect it," John explained, sitting in the fort lobby. The idea was for the brother to reach Italy, make some money, and send it back for the family to invest in their own fishing net. "Even now, it's still a big blow to us. We know what we had planned and put up against the future . . . to make things easier for us over here. It was supposed to be a turning point in our lives, but unfortunately, he couldn't make it." Like John, Simon was a fisherman. With more than twenty years' experience, wherever he went on the sea, he took the position of captain. Their father, too, had been a fisherman, and they both decided to follow in his footsteps at a time when the fishing business was still lucrative and yielding big catches.

John: Fishing is like learning any other kind of profession: you need to be tactful; you have to keep your eyes on the ground and follow in the footsteps of your predecessors. Someone who has very much experience, you need to be close to this person. He doesn't have to show you how to do it; you should just watch him, how he handles the fishing and goes about the particular thing.

John dropped out of school and began fishing professionally, whereas Simon had "a bit of education" and worked simultaneously as a clerk for one of the village canoes. But over the years, the decline in the fishing business made it increasingly difficult to make ends meet. Simon, being the elder, wanted to "relieve the burden of the family" by traveling abroad to look for work. When he finally decided to try for Europe, he had already been to Libya on two occasions and had come back with enough funds to put up a two-bedroom house. John supported the decision to travel abroad; he could see no other option available to them. "Senya is a stagnant kind of town. Life is quite slow and things are not all that favorable. There's no improvement, the majority of us are at the bottom, and only the well-to-do are moving ahead." Before leaving for Italy, Simon called the family from Libya and told them that a boat was leaving and that they should pray for him. "We knew it was the route immigrants use to reach Italy, so we didn't expect anything to happen. But at the time he was supposed to reach Italy, there was no news of him." The family called Simon's friends in Libya and Italy, but there was no information as to his whereabouts. Six months later rumors began circulating in the village that Simon had drowned in the Mediterranean. Still, John and the family couldn't believe it and attributed it to "common hearsay." At the time, John's nephew was on his way to Libya, and "when he reached there, we asked him to make inquires regarding the whereabouts of my senior brother."

The sometimes long and fraught process of obtaining reliable news about a person lost in the desert or on the sea had thus begun. For most

Guan families, the first step in this process is receiving a cassette tape from Libya, recorded by a travel companion, relative, or close friend discussing the whereabouts of the missing person. Cassette tapes are typical mediums of information because many people in fishing communities are illiterate. Moreover, a tape can be listened to collectively, ensuring that all family elders are involved, and it can contain more information than a letter. Finally, a tape recording is "a direct link to the person talking," as John put it. "You feel the person is really alive and kicking, because it's like you're chatting with the person. And also, in Libya, when you come home from work and it's cold, you feel like you're interacting with your family when you talk to them on a cassette."

The following is an excerpt from the tape that John's nephew, Daniel, sent from Libya shortly after his arrival.

Uncle John, I am discussing the whereabouts of our senior uncle with my friend (the one whom I came to meet and whom I am staying with in Libya). Uncle John, you see, I am at a loss for words, and I don't know what to do. I am confused right now. Why is it that for so many months we have heard nothing of our uncle's whereabouts? For instance, Uncle John, if you go and they arrest you, they'll take you to prison in Tunisia or Malta. But in those places you can write a letter or make a phone call. So I don't know whether he's in Spain or what; I can't even sleep. My friend is equally worried because there is no trace of him. We called all his friends in Italy, and they are worried too. We just have to pray hard that soon we will receive good news. Other than that, I can't confirm if he is dead or alive. There is this mixed feeling inside, and I am at the center of the whole situation—I just don't know. I am in Libya now, and I have combed every corner, and I can't trace him. When you travel somewhere, you call back and say that you have arrived safely. So I can't even close my eyes at night; I just don't know what to do. We should just pray—some of us are alive only by the grace of God. Look at when we were coming! My friend is attesting to it. When we were coming, fourteen people from our crew lost their lives. Their bodies where just dumped in the desert. Personally, I didn't think I could make it—it was only by the grace of God. The journey was quite terrible. Some ran out of water, some ran out of food, it was difficult, and I never imagined I would be alive today. The desert is not like an ordinary road where you can have a smooth passage. There is sand throughout the place, and the weather is very, very hot. If you run out of food and water, there is no car coming to help you; you'll lose your life. So, when somebody wants to go to Libya, he should be careful to seek information. It was a horrible experience. I thank God I made it. We have to watch our footsteps well; that is our way of life over here. We just don't know and everybody is putting off the whole issue [of going to Europe]. When we came, we heard that a boat was going with two hundred people and they all drowned. The rate at which they are dying is alarming. I can't figure out if he was part of this crew. I have to rely on the information coming from his friends in Italy. But they are saying that there is no trace of him. So you can't pinpoint the very place he is at now. We have to rely on God. Maybe we'll get information that he's in a different country. But that is not quite possible. The only place he could turn up is Tunisia, and in that place they would arrest him and maybe beat him a while and deport him back to Libya. They wouldn't like to detain him for more than a week. And you also have access to a telephone in that place—you can call home. Uncle, I just don't know if he is dead or alive.

Evident from the tape is the difficulty in obtaining any solid information on migrants lost in the clandestine migration operating out of Libya. Moreover, the reluctance to convey bad news, discussed earlier, also seems to influence this report. Clearly, if we read between the lines, the nephew is leaving little room for Simon being alive; he's careful, however, not to proclaim his death. This reluctance of travel companions to provide candid information, combined with the family's hopes of seeing a loved one again, sometimes brings the process of obtaining information to a standstill. The family of Stephen, for instance, the young man whom Louis and his friend had to leave behind in the Ahaggar Mountains in 2002, would not give up hope that he would one day come back, however unlikely a scenario that appeared given Louis's story. Regrettably, I could not interview Stephen's mother, because, as her grandson Eric explained, "it is one of her greatest pains. Every time she remembers my uncle, she weeps a lot because she doesn't know if he's dead or alive. We don't even talk about it between us." Stephen had just married and had set out looking for work in Europe "to make life easier in the future." He collapsed somewhere on the road. "He was the person everybody loved in the family," Eric said.

Eric: He was a responsible guy—only twenty-seven years old, very hardworking, determined, and very clearheaded. He was someone who was really ready to venture, to do something good in life. Everybody liked him because he was also very jovial and hospitable. When we were around him, he would tell stories and crack jokes for us to laugh, and he was always ready to help and to give out.

Louis eventually told the family that Stephen was extremely weak when they left him on a mountain path in Algeria, but the family was not convinced of his death. "He was alive when they left. They could not stay with him to see what happened, so they cannot confirm his death." Eric believed that Stephen's travel companions were in fact withholding information. "They are afraid to come out with the whole story, because it's difficult to deliver bad news; they'll see you as a bad person. Though, we would prefer to hear the news, whatever it is." Stephen's family continued to hold on to the fact that nobody witnessed his death; as long as Stephen's death has not been confirmed, he might as well be alive somewhere, Eric maintained.

Eric: We strongly hope that he's alive—even I myself; I believe seriously he's alive. I don't have any proof of it, but if they left him on the way, then he might have found someone who could accommodate him and take care of him, and take him along. Perhaps he's not ready to talk to anyone yet because he's such a disciplined guy. He makes certain decisions and then he surprises you. So it's possible—even if it takes ten years—that he's alive in Libya or somewhere else that life has sent him. It's really a fifty-fifty chance . . .

Family members have had dreams about Stephen's fate, but they were inconclusive. "I saw him coming home in a dream," Eric said; "that's why I think he's alive. There's an intersection near our house, and I saw him standing there, holding a bag, and he was coming home." Another family member, a woman, saw him standing on a road with his back turned to her, "which does not carry a good meaning." Eric reluctantly admitted, "That means he's dead." While Stephen's family had postponed a decision on his condition and whereabouts, still waiting for good news from abroad, other Guan families have turned to magical means of obtaining information. Thus, in Senya Beraku, families are likely to consult an *obrew*, the Guan traditional priest, if they sense an imbalance in the spiritual world that needs to be addressed.

Having received no conclusive information on the whereabouts of Simon, his family put the matter aside, waiting for further news from Libya or Italy. But soon they began having a growing sense of unease in the house. "We had a feeling when we entered the house that something had changed," John said. "It was as if someone was following us. That was the experience most of the family had in the house, so we began thinking it might be his soul hovering around." This phenomenon of the soul hovering is likely to happen when a Guan person dies in a far-off place under extraordinary circumstances. As Papa Kweku (who is the late Simon's uncle) explained: "When somebody dies on the sea, his soul will be struggling until he can come home and rest in peace. He struggled before dying, so his soul will keep struggling, and it's important for the elders and those at home to perform the necessary rites to allow the soul to come back to Senya Beraku and find peace." The notion of an imbalance in the spiritual world, as expressed in dreams, vision, sensations, or even mystical sightings, prior to learning of a person's death, is quite common in Guan accounts of people lost to high-risk emigration. And these accounts often, though not always, stress that the family observed these spiritual signs *before* the village rumors began circulating. The shock of death appears somehow easier to bear when one is not the last to know; it is as if the rumors sting less when, in hindsight, one could gather that the soul of the deceased had tried to establish contact and to convey the painful and intimate information that the village rumors so bluntly and publicly administer.

Mary provided another example: she was a young widow who had lost her husband, who was on the sea going to Europe. In her case, the unexplainable physical and psychological suffering she and her baby girl experienced eventually made her believe the rumors that had begun circulating. "We went through a whole lot. At times I felt overwhelmed with some kind of anxiety for no particular reason," Mary explained.

Mary: Also, our child began to fall sick continuously. I was selling soup at that time, and when I was going on my rounds, I would hear people discussing things about somebody drowning on the sea, but whenever I came closer, they would stop talking, like they were telling a secret. I had not formally heard that he was dead, but when my daughter kept falling sick, I began to suspect that something was wrong. My husband was someone who used to call occasionally, but when the calls also ceased, I began to think that maybe it was true what people were saying. Then, I received a cassette from Libya confirming his death.

In Mary's testimony, too, the premonitions of foul play precede the brutality of the rumors, as if to cushion the full blow of loss. But in addition to being insensitive and hurtful in a social and emotional sense, the rumors of migrant deaths perhaps also represent a continuation of the sense of arbitrariness that many experience in the unequal relationship with the powerful circumstances of migration that appear to take or give life on a whim. Indeed, one can lose a relative, and even learn of this terrible incident, in the fragmented and haphazard way that only confirms one's helpless and peripheral position, excluded from the actual events; but the narrative reworking of the loss allows the family to take existential center stage in the unfolding of the events, as the subjects to whom the tragic events were first revealed, thus altering the balance between being victims of happenstance and being active participants in the tragic events. In this sense, any symbolic reworking of the incident "involves making words stand for the world, and then, by manipulating them, changing one's *experience* of the world" (Jackson 2002: 18; emphasis in the original). Thus, the family of a lost migrant may indeed be powerless to decide over actual life or death; but how it happened, how the information was retrieved, and what course of action should be taken next all were for them alone to decide, sidelining the devastating rumors or making them irrelevant and reinstating themselves as principal actors in the narrative of loss.

That being said, we should be careful not to regard narrative as the only way to bear loss. Many, like Stephen's family, choose not to talk about the probably fatal incidents at all. Indeed, being silent, keeping one's worries to oneself, and going about one's normal business while waiting years for information and assuming the hurtful memories will slowly fade away appeared an equally accepted strategy of making life bearable in the face of loss. Methodologically, in talking about death with informants, it became clear that they did not necessarily attribute a therapeutic quality to reliving a painful incident, and some found it more sensible to keep quiet about what could not be reversed. Indeed, why would one want to dwell upon incidents that one knew would cause one pain to recollect? In this sense, the narrative of loss is but one strategy for making life bearable, the question not being so much what really happened on the sea or in the desert, but rather what in any given situation will sustain a subject or a group of subjects. Sometimes silence appears to do exactly that (see also Jackson 2005: 147, 156).

To return to the events surrounding Simon's death, in Ghana, ancestors are generally held in the greatest reverence, and facilitating the soul's ascent to the spirit world of the ancestors, whence they watch over or punish the living, is a major concern of Ghanaian funeral rites (Nukunya 2001: 56). Therefore, a homeless soul hovering about, caught betweens worlds, as it were, is not an acceptable state of affairs. Feeling neglected, the lost soul might turn against its own family and cause accidents or deaths. But because of the uncertainties involved in illegal immigration, the family does not hasten to make a decision unless clear "evidence" of a person's death is presented; thus, if no conclusive cassette tape or reliable witness appears, usually steps will be taken to obtain more information before the burial rite is held. And so, on behalf of the family, John decided to consult Madame Sophia, one of Senya Beraku's *nbrew,* who work with the little people of the bush. These *mmoetia,* or simply "dwarfs," are traditionally used as go-betweens when people need to obtain information about the spirit world. "They are able to go to all corners of the world to look for information," Madame Sophia explained. However, they are mischievous and playful beings, and working with them is not necessarily a blessing. "They took my husband away," Madame Sophia recalls; "he fell sick and died. I asked them about what happened, and they confessed to killing him to make me concentrate on the work. I felt bad about that, but they are helping me too. So now, apart from this work, I don't do anything else." Indeed, when it comes to retrieving information, Madame Sophia is known far and wide.

Madame Sophia began working with the *mmoetia* many years ago when she worked as a fishmonger in Yeji. One day she ventured into the "deeper part of the forest" to cut down firewood when she suddenly heard people laughing from the treetops. "But when I looked around, there was nobody there, eh!" She rushed home with the firewood, feeling a bit uneasy about the unexplainable laughter in the trees, but having smoked the fish and seen that they were "all well smoked," she put what had happened behind her and went on with her business. The following day, however, maggots had eaten up all the fish. "I was surprised and said, 'What is this?' It went on like that for a while; the fish got spoiled even though they had been smoked or cooked perfectly. I got worried because our business was collapsing." She decided to consult an *obrew*, who revealed to her that "it was the dwarfs who were doing it all; they were the ones laughing, and those are the things they do to entertain themselves. She told me that they were sending me a signal; they wanted me badly to work with them." Madame Sophia then underwent a series of rituals, during which the dwarfs confirmed that they had singled her out for further assignments. The *obrew* took her deep into the forest where she mixed a magic potion with herbs and trickled a few drops into her nostrils, causing her to black out and "enter a different world."

Madame Sophia: I saw those dwarfs in multitude; they were more than a hundred. They are very short, their feet are on backwards, and their women have their breasts on their knees—and they are partly bald too. They use white clay over their eyes, over their foreheads, and around the mouth. I felt very heavy—but because of the medicine I was able to see them. If you should see them, you would run away. You cannot withstand the sight of them.

Madame Sophia began working with the little people, following their advice and making a living; people came from afar to consult her. Just as her business began growing, her husband died. "Unless you offend them, they are good people, but you have to worship them truthfully."

Madame Sophia therefore tends to the dwarfs' needs continuously and makes sure they are happy. The little people eat three times a week, Sundays, Wednesdays, and Fridays. They like sweet foods, particularly bananas, and local palm wine; she buys their food in the marketplace and arranges it for them in her visitation room, and when she comes back, the plates have been emptied. Incidentally, the *mmoetia* are both black and white. Thus, Madame Sophia works with five black ones—three females and two males—and two white males. To see them, she washes her face with water from a bowl mixed with secret herbs and then enters into a trance. This has to be done at midday, when the sun reaches its zenith, because the little people prefer to appear when it is hot. When the little people visit the *obrew*, they like to play with a particular nut found in the bush. As another sign of their presence, one can usually observe the strange patterns of nuts they leave on the floor.

John and his elder sister visited Madame Sophia to ask her advice about Simon's disappearance. In a state of trance, Madame Sophia summoned the *mmoetia* and asked them to seek information in the spirit world about Simon's whereabouts. A few days later, as she was going about her duties, the *mmoetia* gave her a piece of information. As always, Madame Sophia was busy talking to clients—people are often sitting outside in her courtyard, perhaps a small group of barren women or some fishermen longing to change their luck—when she went into her visitation room and suddenly received a message. She found a letter addressed to her on the floor, on the back of which was written the name of the late Simon. "The little people had decided to intervene on the family's behalf," Madame Sophia said. "They went to the place where the accident happened to find out the facts, and they came back with the letter." Madame Sophia sent for John and the elders in his house. She presented them with the letter, which stated that Simon had indeed died on the sea on the way to Europe and that they should proceed with his funeral. Still, the family was not convinced, and they sought the help of a Baptist preacher in the Brong Ahafo Region whom Simon himself had consulted prior to leaving. This effort, however, was also inconclusive. A few weeks later, however, Madame Sophia provided additional information that made Simon's family reconsider the situation.

Madame Sophia was in her room conducting a consultation for a group of other people when suddenly the ghost of Simon appeared to her. "He came to stand right here," she said, pointing to a place just inside the entrance of the darkened visitation room. "I asked him what he was doing here. He told me that it was so painful that he had died and yet he was still in the water, feeling cold, when all his friends had been taken away. He felt awful because he was no more in the world. And they were even teasing him that he had no family who could come and take him and perform his funeral." Madame Sophia sent for John and the family elders, and then she went into a trance and summoned Simon's ghost. "This time she was talking directly to the ghost," John said, "and suddenly the room became chilled, as if an air-conditioning system had been switched on." The ghost of Simon appeared to Madame Sophia and repeated his complaints. He explained how he was lingering on in the Mediterranean Sea, dead in the water, when the three little people came asking the truth about his disappearance and what had happened at sea. "I wrote the letter myself," he said. "So why are you still hesitant and postponing my funeral? I am pleading with you to release me from this burden." Madame Sophia explained to John's family that the situation was getting out of hand and required that the proper steps be taken, sooner rather than later.

Madame Sophia: It is not proper to die like this—it's unnatural. Therefore, the ghost of the dead person can create disasters in the home; he can even kill somebody because he is suffering. Sometimes the souls get very agitated and try to force themselves into the world to let people know the truth. They had been to see me three times, yet they had done nothing. Now, he said, he would create havoc in the house, and then they'd surely know that he was dead.

Simon, talking directly to John through Madame Sophia, warned him that somebody was trying to steal some roofing slates he had stashed away in his house, and Simon wanted those people stopped. Later, John discovered that five of the slates had been broken, which he felt was proof of the story's authenticity. "It was an attempt to carry them away, so that made us to believe that the whole thing was true." In the light of the new information that Madame Sophia had produced, and the risk of further enraging Simon's ghost, the family finally accepted his death and went home and began preparing the funeral.

Since Simon had died in a far-off place, the first thing to do "to bring home his funeral" was to see Nkensen, the principal deity, residing at the shrine on the main road entering Senya Beraku, and plead with him to allow the soul of Simon into the spiritual realm of the village. As Papa Kweku explained, "That is the point of transit between the village and the outside world. Nkensen is the king of the lesser gods, so he'll stop all kinds of bad spirits trying to enter town, and he'll arrest them unless they have a proper reason for coming." Simon's family sent an elder to the *osow*, the guardian of the shrine, to conduct the necessary rituals for the soul to be allowed entrance. Then, the actual burial rites could be commenced—the Christian burial administered by the Baptist church at the cemetery on the hilltop, and the traditional rite conducted in Simon's house. Concerning the latter, Madame Sophia had ordered the family to fetch a bucket of seawater, mix it with a certain seaweed, and, while conducting the rituals, sprinkle the house with the water "to trap the soul" in the very element that had killed him; and also to decapitate a white fowl and recite secret incantations to secure the passing of Simon's soul into the spiritual world and thus put an end to his suffering.

From this description of the lengthy process of obtaining information about the death of a Guan captain, including the rituals involved, it is clear that the reception of news of migrant deaths in Senya Beraku, perhaps not surprisingly, contrasts radically with reception of the same news in Europe. There is no air of routine in Senya Beraku about the loss of a life on the Mediterranean or in the Sahara. Although it may not be surprising that families back home are thus shattered, research on the political economy of the globalized world and the casualties it entails could profit from exploring the effort of the bereaved to deal with the situation, to rework the loss and to make sense of it, because it is precisely here that one can find counteraction—not normative but existential—against the absence of recognition that characterizes the unequal encounter with, for instance, the deadly border regimes of the privileged world. The self-evident emotional and psychological stakes aside, it is remarkable that the deaths entailed in illegal immigration are recognized on many different levels of village life and that major efforts are set in motion to sort out the details and make sure that the lost person's soul is socially and politically reclaimed, as belonging not only to a family but to the Guan community of Senya Beraku. Moreover, the soul hovering helplessly about in the forsaken borderlands of Europe is reconfigured in the village's religious cosmology. Again, this form of local counteraction appears to be less a critique of the world political economy than a way of conceding a loss, even the ultimate one, in the face of powers that one has no control over. The body stays behind but the soul returns, and the latter's ascent to the eternal afterlife of the ancestors is meticulously facilitated. In many ways, this process of reclaiming and circumscribing the soul of a person lost on the Mediterranean appears to reverse the figure of *homo sacer*, characterized as leading a "bare life," having value in neither a legal nor a religious sense, who may be killed without committing any offense and yet cannot be offered to the gods (Agamben 1998: 8). Perhaps the African immigrant is nothing but a *homo sacer* in the political economy of the globalized world—a bare life to be dealt with in a mode of social prosopagnosia. But in a local Guan context, the immigrant is a social and political subject belonging to a family and a community, someone whose life and death are recognized.

But the many deaths on the way to Europe—especially from the viewpoint of the young women not only widowed in the process but also quite often made single parents—have dire social and economic ramifications. Thus, in many cases, a child is born only a few months before or even shortly after the departure of the husband-father, demonstrating that having a family does not discourage young men from going to Europe. In fact, it appears to be yet another reason for setting out in search of brighter prospects.

YOUNG WIDOWS, SINGLE MOTHERS

Despite having put the soul successfully to rest, the families of lost Guan captains continue to face emotional and socioeconomic challenges. In this regard, young wives seem to be among the most vulnerable, in that they depend on the husband to help support their child or children. The difficulty of supplying one's family with basic necessities during the decline in fishing is in many cases behind the often joint decision of wife and husband that the latter should travel abroad. The young widows and mothers are left in a precarious situation when that strategy completely fails with the husband losing his life in the effort. As a first sign of distress, the yet unknown fatalities on the Mediterranean and in the Sahara produce physical-bodily correlates. During the wait for news of their fathers, for instance, it is almost always reported that the children of lost captains suffer from inexplicable spells of sickness until the cassette tape arrives from Libya or "evidence" is produced through the spiritual means described above. This happened to Mary's baby girl, as mentioned above, and also to Rachel's baby boy. One afternoon, we sat down with Rachel and talked about how the death of her husband has affected her life.

Rachel received Ebenezer and me outside the family compound and led us through the gate (basically a piece of the wall that appeared to have collapsed) into a courtyard, where her mother sat on a stool at the opposite end, blowing into a small fire on which a small black pot was cooking. The smoke lingered along the walls of the yard before it rose into the sky. A couple of goats foraged under a storage cage that rested on wooden poles up against the north wall. Rachel was a very quiet girl, round in shape, in her early twenties (she could not provide her exact age). Although it pained her to recall the events surrounding the death of her husband, she eventually did so in a quiet, measured way, as if weighing her words carefully. The first sign of something amiss had come suddenly when a big butterfly appeared. (Incidentally, the Guan are not the only people to associate Lepidoptera with the soul; consider, for instance, the Greek goddess of the soul, Psyche, who is often portrayed with butterfly wings [Hogue 1987: 186].) When Rachel tried to kill it, the butterfly disappeared into thin air. Then, one day her son suddenly began crying "very seriously," and she couldn't understand what was wrong with him. It was late afternoon, and the whole house was very quiet.

Rachel: Then I went into the courtyard, and there I saw the figure of my husband at the gate. I nearly passed out; I had goose pimples all over my body. Afterward, I was so shocked that I couldn't do anything. I just went in the room and slept the whole day; I didn't even wake up again until nighttime. The following morning they brought the tape from Libya, confirming his death.

But even after this tape arrived, the boy kept falling sick. Since her husband, Robert, had left when she was seven months' pregnant, he never saw his son, which, as the suffering of the child continued, was considered a possible reason for the baby boy's frequent unexplainable spells of sickness. Rachel consulted an *obrew,* who "called the soul of the child to ask what was wrong," and it was revealed that the boy was indeed missing his father. "He was supposed to be with his father, but he never even saw him after coming into this world," Rachel said. The *obrew* instructed them to make a pillow out of the father's shirt for the boy to sleep on and to tie a part of the shirt around the boy's wrist. Eventually these measures solved the immediate problem.

Many times, the death of a husband to high-risk emigration, however, has long-lasting effects on the life of the young widow. The first thing to happen, when death has been confirmed and the funeral has been conducted, is that the woman undergoes the extensive Guan widow rite. She has to sleep one night in the bedroom with her dead husband—not in the bed but on a floor mat. When there is no dead body, the wife sleeps next to a picture of her husband. The woman is put in the bedroom at dawn and stays there until dawn the next morning. The body of the widow during this period is considered to be unclean; thus she is given a wooden stick to scratch herself if she needs to. "As soon as you lose your husband, your body is engulfed in some kind of filth—it becomes dirty," one widowed fishmonger explained. "You have to perform these rites to cleanse yourself, so that you can return to normal life.

The following day before dawn, at the first crow of the cock, four elderly women from one's family call on the widow; the widow is not supposed to respond with her voice but should only make a sound in the throat. "It's a moment of quietness and soberness, so you don't have to speak out," one woman explained. Then the four elderly women take the widow to the beach at 3 or 4 A.M., where they bathe her in seawater. The women bring a piece of the widow's husband's clothes torn in half and wrap it around her while she is otherwise naked. The widow walks facing the sea, arms crossed and her hands placed on her shoulders. When she reaches the sea, the women walk her into the surf, dunk her in the water three times, and bring her back ashore. The elderly women, having brought along a bucket of freshwater, now wash the widow's whole body thoroughly, "to cleanse her and wash off the filth," as another elderly fishmonger explained. Then the widow is brought home and presented with a special necklace, earrings, traditional slippers in red and black, and a piece of plain black cloth without a design. Moreover, the family elders kill two fowls and prepare food for the woman to eat as her first meal as a widow, with another woman who has gone through the widow rite. Then a libation is poured, and the soul of the late husband is summoned to announce and explain that there shall now be a physical separation between the wife and the husband—he being in the spiritual world and she in the material.

Adhering to the ritual and the instructions of the elder women is important, since otherwise the soul of the late husband will haunt the widow (see also Aborampah 1999: 262). As part of the rite, the soul is instead encouraged to watch over the widow and the children from his position in the spiritual world, where he is believed to intervene should any harm be directed at them. Traditionally, during the mourning period the widow is not supposed to work or handle money, only to give out instructions for other people to help her out or to buy what she needs, such taboos signifying that she is not yet ready to partake in normal life. The period of mourning lasts one year; the widow's discarding of the black cloth, which she is not supposed to keep herself, and donning of a white cloth mark the end of widowhood. Christians also hold a memorial service to mark the end of mourning and signify that the widow has re-entered village social life and that she can, should she choose to, remarry. "You're a different person" a fishmonger explained—"when you lose you're husband, the burden of grief hangs over you, but when you go through the ritual, you come back to your senses."

But for many of the young widows, the elaborate ritual that comes so unexpectedly and early in their lives does not always offer much comfort; in fact, it brings the harsh reality of their husbands' deaths to the fore. "The whole thing really devastated me," Rachel said. "I never thought that I, of all people, should go through this process, because I am too young to be a widow already and to endure all these things. We were only at the start of our lives, and the whole thing still pained me so much." As Mary explained, "It was hell for me. The body was not there, so I had to sit next to the picture of my dead husband until dawn." Outside the room, the old women in Mary's family were holding her newborn; the baby cried for her mother all night, and only stopped when it was brought inside for Rachel to breast-feed. But when the time came for Rachel to go to the beach, she told them that she couldn't do it—she was too afraid to go to the beach at night. "Instead they went and fetched a bucket of seawater, and then the old ladies washed me down right there in the room." The expressed reluctance of the young women to undergo the traditional widow rituals, which ideally should only concern elderly women, is also a reflection of the sociocultural changes taking place in Ghana as a result of "modernization and Westernization," and the fact "that mortuary rituals have not been immune to these changes, but have come to reflect a new meaning of death. The dread once held for the spirit of the deceased has waned" (Aborampah 1999: 268). Mary and Rachel, however, because of their young age, were not expected to go through the full ritual. "I wore the black cloth for eight months," Mary said. "I took it off on a Sunday and went to church all dressed in white." The pastor prayed for her, and she went back to her family house and had a meal with some friends. "We even took a picture while we were eating. After that I began living my normal life again."

Formally, Mary could return to her normal life, but particular things had changed with the death of her husband. Most often, young widows report disagreements with their in-laws over the husband's belongings. Mary, for instance, was told to move out of the room she had shared with her husband, Samuel, in his family compound. "That was the most painful of it all," she recalled. "They came with a truck and took all his belongings. They didn't leave me a penny. His sister even wanted to take the television also, but he had always said that his daughter should be able to watch TV on that when she grew up, so in the end they let me keep the television and the bed." According to tradition, Samuel's family had to appoint a successor—someone who, on behalf of the late husband, takes over his responsibilities—but when appointed, Samuel's elder brother refused, and Mary is now struggling to take care of her child alone.

Mary: Some of his friends come by every now and then and help me out, but his family doesn't support us. I feel bad about that, like they have rejected me. My own family is not helping, either; everybody seems to be minding their own business. I am the last child now staying with my mother, and I help her out. If I could only receive a small amount of money and start selling something on the street, that could generate an income for my daughter and me . . . but nobody's willing to help, which I don't understand. They don't have anything against me, but they won't help. Luckily, one of my husband's friends bought a uniform for my daughter so that she could begin attending school. He wanted her to go to a private school, but I was afraid that I wouldn't be able to pay the fees and she would lag behind, so now she's attending regular school.

Rachel experienced similar disappointment when Robert's family had promised her to pray over his personal belongings, hand them over to his successor, and give her the rest, only to find out that nobody had been appointed to help her out and that suddenly his cousins were wearing his clothing around town; one person was even wearing his favorite shoes. She went to the family to ask what was going on, "but they took offense and pushed me aside. They don't even care for the baby; if they see him in the street, they'll just walk right by him. That makes me feel very bad and rejected. This is the very time that I need some assistance and support, but it seems they do not care at all. So I am just praying to God that things could get better for me soon, and I can take care of the baby." Frequently, however, these disputes echo a more fundamental clash between the lifestyle young couples often seek—living as a monogamous nuclear family—and the interests of the lineage group that often owns the house in which the little family resides. Therefore, having lived together in a room as a married couple does not automatically mean that when the husband dies the widow or her children will inherit that space. On the contrary, in accordance with Guan tradition, the husband's extended family asserts its claim to his property (for a discussion of tradition and change in the marriage institution in Ghana, see Nukunya 2001: 159–169).

Although most wives agree to their husbands' migration plans as a family strategy for getting ahead in life, both Rachel and Mary had reservations. To Mary, the whole idea of traveling abroad placed her in severe doubt, though she acknowledged that emigration to Europe could advance their situation considerably.

Mary: When he told me he wanted to try and reach Europe through these crooked means, I objected to it. But most of the guys in town are very difficult to control. Once their mind has been made up, there is little you can say to deter them from going through with it. He was arguing that his friends were entering Europe and he wouldn't give up without making an effort, and that I shouldn't try to discourage him; he wanted to improve the living conditions of his family. At the time he left, I had just given birth to a baby, and I also wanted things to get better for us. They made one trip to Italy and were arrested on arrival and kept in a cell for some time and then deported back to Libya. He told me he would try again, but not when that would be, and the next thing I knew was that the boat had sunk on the high seas and everybody had drowned.

Rachel learned that Robert was going only three days before he was to leave, which led to an argument. "Although, when one travels outside the country, it is safer to keep one's travel plans to oneself until the time everything is 'intact,' I was worried, and I could not understand why he had waited so long before telling me." Rachel's concern was intensified by a dream she had had about Robert leaving for Libya and facing fatal difficulties on the way. At the time, she had not attributed "any serious meaning" to it, since his travel plans were unknown to her. Now, she felt his decision was a dangerous one. "I told him not to go ahead, because he would face difficulties coming back. But he just joked about it, and told me to go away with my devilish ideas. He wasn't the kind of person who rushed into things, so I think his colleagues persuaded him to go, thinking it was much better in Europe." Now, Rachel's life had come to a halt. Waking at 6 A.M., she prayed and swept the compound. Then she did some washing and tidied up her room. She ran a small roadside tabletop store where she sold oranges and toffees, but business was slow because of the dwindling catches.

Rachel: It is not like it used to be—everything is going down. The decline has really affected us, especially the young people, both men and women. Most of the ladies have taken to traveling to nearby towns to trade, and the guys, too, travel out to look for construction work; others embark on that dangerous trip to Libya. That is the reason why most of the guys are taking these risks.

Every evening except Monday, Rachel went to church around six o'clock; afterward she headed directly home and went to bed by nine at the latest. Emotionally, she was still adapting to the loss of her husband, Robert, and found that she spent a lot of time thinking about him. "He was a humble and hardworking guy, a quiet type. Things weren't all that bad for him; in Libya too, he earned the respect of his colleagues because of his humbleness and meekness. He was not somebody who had to talk a lot and joke about his social responsibilities. I really lost a good person in my life." Considering her difficulties, she found it hard to accept that "most of the young guys are going now, even more people than before. The death of my husband is not a reason for them to stay here. It makes me feel bad because they don't know what they are doing."

Mary also viewed the death of her husband as having put her life on hold. "I am in a standstill position," she said. "I am not following the normal course of life at all. Nothing is moving in my direction. I get very fed up with life sometimes. I see my friends from school living ordinary lives, and I feel bad for myself." Mary eventually became a close informant, and she would often come by Fort Good Hope with her daughter, Priceless, who would traverse the place to collect bottle caps from the tables in the courtyard and the lobby to be used in her math class in school. Although Mary had completed junior secondary school and had been accepted to senior secondary school, she couldn't attend classes "because of financial problems." She was now, at twenty-four, the last child still in her mother's compound, and though they had "a cordial relationship," her mother, because of her own financial troubles, was unable to help Mary with basic necessities. When Mary did manage to find some money, she would use it to pay debts. "Yesterday, a friend of my husband gave me 10,000 cedis, so I went to a cousin's house and paid him 5,000 that I owed, and then I went to the chemist and gave him the rest because when Priceless is not feeling well, he gives us medicine on credit." Although the assistance Mary received did little for her own needs, staying in her mother's compound meant Priceless would at least be fed on a regular basis.

Mary: They will try to give Priceless a little bit of the food whenever somebody is cooking, and Priceless never complains. But me personally, I will not be given anything—and I find it really hard to ask anybody for help. It's really quite horrible. We survive only by God's grace. Sometimes I get only one meal a day, and that's the end of it. But I just pray that I will be able to feed Priceless.

In the wake of her husband's death, Mary appeared to have little hope of pursuing her aspirations; instead she found her life confined to tiresome routines and a sense of moving nowhere. "My mother's place is not very lively and I feel very dull sometimes, and I worry a lot. A young girl of my age should be doing something active." When she woke up in the morning, she prayed and attended to her household duties, such as sweeping the compound; then she prepared breakfast for Priceless and got her up and ready for school. Usually she would walk her daughter to school, then return to the compound and wait until the time Priceless had to be picked up again. In her free time, she read books based on Latin American telenovelas. "My favorite is *The Promise*," Mary told me. "It's about love relationships. The one I am reading now is about a boy who's wooing a girl, but the girl is confused because the boy comes from a rich background." After picking up Priceless from school, Mary stayed in the house and made sure her daughter had a meal and was tucked into bed in the evening. Then Mary would, again, "just relax until nightfall and go to sleep. Sometimes, when I feel too dull, I'll take a stroll up the road to visit my sister. That's all I do for a whole day." For the future, Mary was hoping to establish a little business of her own to avoid the daily uncertainty of finding a meal for herself and Priceless, but she found it difficult to keep her courage up.

Mary: The town is not productive—there's nothing meaningful that we can rely on. The decline is bringing hardships on everybody. Most women are trying to go into other kinds of business—selling plastic cups and plates. Sometimes my husband's friends will give me a little note, but that's not something I can bank my hopes on. I have been trying all angles to get something to trade in so at least I can take care of Priceless. But it's difficult; it seems like people are shunning me. It's difficult to even confide in people. Some people seem to care, but at the end of the day they go away and don't come back.

The death of a Guan captain on the Mediterranean sets in motion a series of developments that inflict difficulty on the families at home, especially the young widows. Here, I have briefly introduced some of the themes brought into play by the fatalities in high-risk emigration, which, if examined in more detail, could further enhance our understanding of the long-term effects on village life. In the event of a migrant's death, the young women are expected to undergo the extensive widow rituals that, to at least some young women, are unwanted and stressful. The death of a husband also entails the immediate loss of his economic support, which is not easy to replace. Moreover, the young widow appears in a weak position in terms of inheritance, which often leads to disputes with the late husband's family over material belongings and property and over support for the deceased's children. These disputes reflect changing patterns of family and married life in Ghanaian society to the extent that the young couple's expectations of living together as a nuclear family collide with tradition and his extended family's interests and claims. Thus, "the extended family, which from all accounts is under threat, while the nuclear family is gaining strength," is still capable of asserting itself (Nukunya 2001: 169). But the fact that widow inheritance is an issue at all—when in a Guan matrilineal context the brother's sister and her children are usually the natural beneficiaries—may in itself imply that change is afoot and tradition is being challenged. Indeed, a more thorough study of changing marital practices and family patterns in Ghana may shed light on this development and how these changes may affect the decision to emigrate. In other words, to what extent are the "great expectations" that characterize emigration to Europe (Van Dalen et al. 2005: 775) influenced by the decline in fishing and that general lack of opportunity, as well as by changing sociocultural ideas of what constitutes good family life?

In discussing the sociocultural themes pertaining to the fatalities of illegal immigration and the challenges those deaths pose to lives and livelihoods—especially for young widows—one should note the moral challenges that conceding a migrant's death poses to the existential balance of give-and-take. For this purpose, the next section focuses on the case of Elizabeth, who lost her beloved son on the Mediterranean and was, when we met her two years later, still struggling to come to terms with the accident that ended her son's life.

VIOLENCE AND MORALITY: THE VORTEX OF GIVE-AND-TAKE

In Senya Beraku, obituaries are posted on houses facing the main road. Usually an obituary briefly summarizes the person's life; identifies the nearest family members (father, mother, wife, children, uncles, and aunts); and details the funeral arrangements; and cites the "chief mourners," typically respected village elders and sometimes people coming from abroad to take part in the service. Although Charles's death notice had all of these attributes, it stood out because of his portrait. In this photograph one saw a young man sitting on a blue plastic chair, wearing a baseball cap and a football jersey, smiling and obligingly leaning his head to one side. He appeared vigorous and ready to take on the world had it not been for his "regrettable sudden death," as the obituary put it. Ebenezer knew him very well; they had been schoolmates. Yet there was no way we could meet his mother, Elizabeth, Ebenezer said. Two years had passed since her oldest son had disappeared on the sea going to Italy, and she was still too distraught to talk about it. Even he, a close friend of Charles, had not attended the funeral, because he could not bear to see the mother weeping uncontrollably. In the end, however, having passed Charles's photo daily for almost three months, Ebenezer asked for an interview, and Elizabeth agreed.

We came in the morning. Elizabeth was sitting on a wooden bench outside the family house, on the main street leading to the west side of the village. She was tending a small fire on which she was preparing food. The house was below street level, giving the impression when you watched the road and the people moving by that you were looking up at a stage. And there was a reverse effect, too: sitting on Elizabeth's wooden bench, one felt submerged in a hole, watching other people go about their business. Although Elizabeth, a fishmonger and mother of five (two of them deceased), never stood up during our visit, it was clear from her long legs partly showing from under her blue dress and her slender arms with which she turned the food, that she was a tall woman. She looked younger than one might expect. Even so, the burdens of grief hung like a black cloud over her head, weighing her down and seemingly making every movement painful and unwanted. "Charles decided to travel after the death of his father," Elizabeth began.

Elizabeth: He was the eldest child and wanted to take a step in life, to be able to take care of his mother and his siblings. There is no regular work here. The decline in fishing is bringing untold hardship to the village. We are finding it hard to feed our families, let alone find money for school fees and medicine. And since this is a coastal community, every business is affected. It makes the living conditions quite difficult here. That motivates the young men to travel. They can see that people who have made it and come back are able to live a more normal life.

Elizabeth did not agree with Charles's travel plans, however, and only reluctantly consented. She wanted him to take up a profession that could sustain him in the future. But Charles argued that many of his friends were going and that he wanted to try also, so he could take care of Elizabeth and his younger siblings. "That is why he would take such a risk; to make sure that we would be safe in the future. We loved each other very much. Though he was my son, we lived almost like brother and sister." After leaving Senya Beraku, Charles called her from Libya to let her know that life there was "very strenuous" and that he wished he had never left. "But he asked me to pray for him and hope things would improve in the future. He also said he would not be able to call often because it was very expensive. I should just continue praying, and hopefully things would get better." Then one morning, Elizabeth suddenly had a sense of disaster.

Elizabeth: I used to listen to the religious programs on the radio at dawn, and one time there was an announcement on the radio that a number of illegal immigrants had washed ashore in Morocco. At that very moment a feeling engulfed me, like something was amiss, even though I had heard no rumors yet that my son had tried to go to Europe. I just started crying and couldn't bring myself to stop.

Three days later I had a dream that Charles had returned from Italy. But he was very quiet and was just standing at the gate. I asked him, "Charles, what is the matter with you? Are you dead?" And he kneeled down and said, "Mother, yes, I am dead. I didn't listen to your advice and I have had to face it all." I was sure that something had gone wrong, and I wasn't myself until the confirmation came.

Then the rumors began to circulate. People were saying that a boat had capsized trying to reach Italy. In my church we fasted and prayed, and I asked God to reveal what was happening so that I could be freed from the ordeal I was going through. I saw myself standing in a river washing a particular bow [hair ribbon] that I am very fond of when suddenly two storms coming from both sides swept up the bow and took it away. God [thus] revealed to me that my precious love had been taken away. And if I should follow, I would also lose my life.

Just the following day, there was a messenger from Libya with Charles's passport. They said he tried to take a boat across to Italy but he couldn't make it. When I saw the passport, I knew he was truly dead. I just started weeping and there was chaos in the house.

Elizabeth began to cry. To avoid glances from passers-by and the women on the other side of the street, she kept her eyes firmly fixed on the pot simmering on the fire, while tears welled in her eyes, eventually running down her cheeks and onto the blue dress. "Charles was the most important person to me since his father died," she said. "Whenever he had been to sea, he would pass by the house and give me some fish for cooking, and if I needed money, I could just tell him and he would make sure to look for some." We stopped the interview, and Ebenezer offered words of comfort while I put away my tape recorder and notepad. Ebenezer talked for about five minutes while Elizabeth listened in silence, nodding stoically every now and then. Eventually, Elizabeth declared herself ready to resume the interview.

She recollected that, like many other Senya Beraku fishmongers, she had gone to live in Liberia prior to the outbreak of the civil war. Because of the fighting, she had fled to Guinea, eventually returning to Senya Beraku to meet up with her husband. But while she was gone, her husband had fallen ill, and before she had the chance to see him, he was dead and buried. "That is what pains me the most," she said. "Charles took his place, and now he has died also. So I always feel hurt. Whenever I sit down and have a moment to myself, I start grieving. It's like the world has not been fair to me. But I accept it to be God's will and pray that one day he will interpret the whole thing for me." Now her daily routine began by getting up early and getting the kids in the house ready for school. When they were gone, she would relax and listen to a gospel program on the radio. In the evening, Elizabeth prepared food for the children, listened to the radio again, and went to bed. "The future here is bleak. It is difficult to have a normal life, especially if you're relocated to the village like me, and you don't understand the pattern of life here. There's no happiness in my life. Whenever I sit and think, I become saddened by the events that have befallen me." Concerning the decline in fishing, she was biding her time. "I am staying in the fishing business for now because it is the work I know. But if everything gets out of hand with the fishing business, I would like to go into trading." Approaching the end of the interview, Elizabeth summed up her struggle to come to terms with the events. "Now that Charles is gone, who is going look after us?" she said. "I am just praying that God in his own way will interpret these events for me."

Walking home, I asked Ebenezer what he had said to Elizabeth. He responded as follows:

Ebenezer: When she started crying—to be able to continue with the interview—I was trying to give her some words of encouragement. I said to her that she had to accept the situation as one of those setbacks in life that God allows to happen and only he knows the reason for. I cited an example from the Bible, where God asks Abraham to sacrifice his only son, Isaac, to him. Even though he had only the one son, Abraham had the brave courage to go ahead and do that. It was in the course of the sacrifice that God revealed to Abraham that he should not kill Isaac but replace him with a ram. That was how God saw that Abraham really had faith. So, if she would be able to have that courage herself, maybe things would also open up to her in the future.

Bearing the story of Abraham and Isaac in mind, one can appreciate Elizabeth's two references to God's will and the hope that he would one day "interpret" the events for her. Having said that, when Ebenezer demanded the same composure of Elizabeth that characterizes Abraham, that quite sinister character of the Old Testament, ready to kill his only son, he was clearly asking too much of her. First, the events are different in the obvious sense that Elizabeth lost Charles unknowingly to an accident in the Mediterranean, whereas Abraham was ready to sacrifice Isaac by his own hand at God's command. Second, Ebenezer was asking for something that, on the face of it, was not only practically impossible but also humanly impossible and even ethically wrong, namely that Elizabeth should sacrifice her own son.

Nevertheless, the incidents have certain important similarities. I have discussed how dead captains, "bare life" to the political economy of the globalized world, are meticulously reclaimed and circumscribed locally—socially, politically, and religiously. I now suggest that Ebenezer's somewhat misguided advice can shed light on the critical existential theme of conceding a loss, the ultimate one at that, in the face of powers over which one has no control. Briefly, the story of Abraham and Isaac from the book of Genesis, chapter 22 (central, mutatis mutandis, to all the Abrahamic religions), begins with God asking Abraham to sacrifice his only son, Isaac, on the mountain of Moriah. Without questioning the demand, Abraham rises early, saddles his ass, and sets out on a three-day journey, bringing along two men and his beloved son, given to him in his old age (when Isaac was born, Abraham was one hundred and his wife, Sarah, was ninety). They reach the mountain and Abraham and Isaac begin the ascent, leaving the two men behind. Upon reaching the top, Abraham builds a fire and binds his son to a stone alter. He then raises the knife over Isaac to cut his throat, when suddenly an angel intervenes and tells him not to lay his hand on the boy. Abraham then lifts up his head and sees a ram trapped in the nearby bushes, and he sacrifices the animal in Isaac's place. Because Abraham did not hesitate to obey the command to sacrifice his only son, God blesses Abraham and his lineage and, through Abraham, all the nations of the earth.

Leaving the normative theological questions aside, I argue that Abraham's willingness to sacrifice Isaac translates into everyday, secular existence as a powerful allegory for the (im)moral economy of existential reciprocity—that is, the challenge of coping with devastating loss in the form of sacrifice while retaining hope that the outside world will provide something of commensurable worth, keeping in mind, as I have argued earlier, that experientially, giving up is also a form of giving. Thus, Kierkegaard, in *Fear and Trembling* (1985 [1843]), understands the challenge of the Abraham and Isaac story as lying beyond any reason or moral, as the demand to resign everything infinitely, only to take it back on "the strength of the absurd" (Kierkegaard 1985 [1843]: 65). In other words, the challenge is to give up everything, even what cannot be given—one's most private affairs and what one loves the most—in the absurd belief that one way or another, in one shape or another, it will come back.

Without question, the story of Abraham and Isaac is remarkable in that in asking for Isaac, God demanded much more of Abraham than anyone could ever be asked to give up. In suspending all reason and morality, Abraham becomes a terrible and enigmatic figure, one humanly impossible to follow. As Kierkegaard says again and again, "Abraham, I cannot understand," only to add, "Even though in a certain lunatic sense I admire him more than all others" (Kierkegaard 1985 [1843]: 66, 86). Unlike Abraham, Elizabeth is understandably reluctant to give up her son, though she has accepted his death to be a fact; that is, she's reluctant to let the person nearest and dearest to her become part of the give-and-take of life or, purely and simply, to sacrifice him. Furthermore, she appears to doubt that after giving him up, he will be replaced with a ram and death be overturned. At the very least, having lost Charles already, Elizabeth is impatient to know when God will "interpret" the events for her—when the incident may be reversed and Charles returned to life. Only then, it appears, will she give him up. As a consequence, anticipating the growing unlikelihood of Charles's coming back, Elizabeth seems to question the very morality of this exchange, arguing, "It's like the world has not been fair to me." Yet the comparison with the Abraham and Isaac story is not completely inapropos, whatever the reasons, perhaps even dubious ones, Ebenezer may have had for bringing it up. The everyday demands of the existential give-and-take of life, at once sustaining and depriving a person, also lie beyond reason and morality. Sometimes they appear to make people give up more than can be reasonably or ethically asked, and give no insurance that life will be restored to a bearable state, except perhaps for the comfort one can find in the extramundane conviction of mythical figures who, like Kierkegaard's Abraham, resign everything infinitely and take it back on the strength of the absurd. Less devout people, and even strong Christian believers like Elizabeth, may feel that generally speaking, the world should be declared bankrupt because it has taken so much and given so little that it will never in a lifetime be able to repay what it owes (Emerson 1997 [1844]: 25).

Yet the story of Abraham and Isaac reveals a paradox about both existential reciprocity and the concession of loss Elizabeth is finding thoroughly unacceptable: if giving up is also a form of giving, then, to paraphrase Kierkegaard's teleological suspension of the ethical (1985 [1843]: 95), there appears to be a reciprocal suspension of the ethical. In other words, certain symbolic gifts violate the ethics of the moral world they are supposed to sustain. Indeed, Abraham *had* consented to give up Isaac, without knowing, without calculating, without investing—beyond any economy. Therefore, the sacrifice of Isaac is also the sacrifice of "the *oikonomia*, namely of the law of the home (*oikos*), or the hearth, of what is one's own or proper, of the private, of the love and affection of one's kin" (Derrida 1995: 95; italics in the original). Thus, Derrida argues that the sacrifice of Isaac can be read as the paradox of absolute duty and responsibility to the absolute other—"God, if you wish"—which demands that one behave "in an irresponsible manner (by means of treachery or betrayal), while still recognizing, confirming, and reaffirming the very thing one sacrifices, namely, the order of human ethics and responsibility. In a word, ethics must be sacrificed in the name of duty" (Derrida 1995: 66–67, 69). As a consequence, only when God has seen that Abraham knows absolute responsibility, fears and trembles before it, and not only knows it but acts on it by offering *the gift of death*, does God send an angel to intervene. Abraham is stopped when there is no longer a moment of time between the knife and Isaac, when he had resolved to kill Isaac and the sacrifice therefore was consummated; only then is the world of human ethics restored (Derrida 1995: 72). Thus, having made sure that such a gift, "outside of any economy, the gift of death—and of the death of that which is priceless—has been accomplished without any hope of exchange, reward, circulation, or communication," God decides to give back: he restores Isaac to the world of the living. In this sense, through the sacrifice of that which cannot be sacrificed, the economy of the hearth is substituted with the "*an*economy of the gift"; that is, God, the absolute other, gives the gift of life in return for Abraham's gift of death (Derrida 1995: 96–97). From the perspective of secular, everyday existence, one may conclude that at the very heart of the moral world of existential reciprocity one finds not economy or the moral ethics of the social world, but the system of gift-giving with all its perils and ambiguities, including, apparently, a suspension of the ethical to the demands of the absolute other. But what is the point of this substitution of the economy of the hearth with the noneconomy of gift-giving?⟩

Kierkegaard wonders why the proverb "Only one who works gets bread" does not pertain to the actual world it proposes to describe. "The outside world is subject to the law of imperfection; there it happens time and time again that one who gets bread is one who does not work, that one who sleeps gets in greater abundance than one who labors. In the outside world everything belongs to whoever has it, the outward world is subject to the law of indifference and the genie of the ring obeys the one who wears it" (Kierkegaard 1985 [1843]: 57). But things are different in "the world of spirit," Kierkegaard argues. Here, "it does not rain on the just and the unjust alike, here the sun does not shine on both good and evil, here only one who works gets bread, and only one who knows anguish finds rest, . . . only one who draws the knife gets Isaac" (57). In this moral world, reality is a permanent, reliable, and substantial whole (Laing 1973: 39) in which one has the attention and responsiveness of the powers that sustain one and, thus, a sense of leverage in terms of choosing the direction of one's life. But this moral world is also a world of "anguish," a world where, unbelievably, "only one who draws the knife gets Isaac." This is paradoxical indeed, but it is only in a mode of existential reciprocity, which guarantees the practical and moral structure of the world one longs to preserve, that demands can be made that take one outside the reason and ethics of the social world. This is because adhering to the give-and-take of life is adhering to the absolute other over the economy of the hearth, which cannot be of its own making. In the same way that a place where the obligation to exchange with outside forces beyond one's control is a place "eternally denied social man" (Lévi-Strauss 1969: 497), the requirements of what one should give, and in what manner and how much, are not subject to the ethics of "social man." Rather, "social man," to remain just that, has to sacrifice the social. Thus, although such a form of reciprocity could correctly be viewed as an "unsociable extreme," the derived concept of "negative reciprocity" (Sahlins 1972: 195) is not helpful in trying to grasp it. The obligation to give, which includes the obligation to give up, does not respond to the ethics of the horizontal social world one longs to preserve, but demands a sacrifice of this dimension, or of the hearth and the ethics of human life it entails, only to reaffirm it. So, in this extreme mode of reciprocity, one finds not necessarily negative reciprocity but a form of reciprocity that transcends the social world in order to constitute it "on the strength of the absurd." Such a form of reciprocity is perhaps better described as, respectively, "all-taking" and "all-giving" (Jackson 2005: 43). This organization, however, entails anguish and sacrifice; sometimes, argues Annette B. Weiner, the fear of losing what cannot be given up, or the hope of approaching what is beyond exchange, motivates the exchange itself. Weiner finds the dynamic of reciprocity to consist of protecting one's "inalienable possessions" from entering into exchange, that is, to arise from "the desire to hold something back from the pressure of give and take" (Weiner 1992: 43). Weiner is right, of course. But in keeping with the argument above, this is also a project doomed to failure, because affirming social worlds paradoxically brings one into the realm of sacrifice. ⌉

In this sense, as Derrida argues, though the Abraham and Isaac story is "monstrous, outrageous, barely conceivable," it still reflects "the most common thing," or "what the most cursory examination of the concept of responsibility cannot fail to affirm," when taken to its ultimate expression.

> As soon as I enter into a relation with the other, with the gaze, look, request, love, command, or call of the other, I know that I can respond only by sacrificing ethics, that is by sacrificing whatever obliges me to respond, in the same way, in the same instant, to all others. I offer a gift of death, I betray, I don't need to raise my knife over my son on Mount Moriah for that. Day and night, at every instant, on all the Mount Moriahs of this world, I am doing that, raising my knife over what I love and must love, over those to whom I owe absolute fidelity, incommensurably. (Derrida 1995: 67–68)

Certainly, Elizabeth is torn between the will of God and the love for her son. Thus, in a vision, Elizabeth is warned to let go of the precious bow that is swept away from her in the river and is asked to give Charles up and not to follow him; otherwise she herself will be lost. One can appreciate what is at stake. It is not that Elizabeth is encouraged to trade off Charles in order to save her own life. No such option appeared in her vision. Rather, the challenge concerned something extraordinarily dear to her, quite possibly more dear than her own life. So the vision means that unless Charles is given up, he will not come back, and then both will be, in truth, lost. Having said that, I do not pretend to know what Elizabeth is going through. Here, I attempt no psychological analysis of her loss or her obvious emotional strain. Instead, I focus on certain critical existential dilemmas. Although one may approach an understanding of this paradoxical ordeal, to live it is, of course, a very different challenge. That is why, to Kierkegaard, the Abraham and Isaac story is not an example one can follow. Each human being has to take this step on his or her own, continuously resigning everything infinitely and taking it back on the strength of the absurd— something that Kierkegaard declares he is unable to do himself. "To be able to lose one's understanding and with it the whole of the finite world whose stockbroker it is, and then on the strength of the absurd get exactly the same finitude back again, that leaves me aghast" (Kierkegaard 1985 [1843]: 65–66). But in resigning everything infinitely, one is reconciled with existence by the pain of making this move, Kierkegaard argues. "Infinite resignation is that shirt in the old fable. The thread is spun with tears, bleached by tears, the shirt sewn in tears, but then it also gives better protection than iron and steel. A defect in the fable is that a third party is able to make the material. The secret in life is that everyone must sew it for himself" (Kierkegaard 1985 [1843]: 74). To have to give up what matters most, therein lies the constant danger that threatens one's moral world. One could argue, echoing Emerson, that the reason that the world is still in business at all, and not already declared bankrupt, is that the investors perhaps sense that they may be in for a loss if the property were to be divided, disposed of, and eventually measured against the enormous investments and sacrifices made. In other words, to appropriate the system of the gift, which governs moral worlds, into the economy of the hearth would radically increase the risk of insolvency already pressuring the world— how could one's reason and morality have it any other way? So, whether one in the midst of it all makes life bearable, or whether one reaches a breaking point "beyond which adversity comes to be experienced as unbearable" (Jackson 2007: 126), the challenge of existential reciprocity remains: not only to keep one's "inalienable possessions" from circulating but also to deal with the fact that they will, eventually, by one's own hand, circulate, given the shakiness of life and the encroachment of the other.

One conclusion that can be derived from this argument is that existential reciprocity, as discussed in chapter 3, is not well represented by the circle of the Three Graces. It goes against the social grain to exchange only with close kin; in fact, in order to constitute the social, existential reciprocity reaches beyond the social, beyond economy, reason, and ethics. Therefore, this form of exchange does not conform to the trope of a circle, which has no beginning and no ending but closes upon itself in harmony. Rather, existential reciprocity is haunted by an undercurrent of violence and the fact that "the separation between acts that sustain a moral life and inhuman ones that destroy it is thin" (Kleinman 2006: 26). This theme of destruction is also prevalent in Marcel Mauss's description of the "monstrous" Kwakiutl potlatch. "In certain kinds of potlatch one must expend all that one has, keeping nothing back. . . . In a certain number of cases, it is not even a question of giving and returning gifts, but of destroying. . . . Whole boxes of olachen (candlefish) oil or whale oil are burnt, as are houses and thousands of blankets. The most valuable copper objects are broken and thrown into the water. . . . In this way one not only promotes oneself, but also one's family, up the social scale" (Mauss 1990: 37, 42). Here, the sacrifice of the economy of the hearth made to reaffirm, even strengthen, one's moral world stands out clearly. But is Mauss correct to suggest that the system of gift-giving, as the functional principal of society, will reach its peak of "wisdom and solidarity" when "by opposing reason to feeling, by pitting the will to peace against sudden outbursts of insanity," peoples of the world "have learnt how to oppose and to give to one another without sacrificing themselves to one another" (Mauss 1990: 82–83)? Probably not. Rather, reciprocity is monstrous at heart, all-taking and all-giving.

Thus, following Kierkegaard and Derrida, the moral basis of the economy of the hearth is violence committed against one's own, the very sacrifice of what one holds dearest, with a view to sanctioning the fabric of one's moral world. Existential reciprocity in this ultimate form cannot be translated into economy, reason, or ethics. Perhaps, then, Mauss is closer to the true nature of reciprocity when he describes the form of exchange that a civilized world has to abandon in order to progress to peace and prosperity: "Men approached each other in a curious frame of mind, one of fear and exaggerated hostility, and of generosity that was likewise exaggerated. . . . There is no middle way: one trusts completely, or one mistrusts completely; one lays down one's arms and gives up magic, or one gives everything, from fleeting acts of hospitality to one's daughter and one's goods" (Mauss 1990: 81). Indeed, according to Emerson, "the only gift is a portion of thyself. Thou must bleed for me. This is right and pleasing, for it restores society in so far to its primary basis, when a man's biography is conveyed in his gift, and every man's wealth is an index of his merit" (1997 [1844]: 26).

Returning to something Elizabeth said, we may explore this notion of reciprocal violence further by comparing it to the trope of the circle, as expressed in the dance of the Three Graces. Elizabeth explained that after she saw Charles in a dream, her church arranged a fasting and praying session where she asked God to reveal what had happened. Then, "I saw myself standing in a river washing a particular bow that I am very fond of," she said, "when suddenly two storms coming from both sides swept up the bow and took it away. God revealed to me that my precious love had been taken away. And if I should follow, I would also lose my life." Those two storms, converging in a vortex to sweep up Charles, in many ways provide a better visual understanding of the existential give-and-take than the circle of the Three Graces. Incidentally, in an analysis of the vortices in the work of Turner, the art historian W. J. T. Mitchell (1983) associates the vortex (belonging to a group of transitional and dynamic forms ranging from the two-dimensional S-curve to the cylindrical helix to the conical vortex, or from the trail of the snail and the winding road, to smoke coiling upward and the double helix of the DNA-string, to the maelstrom and the nebula) with both destructive and creative powers, citing such phenomena as whirlpools and whirlwinds; scenes of destruction, instability, and disintegration; finding vortices "literally in natural disasters, metaphorically in the 'whirlwinds' of political revolution or psychological disorientation." The vortex suggests "vast dangerous patters of energy." Mitchell continues, "The vortex is the vast, stable, sublime form of instability itself, the image of forms, like hopes and empires, being created and destroyed" (Mitchell 1983: 127–129, 144). Turner wanted to record this natural phenomenon, or to "glimpse into the eye of annihilation, and attempt to explore the boundary between form and chaos"; and so, at the age of sixty-five, he allegedly had himself tied to the mast of a ship sailing the English Channel in a January winter storm. The result was the famous painting *Snow Storm: Steam-Boat off a Harbour's Mouth* (1842; Tate Gallery, London), which depicts a small vessel in distress, fighting to escape a powerful storm that whirls outward, out of the frame and toward the spectator. (This painting immediately reminds one of the smuggling boats on the Mediterranean caught in rough weather, at the point when, as one captain cited earlier put it, it is decided whether "we were either going to be dead or to be alive.") According to Mitchell, the outward motion of the vortex articulates at once the energy of the storm and the vertigo induced in a person subjected to a whirling motion. "That is, the picture tries to show what it was like to be in the scene, enveloped by its energies, and not to be detached from that experience by the security of a cabin, a frame, or a secure sense of perspective" (Mitchell 1983: 140).

In Elizabeth's case, the two storms that converged to sweep her precious bow away exhibited all the uncontrollable powers of the vortex, powers of both annihilation and creation, causing her to lose her footing as well. Thus, in the aftermath of the vortex, Elizabeth still appears disoriented, waiting for God to "interpret" the events that so brutally turned her life upside down. Elizabeth's recollection that, after Charles's death was confirmed, "there was chaos in the house," seems appropriate given that the etymological root of the word *chaos* is the Greek *khaos*, "void" or "chasm." Indeed, the vortex of give-and-take, violently insensitive to human wants and desires, seems to exist on a fine line between order and disorder. Returning to the trope of the circle, in the real world, should the Three Graces for a moment let go of one another's hands, they would risk being whirled away; whereas should they choose to cling to each other's hands forever, lost in their eternal dance, under no obligation to sustain their existence outside their own circle, they would, admittedly, prove their divine nature.

A PLACE TO LAY DOWN ONE'S HEAD

As we talked to Michael about the death of his nephew, Alex, on the Mediterranean, the question resurfaced of risking everything to reach Europe, weighed against the gains one hoped to make in the process. The nephew had been very dear to Michael. During his time in junior secondary school, Alex stayed with him, and often came back to visit after he took up an apprenticeship as a mason in Accra.

Michael: I was his uncle, taking care of all his needs. He always sought advice from me, so that it had to happen like that [drowning at sea] makes me feel very bad; even now I feel the pain of it. Anytime he came for weekend trips, he would come and greet me and maybe share a drink; he was almost like a son to me.

Because things were slow in Ghana, Alex went to Libya and stayed there for almost three years, remitting wages to his family regularly. He then decided to try to reach Europe. He rang them from Libya and explained that he had found a connection to Italy. That was the last they ever heard of him. "It really disturbed me; it wore me down" Michael told us. "Most importantly, he had a ten-month-old baby, and it has shattered his wife so much, because it was a nice opportunity for a young man, and now . . . He was a very hardworking guy, full of energy, so for him to lose his life like that was terrible." Yet, having lost his nephew, Michael did not disapprove of illegal immigration and was reluctant to advise others against going.

Michael: They have to take these risky adventures. Though it's a big tragedy to lose your life when you're in your prime, one shouldn't blame them too much. They are reaching maturity, reaching their peak, and they should take a step ahead. When you see these guys coming home from Europe, you feel pity for yourself; you feel hurt in your soul. Because we started with these people, and after two or three years in Europe they are able to make money and raise themselves to a certain level, and choose to move around with friends who are also at that same level; they reject us. That makes us feel very bad; it dampens our spirits. It makes you think that you also need to make a move.

The risk of death is commonly talked about as the price one has to pay to "take a step ahead"—as if one can better afford to lose one's life by taking a step ahead than through the slow but inevitable demise of village life. "We know if we reach those places, we'll be able to make it and make some money that can be invested at home," Michael said. "That's what encourages everybody to take this perilous route. If we're able to make it, our lives are never going to be the same." Michael expresses the painful realization that, in a difficult situation in which resources are drying up and growth appears impossible, to sustain one's life, one has to part with one's friends and family, even risk losing them. In the effort to take back that which is already drifting away from under one's feet, namely the very order and nature of life one holds so dear, one must abandon it. In this sense, high-risk immigration is an effort to substitute a world where everything belongs to whoever has it (which so-called globalization has done little to change despite the promises made for it to the contrary) with a moral world, a world in which "a man's wealth is an index of his merit" (Emerson 1997 [1844]: 26). But, apart from the many deaths, how does this migrant world of sacrifices manifest itself in the village of Senya Beraku? Because of the generally miserable state of affairs in Naples, few Guan migrants made any real progress in terms of establishing themselves materially, and none of them had been able to return to the village yet—because of either financial or legal problems. Nevertheless, they were making some small but significant advances. Thus, I was one day invited to see Samuel's hard-earned plot of land in Senya Beraku, where he was planning to build a house and to one day come and stay, returning from the brink of disaster to the warmth of the hearth.

It was clear from staying with Samuel in Naples that his sister, Mercy, was the most important person in his life next to his mother. According to matrilineal descent, his mother and his sister, and the children his sister would eventually have, were Samuel's nearest and dearest, and Mercy therefore had every interest in seeing him succeed in life. Moreover, the family's hopes of advancing socially were invested in Samuel. Thus, Mercy was the one he consulted before making big decisions, such as leaving for Libya, and she in turn gave him the golden key he carried around his neck to unlock the doors of opportunity and keep adversity at bay. Mercy and Samuel had the same mother and father; consequently, she bore an uncanny resemblance to him, except that she was slenderer and perhaps a bit taller. She was quite a devout woman, a frequent churchgoer and involved in one of the many Pentecostal congregations in Senya Beraku. (Having found a suitable husband through the church, she was expecting to marry in the fall.) Mercy came across as an industrious and hardworking person who had little time for the notorious drinking and reckless lifestyle of the fishermen. She had her own hair salon in her mother's house, and seeing the way the fishing business was going down, she had given up life as a fishmonger and had reverted to making batik that she sold in the marketplace.

In the village, Mercy was the one Samuel had entrusted with overseeing his plot of land. One day, she agreed to show it to me on condition that my assistant not be informed. Indeed, we had to leave early, she said in her quiet but resolute manner, so people wouldn't talk. Mercy didn't want to draw attention to the place by walking around it with a white man, because she generally didn't like people poking their noses in her business, and because such attention might arouse envy in others, perhaps leading someone to curse her and thus try to end the progress the family was making. So one early morning, we walked out of town on the main road, passing by the big houses being built two or three hundred meters outside the village perimeter. They were, Mercy explained, commissioned by people living abroad or in Accra, who wanted a private place to stay when they came to Senya Beraku to visit family or friends. When we came to a slight bend in the road, Mercy stopped and pointed into the rough bush. "That is Samuel's plot of land," she said. "Those blocks over there belong to Sammy's friend who is also in Italy. They are four of them in Italy, who all bought a plot of land at the same place." Although there was not much to see as yet—a pile of bricks by the roadside, a backdrop of heavy vegetation—there was a certain sense of urgency and preciousness about this otherwise insignificant piece of land and the imaginary house on it, as I thought of Samuel's long journey to Europe, the difficulties he faced, and the challenges of migrant life in Naples.

Mercy: The very moment I heard that Sammy had bought a plot of land, I was very happy. He called me from Italy and told me he had acquired a plot of land, and that I should go for the receipt. And now I'm getting ready to put pillars down at the corners, as soon as the surveyor has been here to measure up the land.

H.L.: What kind of house do you see being raised here?
Mercy: I like cream colors, and at the bottom, a darker color. So, when it rains, the mud will not stain the walls. It should contain a television, a fridge, and a fan, so that when you're coming down [here], you shouldn't have to carry those things. It should not be a very big house, about two, three, four bedrooms, kitchen, and bathroom.

You would not be staying here for the rest of your life, something little, something neat. You have to go from one place to another. So, from a very humble beginning, people will have to see you are developing. They should see a big difference, something nicer than my mother's house. Maybe a friend would like to come and stay too. And I would be very proud: "Look at my brothers house!"

H.L.: What did you think about Samuel leaving for Libya?
Mercy: Sammy always used to tell me, "Sister, I'll travel," but he had nobody to help him to go through the normal way, so he had to go through the desert and across the sea. Sammy went through a lot. It's wonderful that he has succeeded. I hope that whatever his aim in life is, he'll be able to obtain it. You have to have a place to lay down your head. That's the reason why they are all there [in Europe], looking for somewhere to lay down their heads, you and your family.

If Sammy had stayed here, I don't think he would have been able to buy a plot of land like this.

H.L.: Why not?
Mercy: Life here is difficult—seriously difficult—because what are we doing here? What are we doing here? We are not doing anything. The only way you can make it is to travel out. So, if you have the means whereby you can go through the normal channels to Europe, then you'd do it. Though it's not easy over there, the little that you can bring home can do something good. So we always pray that God will help them to find a good job and they can come back and do something good with the money. A guy in our neighborhood went abroad, and very soon he was able to send money back for the family to put up a house. Now, he's very respected—before he hustled at the beach.

H.L.: This place [Samuel's plot] is a bit far from Senya Beraku?
Mercy: It's good. I like this place. The place is very quiet; you don't have a lot of people disturbing you.

Me, personally, I don't like noisy places. Somewhere calm, that is what I like. I don't know for him. I like a very quiet place, that's how I am. I am even planning, if God helps me, to have a place like this myself around here, putting up my own structure. When I come down [after the marriage], I'll be able to stay here and send for my mother, and if there's something I have for her, I'll be able to give it to her and go back, so I wouldn't have to live in the village. I wouldn't let people know much about me, because sometimes people get jealous.

H.L.: Have you considered traveling to Europe yourself?
Mercy: Young women are not able to travel. Look at the process that Samuel went through. Can I go through that? No, I have to stay. Those of us who are here, we are trying and planning to own something, to be called an owner of something. But if God permits you to go to Europe, you should fight hard and come down and put up something, instead of running around behaving like somebody when you're nobody. You really have to try hard—to fight really hard.

This plot of land on the outskirts of the village was the material expression of the hard-fought success of Sammy's emigration story, which would eventually see the family move ahead in life, socially and economically: a modest house but with enough rooms for each individual to have privacy and with the modern conveniences that their mother's small house in the step-father's compound did not offer. Ideally, this development would allow the family to earn the respect of the community, which would recognize that this family was moving ahead in life, "going from one place to another." But the house and land also represented something more: the fishermen's successful attempt to reposition themselves within the circulation of goods, symbolic as well as material, by traveling illegally to Europe, thereby pursuing a strategy of retrieving their lives and livelihoods from a discouraging future. In so doing, the fishermen have substituted the law of indifference (whether the political economy of the globalized world or the declining marine environment) with the give-and-take of a moral world, with a world in which one's actions make a difference and one's appeals are accommodated. Michael Jackson (2002) has described this as "a world that is felt to be as much one's own as it is beyond oneself" (126). I argue here that such a continuous sense of reciprocity with the environment by which one is sustained, and the power one is hereafter able to exert on the direction of one's life, produces a sense of existential control. This, I suggest, is existential reciprocity. It is a sense of connectedness in the life-world, a sense that thrives on the "psychological oxygen" of responsiveness, to follow Heinz Kohut (1984: 18). The challenge, however, as described in the previous section, lies in the fact that reaching beyond one's own circle is always to risk the violence of the vortex of give-and-take. In the case of the fishermen of Senya Beraku, this challenge appears more literal than in most other cases. To be sure, West African smuggling-boat captains, taking matters into their own hands, do not have the privilege of watching the storm from the safety of the shore but are rather working on deck, navigating a ramshackle boat to Europe in one piece. That they do so, knowing beforehand the dangers, seems a testimony to the existential importance of this endeavor. Although what they seek is inseparable from the socioeconomic advances that it articulates, it is yet not reducible to them. Rather what is at stake is the reaffirmation of one's moral world against growing arbitrariness and unresponsiveness. It is the need to "put something up against the future," as John expressed it. More than presenting a realm of possibility and growth, the future for the fishing community resembles a blind force of nature that one has to protect oneself against and otherwise accept and endure. As Mercy put it herself, "You have to have a place to lay down your head. That's the reason why they are all there [in Europe], looking for somewhere to lay down their heads, you and your family." What better expression of the desire for ontological security in a changing world could one possibly imagine?

Conclusion

Although this book emphasizes the life-worlds of the Guan fishermen, it does not focus solely on subjective experiences, if one thereby means drawing on data pertaining to inner states, thoughts, feelings, or the like. Instead, this book attempts to simultaneously describe various social, psychological, political, and existential demands on the lives of the West African informants and how these challenges both inform and give shape to subjective experiences. To capture this perennial tension, the notion of "critical phenomenology" is employed: by addressing broader social and political issues in accounting for subjective realities, I seek an understanding of the ways these different forces intersect with and challenge migrant life-worlds (Desjarlais 1997: 24–25).

Concerning the political realities framing the movement of undocumented migrants, scholars on globalization and migration have argued that it would be difficult, if not impossible, to stop people from poorer countries from moving to richer countries (Hansen and Stepputat 2005: 18); at least it would be difficult to stop them "without drastically curtailing civil and human rights, which would be at odds with enlightenment values and the open nature of modern capitalist economies" (de Haas 2007: 826). But what appeared impossible only a few years ago seems perhaps possible today. Migration out of Libya has apparently been halted, following the so-called "friendship pact" between Libya and Italy. Libyan official sources report that, in 2009, up to 90 percent of refugees, asylum seekers, and migrants were stopped before they reached Italy. As a consequence, rather than assuming that European nation-states cannot stop people from moving, one should perhaps be asking how far they are prepared to go, including pushing migrants back to countries where their life and freedom will be threatened, in clear violation of conventions and international human rights law.

As yet, we know little of the human consequences this course of action entails. In the case of Libya, however, one recent report by the Jesuit Refugee Service in Malta (2009) that focused on the circumstances of people handed over to the Libyan authorities after being picked up by Italian vessels on the high seas, or apprehended by Libyan authorities en route to Europe, confirms that outsourcing of migration control and pushing back asylum seekers, refugees, and migrants have serious implications for the detained. These implications appear irreconcilable with the legal, political, and humanitarian values that many European countries are not only proud of but also seek to promote in the rest of the world. Africans kept in Libyan prisons on behalf of Italy are detained without legal process and for an undisclosed period of time; they are not recognized as potential refugees, and their claims for asylum are not heard, as no system or legal framework allowing for such identification is available. They are kept under congested and unsanitary conditions, and many suffer from scabies, dermatitis, and respiratory problems. They do not receive adequate food and water and have no access to medical facilities. In fact, some report that asking for medical assistance, even for pregnant women, can result in mocking and beatings by the guards. Indeed, the Libyan immigration system, many migrants report, is characterized by the use of violence, the incarcerated "brutally beaten," sexually harassed, and punished with electroshock stun weapons. One woman reported that her uncle was left for dead in a pile of garbage after being badly beaten and tortured with electroshock guns; two days later, somebody happened to notice that he was still alive (JRS Malta 2009: 2–11).

Despite the apparent temporary cessation of the profitable business of smuggling, a new form of corruption has appeared. Many would-be migrants in Libyan jails are reportedly extorted by the detention officers and only let go if they agree to borrow more money and have it sent via Western Union. Some even report that they are sold back to the human smugglers, who facilitate another attempt to reach Europe, then add the cost of buying the passengers to the price. One migrant reported in an Italian documentary film that he was arrested seven times and sold five times before finally reaching Europe (Segre et al. 2009).

Those who make it to Italy find themselves doing so-called "dirty work," jobs unwanted by Italians. Indeed, the data show that while there is a strong Italian political desire to keep the migrants out, the structure and dynamics of the Italian labor market—supporting the lifestyles many Italians have become accustomed to—has a place reserved for a vulnerable low-paid workforce. Here, one could perhaps draw a parallel to the situation of Latin American undocumented migrants in the United States, whose lives are also characterized by their "deportability" and the fact that such a category of people—removable from the territory of the nation-state at any time, such as when the economy has less need for them—accounts for a "profoundly useful and profitable . . . reserve of labour" (De Genova 2002: 439–440).

In this light, it remains to be seen how the financial crisis and the recent tightening of migration control measures in Italy will affect the work situation of the new immigrants. There are signs that migrants are finding it increasingly hard to sustain their existence in Italy. In the spring of 2010, I was contacted by a Christian homeless shelter in Copenhagen asking for advice on how to deal with the relatively large number of young West Africans suddenly seeking their assistance. The young Africans had begun arriving around Christmas and had now almost "pushed out" the regular clients, including former psychiatric patients, alcoholics, and substance abusers. Preliminary interviews suggest that many of the young men are Ghanaians and Nigerians, and the rest come from various other countries in West and Central Africa. They report struggling to find work in Italy and Spain because of the financial crisis and have decided to try their luck in Denmark—but so far with little success; many claim to be hanging out in public libraries, waiting for the shelters to reopen.

For the Guan who work in the Naples underground economy, it is a hard, risky life standing by the roadside waiting to be picked up; nevertheless, it is a life that offers certain possibilities and forms of action for migrants, though it also means exclusion from participation in many areas of Italian life. Even though the underground economy grossly exploits the West African migrant workers, and often significantly intensifies the precariousness of their situation by subjecting them to dangerous work situations and abuse, the underground economy also provides a source of income, sustaining the migrants as they struggle to gain a foothold in Europe—which appears to be why migrants head for Naples in the first place. Even under very difficult circumstances, the Guans seem to find ways of making life bearable.

The structure of the labor market in Naples provides three basic work situations for the Guan migrants that entail quite different experiences and strategies: day-laboring, the most risky and stressful form of work; semi-regular work with a regular boss, or *capo*; and the regular work situation, which is quite rare for these migrants in Naples. Although all of these work situations entail some degree of precariousness, day-laboring poses the greatest challenge in that migrants are subjected to arbitrary acts of exploitation, abuse, and even robbery and do not know who will pick them up and what will happen to them. Working with a steady employer and developing a relationship based on mutual dependency provides better protection, the data suggest, though, as Samuel explained, there's no guarantee that the work situation is safe or manageable or that one's salary will be paid according to the work agreement. Finally, regular work, though largely unattractive and unsafe compared to jobs that Italians hold, has a different meaning for migrants than the two other types of work in that it represents an important step forward, allowing migrants to establish themselves in Italy and at home. But since it can be obtained only if one has documents, it is not common among the Guan migrants of Naples.

Moreover, the precariousness of migrant lives that depend on the underground economy appears to be intensified by the fact that migrants confront blatant racism on a daily basis. In occupying the only positions available to them, migrants seem to confirm in some Italians' minds certain discriminatory ideas about them as inherently inferior, which in turn facilitates certain kinds of hurtful discourses and actions, limiting options even further. "Our lives are shaking in the hands of these people," as Francis described the uncertainty and anxiety surrounding migrant lives. But rather than condemning Italy as an unchanging mass of essentially "wicked people," which was the understandable interpretation many informants offered, this book attempts to show how the reception of migrants reflects certain Italian sociopolitical and historical developments that cannot be disregarded when trying to grasp what may be at stake for Italians.

But why do the migrants risk their lives by coming to Europe, and why do they choose to substitute their friends and families at home with such a difficult and even hostile environment? To understand the choices Guan migrants made in risking everything for Europe, I explore the disconnectedness revealed in recent developments in the political economy of the globalized world. Viewing high-risk migration as either a matter of obtaining material gains or the result of sheer thoughtlessness, with all its biased connotations, is not a satisfactory explanation. To be sure, material gains often articulate social and existential needs, but these needs cannot be reduced to the gains themselves. Moreover, the Guan migrants have relatively deep knowledge about the dangers and hardships of the journey at the time they decide to take their chances, suggesting that they knowingly put their lives at risk and willingly endure the hardships of migrant life in Naples—because the feel they have no other option.

Following social theorists (Appadurai 2006; Bauman 2004; Cohen 2006; Ferguson 2006) who argue that globalization does not necessarily deliver the interconnected world it promises (on the contrary, it provides a world of exclusion), the book suggests that it is precisely this lack of responsiveness to one's wants and needs that yields a sense of desperation in those parts of the world cut off from the circulation of goods, symbolic as well as material, leading people to take drastic measures. To understand what is at stake, the book stresses the need to address this devastating experience of disconnectedness anew. For this purpose the concept of *existential reciprocity* is employed; that is, a form of connectedness that involves all of the constituents of the lifeworld, both human and extrahuman and sustains individuals, bringing them into existence. Existential reciprocity is a form of responsiveness from the powers that sustain one, powers that, regardless of their ontological status, support the fabric of everyday life and entail, subsequently, a secure sense of being. Moreover, existential reciprocity, in the tradition of existential anthropology, addresses the need to strike a balance between where one wants to go and where one is taken by the world (Jackson 2005: xi; Kleinman 2006: 17). By giving one's time, effort, attention, and hard work, one obliges the world to provide something of commensurable worth, or at least to refrain from unfavorable actions; one experientially makes the external world responsive to human needs, thus drawing it into one's sphere of influence. The migrant experience in Naples, however, does not necessarily entail this sense of connectedness; instead most migrants endure many severe setbacks. When real participation in desired social and political fields is denied them, I argue, migrants turn to symbolic action and to the reinvention of their worlds in order to obtain a sense of control in a hostile environment.

The journey to Europe and the role Guan fishermen play in Libyan transit migration to Italy is considered in part 2. Because of growing European pressure on the Mediterranean transit connections, smugglers no longer pilot the boat themselves but leave it up to selected migrants with seafaring experience to handle the boats, and this is where Guan migrants come into the picture. As it happens, the fact that many of them are seasoned fishermen gives them a window of opportunity. Thus, by taking a boat across to Europe from Libya, they get a free ride if they make it. However, their capabilities are pushed to the limit because they are often presented with unseaworthy boats that are dangerously overloaded. Although many Guan captains make it, drawing on their seafaring skills, a large number of captains have perished on the way, along with them hundreds of passengers in some cases. As mentioned above, the controversial new deal between Libya and Italy has temporarily halted this traffic (though the stormy history of relations between the two countries should discourage the assumption that this deal will stand forever), and it remains to be seen what will happen in the Mediterranean. Alternative routes may open; Libya could make new demands; the political landscape may change in Italy. One thing is for sure: the many deaths on the doorstep of Europe, and the testimonies of Africans being detained in Libya, challenge the moral values normally applied to human lives in a European context.

Drawing on Agamben's work, I suggest viewing the Mediterranean borderland as a gray zone where political rule operates outside the law. The human beings caught in this "state of exception" can be understood as *homini sacri*, or "bare lives," to state power—lives that have no value in a legal or political sense (Agamben 1998: 8). This gray zone, however, includes the lesser-known, yet equally dangerous, desert portion of the journey. Although little is known about trans-Saharan migration, testimonies from the desert appear to confirm the brutal nature of this form of migration and the lack of regard for human life. Whether migrants choose the Ahaggar Mountains or the Ténéré Desert route, death is ever present. In fact, many Guan captains prefer the sea journey to the desert leg of the journey because on the sea they can take action if something goes wrong, whereas in the desert they are completely at the mercy of circumstance. Overall, this book takes the perilous journey to Europe as a glimpse at life in the shadows of globalization, and at how the less privileged find surprising ways of pursuing their aspirations—with disappointing results, more often than not—though great efforts are made to stop them.

To reach a more complete understanding of high-risk migration, I also discuss the declining state of West African fisheries. From a regional perspective, the controversial fishing agreements between the EU and

West African coastal countries may be intensifying the very illegal migration process the EU is allocating so many resources to end. On a local level, the growing pressure on marine resources has had immediate social and economic consequences for the fishermen of Senya Beraku. Because fishing is the all-important industry, the decline has affected all corners of the community, and as the fishermen reported failing catches in 2009 for the third year in a row, the village struggled to cope with the consequences. The families that depend on catches for their basic necessities see sending children away for a fee as a strategy of cutting expenses, though this practice has now been made illegal. Other fishermen are experimenting with new technologies such as light fishing, though with disappointing results thus far, while others are moving to bigger cities to look for work—though the general economy of Ghana offers little relief and the fishermen find few opportunities for work outside the fishing industry. The miserable situation is also taking it's toll on an existential level, causing fishermen to lose their hold on the future and creating a sense of environmental disintegration, as the once rich and fertile marine environment is reported to have become "transparent" and "swift," or simply devoid of the promise of life it once contained. This decline, the book suggests, is a result of diminished responsiveness, and I show how such diminished responsiveness alters one's understanding of the external world, leading to the conclusion that existential reciprocity is important not only for sustaining individuals and bringing them into existence but also for maintaining a sense of the outside world as a permanent, reliable, and substantial whole (Laing 1973: 39). To deal with their situation, the young men's main strategy is emigration to Europe via Libya by the dangerous means available. I should mention, however, that another, equally controversial way of traveling may be on the horizon. One young Ghanaian man, who had been deported back to Ghana in 2007, recently informed me that he was enrolling in the British Army in order to claw his way back onto European soil while avoiding the dreaded clandestine journey via Libya. In fact, the number of young Ghanaians enrolled as Commonwealth recruits in 2009 was up by 40 percent since

2006, to 740, and overall "foreign legions" constituted nearly 11 percent of the British Army's full-time troops; these sources help compensate for the problems in recruiting British-born soldiers for, among other things, the war effort in Iraq and Afghanistan (Foggo and Waite 2009). Moreover, emerging ethnographic fieldwork focuses on private security companies, like Sabre International, that recruit young Anglophone West Africans, especially from postconflict areas, and dispatch them to international military operations (Christensen 2010).

Taking into consideration particular characteristics of the various empirical fields studied here (the organization of the Italian underground economy and its need for cheap labor, the organization of Libyan human smuggling and its response to EU pressure, the decline in the Guan fishing industry and the well-established patterns of labor migration to Libya), it is now possible to appreciate that the migration route between Ghana and Libya did not appear out of the blue. Rather, these chains of interdependence, or figurations (Elias 1970: 132), have carved out a special role for West African canoe fishermen in Libyan transit migration, one readily performed by the Guan migrants. This opening, however, is dangerous for those who follow it. After discussing the organization of illegal immigration and the perils it involves, the book turned to an examination of how migrants' deaths are received in the village. A major challenge for surviving family is gathering information as to the whereabouts of members lost in the desert or at sea. In many cases families wait for years while hope fades of seeing their sons, brothers, and husbands again. Although the Guan captains may be "bare lives" in the globalized political economy, their lives and deaths are recognized in Senya Beraku. Therefore, information on the dead having been obtained, one way or the other, the lost family members are reclaimed and again included in the social, political, and religious life of the village. I argue that this is a form of existential counteraction in the sense that a family may be powerless to change what happened, but not how the loss is dealt with. Great attention is devoted to securing the ascent of the soul to the eternal world of the ancestors, thus reinstating the lost person in the moral order.

Even so, the many deaths have serious economic and emotional implications for the families in the village. The book discusses these consequences by focusing on the young widows who find themselves in a very difficult situation, having suddenly lost their husbands and the fathers of their children. Then I explore further the challenges to the existential give-and-take of life that conceding such a loss entails for the bereaved. Returning to the concept of existential reciprocity, I argued that if, experientially, giving up is also a form of giving, then certain symbolic gifts violate the very moral worlds they are supposed to sustain. Taking my cue from Kierkegaard's interpretation of the Abraham and Isaac story, I suggest that existential reciprocity is a form of connectedness that guarantees the morality of the life-world but is paradoxically constituted by actions that take one outside the order of reason and human ethics. Thus, in the everyday demands of life's give-and-take, people are made to give up more than can reasonably or ethically be asked of them, and given no assurance that life will be restored to a bearable state. But what is there to be gained from this noneconomy of gift-giving that demands the sacrifice of the things one holds dearest? Following Kierkegaard, I argue that the attraction is precisely the substitution of the arbitrariness of the external world with a moral world, a responsive world organized by the principal of existential reciprocity, which is, nevertheless, violently insensitive to human ethics (Kierkegaard 1985 [1843]: 57). Thus, giving up what cannot be given up threatens the moral order—and may cause it to collapse—before strengthening it. Indeed, existential reciprocity in this extreme mode treads a fine line between order and chaos.

Finally, the book addresses the fruits of immigration—namely, the rewards that the young men of Senya Beraku continuously risk their lives for. To be sure, the group of Guan immigrants discussed in chapter 1 were making little, if any, progress in Naples. Rather they had escaped the "social death" of West African village life only to face "a much denser form of marginalization" as new immigrants in Southern Europe—a situation in which "the impossibility of gaining a worthy life becomes consolidated and existential uncertainty heightened by a deterioration of established social relations and obligations" (Vigh 2009: 105). Consequently, the village of Senya Beraku exhibited few signs of advancement. However, the book concludes, a small plot of land on the outskirts of town with a pile of blocks on it articulated well the desire to protect oneself against a future that no longer harbors one's aspirations, but rather threatens to sweep destructively across the community like a natural disaster.

Epilogue

Sammy had agreed to show me his place of work. Having obtained documents in Italy, he finally made it out of Naples and found his way to Denmark. It was well past midnight as I sat in my in-law's car in a big deserted parking lot on the outskirts of Copenhagen. The shoppers had all gone, and bright neon signs advertising the goods you could buy at the shops surrounding the parking lot illuminated the open space. There was an ambivalence about the place: the cold, windy weather outside contrasted sharply with the warmth the neon signs radiated, like mesmerizing electric flowers. Sammy had asked me to wait until his boss had finished adding up the day's receipts in the back room. I had parked the car next to a petrol station at the opposite end of the parking lot, so that if someone should ask, I could say that I was about to buy petrol. From the front seat of the car I watched the tiny figure of Sammy through the windows of the McDonald's restaurant, going back and forth between the counter and the food-processing area.

I was about to doze off while listening to a foreign political radio show, when Sammy called me on my mobile phone and told me to go to the back door—the boss had finally left. I drove the car around to the McDonald's parking lot, got out, and walked to the back entrance, where Sammy was waiting in his dirty uniform. Another guy was working with him, a skinny Pakistani boy who had only been in the country ten months. His job was to take care of the grill and the French fry oil, but Sammy complained that he was mostly interested in smoking cigarettes and relaxing. We passed the frozen figure of the smiling Ronald McDonald clown, reaching out his hand as in a greeting, and moved behind the counter. The food-processing area reeked of incinerated meat and the floor was slippery with grease. Sammy's job was to clean up the whole place before daybreak. Then he would move on to an office building in the city, where he emptied dustbins and washed the floors. He explained that they were ripping him off; the subcontractor who hired him paid him for six hours, but was docking him two hours and giving the money to the useless Pakistani helper. Still, Samuel made twice as much as he had in Naples. The Pakistani, who didn't appear to understand English, made coffee and handed out cigarettes.

Sammy and I sat for a while and talked, but the feeling of defeat inherent in the situation, combined with the desolate behind-the-scenes view of the fast food industry, made it hard to concentrate. Sammy had made it out of Naples, but here he was in his dirty McDonald's uniform, invisible, underpaid, unrecognized, working in the middle of the night while the Danes were resting comfortably in their beds. As I was getting ready to leave, Sammy handed me a brown paper bag he had prepared with ice cream, fruit, and some McDonald's toys for my daughter. Driving home to Copenhagen, I warned myself that what might constitute unacceptable terms of existence to a white Scandinavian middle-class person might constitute a new beginning to someone less privileged, a plot of land with blocks on it. Still, I was also recalling something my wife had said to me in Naples. Coming home from field-work one evening and recounting some of the things I had seen and heard about the plight of the illegal immigrants, she commented that though we didn't live far from each other, Sammy might as well live on the moon. Driving back I was overcome by the same feeling that Sammy, though finally at the end of the journey that he imagined would change his life, was still living on the moon.

References

Aborampah, Osei-Mensah. 1999. "Women's Roles in the Mourning Rituals of the Akan of Ghana." *Ethnology* 38 (3): 257–271.

AFP. *See* Agence France-Presse. Agamben, Giorgio. 1998. *Homo Sacer: Sovereign Power and Bare Life.* Stanford: Stanford University Press.

Agence France-Presse. 2009. "EU Wants Turkey, Libya to Help Fight Illegal Immigration." July 17. www.google.com/hostednews/afp/article/ ALeqM5gbe-kxWEV_VNW3lrdBmmrPfrEmwg.

Albahari, Maurizio. 2006. *Death and the Moral State: Making Borders and Sovereignty at the Southern Edges of Europe.* CCIS Working Paper 136. San Diego: University of California.

Alder, Jacqueline, and U. R. Sumalia. 2004. "Western Africa: A Fish Basket of Europe Past and Present." *Journal of Environment and Development* 13 (2): 156–178.

Ammendola, C. F., et al. 2005. *Irregular Migration in Italy: Illegally Resident Third Country Nationals in Italy; State Approaches toward Them and Their Profile and Social Situation.* Rome: IDOS–European Migration Network.

Anthias, F., and G. Lazaridis. 1999. *Into the Margins: Migration and Exclusion in Southern Europe.* Aldershot, UK: Ashgate.

Appadurai, Arjun. 1996. *Modernity at Large: Cultural Dimensions of Globalization.* Minneapolis: University of Minnesota Press.

Appadurai, Arjun, 2006. *Fear of Small Numbers: An Essay on the Geography of Anger.* Durham, NC: Duke University Press.

Arendt, Hannah. 2006. *Eichmann in Jerusalem: A Report on the Banality of Evil.* London: Penguin Classics.

Aristoteles [Aristotle]. 1995. *Den Nikomacheiske Etik.* Oversat af Niels Møller. Frederiksberg, Denmark: DET lille FORLAG.

Arthur, Peter. 2006. "The State Private Sector Development, and Ghana's 'Golden Age of Business.'" *African Studies Review* 49 (1): 31–50.

Atta-Mills, John, et al. 2004. "The Decline of a Regional Fishing Nation: The Case of Ghana and West Africa." *Natural Resources Forum* 28: 13–21.

Augé, Marc. 1995. *Non-places: Introduction to an Anthropology of Supermodernity.* London: Verso.

Baldwin-Edwards, Martin. 2006. "Between a Rock and a Hard Place: North Africa as a Region of Emigration, Immigration, and Transit Migration." *Review of African Political Economy* 108: 331–324.

Bannerman, Paul, and Richmond Quartey. 2004. *Report on the Observation of Commercial Light Fishing Operation in Ghana, February–June 2004.* Tema, Ghana: Marine Fisheries Research Division.

Bauman, Zygmunt. 1989. *Modernity and the Holocaust.* Cambridge: Polity Press.

Bauman, Zygmunt. 1998. *Globalization: The Human Consequences.* Cambridge: Polity Press.

Bauman, Zygmunt. 2004. *Wasted Lives: Modernity and Its Outcasts.* Cambridge: Polity Press.

BBC. *See* British Broadcasting Corporation.

Beck, Ulrich. 1997. *Risk Society: Towards a New Modernity.* London: Sage.

Beck, Ulrich. 2000. *What Is Globalization?* Cambridge: Polity Press.

Biehl, J., et al. 2007. "Introduction: Rethinking Subjectivity." In *Subjectivity: Ethnographic Investigations.* Ed. J. Biehl, B. Good, and A. Kleinman. Berkeley: University of California Press.

Bompard, Paul. 2007. "Shipwrecked Africans Saved after Clinging to Tuna Nets for 24 Hours." *The Times.* May 28. www.timesonline.co.uk/tol/news/world/europe/article18481 48.ece

Bourdieu, Pierre. 1990. *The Logic of Practice.* Cambridge: Polity Press.

Bourdieu, Pierre. 2000. *Pascalian Meditations.* Stanford: Stanford University Press.

Bourgois, P. 1995. *In Search of Respect: Selling Crack in El Barrio.* Cambridge: Cambridge University Press.

Brashares, Justin S., et al. 2004. "Bushmeat Hunting, Wildlife Declines, and Fish Supply in West Africa." *Science* 306: 1180–1183.

Briggs, P. 1998. *Guide to Ghana*. Chalfont St. Peter, UK: Brad Publications.

British Broadcasting Corporation. 2005. "Italy Warns Morocco on Migrants." http://news.bbc.co.uk/go/pr/fr/-/2/hi/europe/4570714.stm.

British Broadcasting Corporation. 2006a. "Gaddafi: Migration 'Inevitable.'" http://news.bbc.co.uk/2/hi/africa/6176720.stm.

British Broadcasting Corporation. 2006b. "Ten Die in Libya Cartoon Clash." http://news.bbc.co.uk/2/hi/africa/4726204.stm

British Broadcasting Corporation. 2009a. "Italy Adopts Law to Curb Migrants." http://news.bbc.co.uk/2/hi/europe/8132084.stm.

British Broadcasting Corporation. 2009b. "Greek Police Flatten Migrant Camp." http://news.bbc.co.uk/2/hi/europe/8146597.stm.

British Broadcasting Corporation. 2010. "EU and Libya Reach Deal on Illegal Migrants." http://news.bbc.co.uk/news/world-europe-11484192.

Buah, F. K. 1998. *A History of Ghana*. London: Macmillan Education.

Calavita, Kitty. 2005. *Immigrants at the Margins: Law, Race, and Exclusion in Southern Europe*. Cambridge: Cambridge University Press.

Camilleri, Ivan. 2008. "Frontex Chief Admits Failure." *Times of Malta*. September 21. www.timesofmalta.com/articles/view/20080921/local/frontex-chief-admits-failure.225630/comments:4.

Canetti, Elias. 1984. *Crowds and Power*. New York: Farrar, Straus, and Giroux.

Caritas Europa. 2006. *Migration, a Journey into Poverty? A Caritas Europa Study on Poverty and Exclusion of Immigrants in Europe*. Brussels: Caritas.

Caritas/Migrantes. 2006. *Dossier Statistico Immigrazione: XVI Rapporto sull'immigrazione*. Rome: Caritas.

Caritas/Migrantes. 2007. *Dossier Statistico Immigrazione: XVII Rapporto sull'immigrazione*. Rome: Caritas.

Carrier, James G. 1992. "Occidentalism: The World Turned Upside–Down." *American Ethnologist*. 19 (2): 195–212.

Carroll, Michael P. 1981. "Lévi–Strauss, Freud, and the Trickster: A New Perspective upon an Old Problem." *American Ethnologist* 8 (2): 301–313.

Carter, Donald M. 1997. *States of Grace: Senegalese in Italy and the New European Immigration*. Minneapolis: University of Minnesota Press.

Chalof, Jonathan. 2003. "Country Report." In *EU and US Approaches to the Management of Immigration*. Ed. Jan Niessen, Yongmi Schibel, and Raphaële Magoni. Brussels: Migration Policy Group.

Choate, Mark I. 2003. "From Territorial to Ethnographic Colonies and Back Again: The Politics of Italian Expansion, 1890–1912." *Modern Italy* 8 (1): 65–75.

Christensen, J. B. 1997. "Motor Power and Women Power: Technological and Economic Change among the Fante Fishermen of Ghana." In *Those Who Live from the Sea*. Ed. E. M. Smith. St. Paul, MN: West.

Christensen, Maya M. 2010. "Lejemordere eller unge i arbejde." *Kristeligt Dagblad*. 9 April. www.kristeligt-dagblad.dk/artikel/361883:3—verden—Lejemordere-eller-unge-i-arbejde.

Cohen, Daniel. 2006. *Globalisation and Its Enemies*. Cambridge, MA: MIT Press.

Cole, Jeffrey E., and Sally Booth. 2007. *Dirty Work: Immigrants in Domestic Service, Agriculture, and Prostitution in Sicily*. Lanham: Lexington Books.

Coluccello, S., and S. Massey. 2007. "Out of Africa: The Human Trade between Libya and Lampedusa." *Trends in Organized Crime* 10: 77–90.

Collyer, Michael. 2006. "Undocumented Sub–Saharan African Migrants in Morocco." In *Mediterranean Transit Migration*. Ed. Ninna Nyberg Sørensen. Copenhagen: Danish Institute for International Studies.

Comaroff, J., and J. L. Comaroff. 1999. "Occult Economies and the Violence of Abstraction: Notes from the South African Postcolony." *American Ethnologist* 26 (2): 279–300.

Csikszentmihalyi, Mihaly. 1991. *Flow: Optimaloplevelsens psykologi*. Copenhagen: Munksgaard.

Csikszentmihalyi, Mihaly. 2005. *Flow of engagement i hverdagen*. Virum, Denmark: Dansk Psykologisk Forlag.

Daly, F. 1999. "Tunisian Migrants and Their Experience of Racism in Modena." *Modern Italy* 4 (2): 173–189.

Das, Veena. 1995. *Critical Events: An Anthropological Perspective on Contemporary India*. Oxford: Oxford University Press.

Davidsen, Lisbeth. 2005. "Minister undersøger forhold i fangelejr." *Politiken*. October 10. http://politiken.dk/udland/ECE125744/minister-undersoeger-forhold-i-fangelejr.

Davis, Natalie Zemon. 2000. *The Gift in Sixteenth-Century France*. Oxford: Oxford University Press.

De Genova, Nicholas. 2002. "Migrant 'Illegality' and Deportability in Everyday Life." *Annual Review of Anthropology*. 31: 419–447.

De Haas, Hein. 2007. "Turning the Tide? Why Development Will Not Stop Migration." *Development and Change* 38 (5): 819–841.

Derrida, Jacques. 1995. *The Gift of Death*. Chicago: University of Chicago Press.

Desjarlais, Robert. 1997. *Shelter Blues: Sanity and Selfhood among the Homeless*. Philadelphia: University of Pennsylvania Press.

Devereux, George. 1967. *From Anxiety to Method in the Behavioral Sciences*. The Hague: Mouton.

DFMFA. *See* Directories of Fisheries, Ministry of Food and Agriculture.

Directories of Fisheries, Ministry of Food and Agriculture. 2003. *Ghana: Post–Harvest Fisheries Overview.* Accra, Ghana: DFMFA.

EC. *See* European Commission. Elias, Norbert. 1970. *What Is Sociology?* New York: Colombia University Press.

Ellen, R. F., and David Hicks. 1984. "Field Assistants" in *Ethnographic Research.* Ed. R. F. Ellen, 209–210. London: Academic Press.

Emerson, R. W. 1997 [1844]. "Gifts." In *The Logic of the Gift.* Ed. Alan D. Schrift, 25–27. New York: Routledge.

Ephirim–Donkor, Anthony. 2000. *The Making of an African King: Patrilineal and Matrilineal Struggle among the Effutu of Ghana.* Trenton: African World Press.

EU. *See* European Union.

European Commission. 2005. "Technical Mission to Libya on Illegal Immigration 27 Nov–6 Dec 2004: Report." www.statewatch.org/news/2005/may/eu-report-libya-ill-imm.pdf.

European Union. 2007. EU General Affairs and External Relations Council Conclusions. October 16. www.europa-eu-un.org/articles/en/article_7409_en.htm.

FAO. *See* Food and Agriculture Organization of the United Nations.

Ferguson, James. 2003. "Global Disconnect: Abjection and the Aftermath of Modernism." In *The Anthropology of Globalization. A Reader.* Ed. J.X. Inda and R. Rosaldo, 136–153. Malden, Mass.: Blackwell.

Ferguson, James. 2006. *Global Shadows: Africa in the Neo–liberal World Order.* Durham, NC: Duke University Press.

Foggo, Daniel, and Roger Waite. 2009. "Commonwealth Cousins Prop Up the British Army." *Sunday Times.* 26 April. www.timesonline.co.uk/tol/news/politics/article6168981.ece.

Food and Agriculture Organization of the United Nations. 1995. *The State of the World Fisheries and Aquaculture.* Rome: FAO.

Friedman, Jonathan. 1999a. "Indigenous Struggles and the Discreet Charm of the Bourgeoisie." *Australian Journal of Anthropology* 10 (1): 1–14.

Friedman, Jonathan. 1999b. "The Political Economy of Elegance: An African Cult of Beauty." In *Consumption and Identity.* Ed. Jonathan Friedman, 167–187. Amsterdam: Harwood Academic.

Frontex. 2007a. *Frontex—Facts and Myths.* www.frontex.europa.eu/newsroom/news_releases/art26.html.

Frontex. 2007b. *Hera III Operation.* www.frontex.europa.eu/newsroom/news_releases/art21.html.

Gammeltoft-Hansen, T. G. 2006. "Outsourcing Migration Management: EU, Power, and the External Dimension of Asylum and Immigration Policy." Working Paper (1). Copenhagen: Danish Institute for International Studies.

Gatti, Fabrizio. 2005. "Io, clandestino a Lampedusa." *L'espresso*. October 7.

Geissler, P. W. 2005. "Blood–Stealing Rumours in Western Kenya: A Local Critique of Medical Research in its Global Context." In *Managing Uncertainty*. Ed. Richard Jenkins et al. Copenhagen: Museum Tusculanum Press.

Giddens, Anthony. 1992. *Modernity and Self–Identity. Self and Society in the Late Modern Age*. Cambridge: Polity Press.

Giddens, Anthony. 2000. *En løbsk verden. Hvordan globaliseringen forandrer vores tilværelse*. Copenhagen: Hans Reitzels Forlag.

Giddens, Anthony. 2003. *The Consequences of Modernity*. Stanford: Stanford University Press.

Glick-Schiller, Nina, et al. 1995. "From immigrant to Transmigrant: Theorizing Transnational Migration." *Anthropological Quarterly* 68 (1): 48–63.

Gluckman, M. 1961. "Anthropological Problems Arising from Industrial Revolution." In *Social Change in Modern Africa*. Ed. A. Southall, 71–82. London: Oxford University Press.

Grillo, Ralph. 2002. "Immigration and the Politics of Recognizing Difference in Italy." In *The Politics of Recognizing Difference: Multiculturalism Italian–Style*. Ed. Ralph Grillo and Jeff Pratt, 1–24. Aldershot, UK: Ashgate.

Grillo, Ralph, and Bruno Riccio. 2004. "Translocal Development: Italy-Senegal." *Population, Space, and Place* 10: 99–111.

Guthrie, Stewart. 1995. *Faces in the Clouds: A New Theory of Religion*. New York: Oxford University Press.

Hamood, Sara. 2006. *African Transit Migration through Libya to Europe: The Human Cost*. Cairo: American University in Cairo.

Hansen, Mikkel Jes. 2007. "Konstruktionen af det illegale menneske." MA thesis, Department of Anthropology, University of Copenhagen.

Hansen, Thomas B., and Finn Stepputat. 2005. "Introduction." In *Sovereign Bodies: Citizens, Migrants, and States in the Postcolonial World*. Ed. Thomas B. Hansen and Finn Stepputat, 1–36. Princeton: Princeton University Press.

Harder, Thomas. 2006. *Italien: Fra Mazzini til Berlusconi*. Copenhagen: Gyldendal.

De Haas, Hein. 2008. "Turning the Tide? Why Development Will Not Stop Migration." *Development and Change* 38 (5): 819–841.

Heidegger, Martin. 1999. *Hvad er metafysik?* Frederiksberg, Denmark: DET lille Forlag.

Hogue, Charles L. 1987. "Cultural Entomology." *Annual Review of Entomology* 32: 181–199.

Human Rights Watch. 2009. *Italy/Libya: Gaddafi Visit Celebrates Dirty Deal*. www.hrw.org/en/news/2009/06/09/italylibya-gaddafi-visit-celebrates-dirty-deal.

ICMPD. *See* International Centre for Migration Policy Development.

IEEP. *See* Institute for European Environmental Policy.

Inda, J. X., and R. Rosaldo. 2003. *The Anthropology of Globalization.* Malden, MA: Blackwell.

Ingold, Tim. 1992. "Culture and the Perception of the Environment." In *Bush Base, Forest Farm: Culture, Environment, and Development.* Ed. E. Croll and D. Parkin, 39–56. London: Routledge.

Ingold, Tim. 2000. *The Perception of the Environment.* London: Routledge.

Ingold, Tim. 2006. "Rethinking the Animate, Re–animating Thought." *Ethnos* 71: 9–20.

Institute for European Environmental Policy. 2002. *Fisheries Agreements with Third Countries—Is the EU Moving Towards Sustainable Development?* London: IEEP.

Jackson, Michael. 1998. *Minima Ethnographica: Intersubjectivity and the Anthropological Project.* Chicago: University of Chicago Press.

Jackson, Michael. 2002. "Familiar and Foreign Bodies: A Phenomenological Exploration of the Human-Technology Interface." *Journal of the Royal Anthropological Institute* 8: 333–346.

Jackson, Michael. 2005. *Existential Anthropology: Events, Exigencies, and Effects.* New York: Berghahn Books.

Jackson, Michael. 2006. *The Accidental Anthropologist: A Memoir.* Dunedin, New Zealand: Longacre Press.

Jackson, Michael. 2007. *Excursions.* Durham, NC: Duke University Press.

JRS Malta. *See* Jesuit Refugee Service Malta.

Jesuit Refugee Service Malta. 2009. *Do They Know? Asylum Seekers Testify to Life in Libya.* Malta: JRS.

Jørgensen, Carsten René. 2002. *Psykologien i senmoderniteten.* Copenhagen: Hans Reitzels Forlag.

Kaczynski, V. M., and D. L. Fluharty. 2002. "European Policies in West Africa: Who Benefits from Fisheries Agreements?" *Marine Policy* 26: 75–93.

Kearney, Michael. 1996. *Reconceptualizing the Peasantry: Anthropology in Global Perspective.* Boulder, CO: Westview Press.

Kierkegaard, Søren. 1985 [1843]. *Fear and Trembling.* London: Penguin Books.

Kleinman, Arthur. 1992. "Pain and Resistance: The Delegitimation and Relegitimation of Local Worlds." In *Pain as Human Experience: An Anthropological Perspective.* Ed. M.-J. D. Good et al., 169–197. Berkeley: University of California Press.

Kleinman, Arthur. 2006. *What Really Matters. Living a Moral Life amidst Uncertainty and Danger.* Oxford: Oxford University Press.

King, Russel. 2001. "The Troubled Passage: Migration and Cultural Encounters in Southern Europe." In *The Mediterranean Passage: Migrations and New*

Cultural Encounters in Southern Europe. Ed. Russel King, 1–21. Liverpool: Liverpool University Press.

Kohut, Heinz. 1984. *How Does Analysis Cure?* Chicago: University of Chicago Press.

Kyle, D., and Koslowksi, R. 2001. *The Global Human Smuggling*. Baltimore: Johns Hopkins University Press.

Laing, Ronald D. 1973. *The Divided Self: An Existential Study in Sanity and Madness*. Harmondsworth, UK: Penguin Books.

Laing, Ronald D. 1976. *The Facts of Life*. New York: Pantheon Books.

Lauritzen, Thomas. 2007. "Giv en hånd til Afrika—ellers gør Kina det." *Politiken*. December 8.

Levinson, Amanda. 2005. *The Regularisation of Unauthorised Migrants: Literature Survey and Country Case Studies*. Oxford: Centre on Migration, Policy, and Society, Oxford University.

Lévi–Strauss, Claude. 1963. *Structural Anthropology*. New York: Basic Books.

Lévi–Strauss, Claude. 1969. *The Elementary Structures of Kinship*. London: Eyre & Spottiswoode.

Lucht, Hans. 2003. "Three Aspects of Reciprocity: Strategies of Dealing with the Sea in a Ghanaian Fishing Village." MA thesis, Department of Anthropology, University of Copenhagen.

Luhmann, Niklas. 1999. *Tillid—En mekanisme til reduktion af social kompleksitet*. Copenhagen: Hans Reitzels Forlag.

Maher, Vanessa. 1996. "Immigration and Social Identities." In *Italian Cultural Studies: An Introduction*. Ed. D. Forgacs and R. Lumley. Oxford: Oxford University Press.

Mai, Nicola. 2003. "The Cultural Construction of Italy in Albania and Vice Versa: Migration Dynamics, Strategies of Resistance, and Politics of Mutual Self-Definition across Colonialism and Post-colonialism." *Modern Italy* 8 (1): 77–93.

Marcus, George E. 1995. "Ethnography in/of the World System: The Emergence of Multi-sited Ethnography." *Annual Review of Anthropology*. 24: 95–117.

Marquette, C.M., et al. 2002. "Small–Scale Fisheries, Population Dynamics, and Resource Use in Africa: The Case of Moree, Ghana." *Ambio* 31 (4): 324–336.

Mauss, Marcel. 1990. *The Gift: The Form and Reason for Exchange in Archaic Societies*. London: Routledge.

Mbembe, Achilles. 2003. "Necropolitics." *Public Culture* 15 (1): 11–40.

Melville, Herman. 1994. *Moby-Dick*. London: Penguin Books.

Merleau-Ponty, Maurice. 1976. *Phenomenology of Perception*. London: Routledge & Kegan Paul.

Ministero dell'Interno. 2007a. *Immigrazione clandestina e irregolare*. www.interno. it/mininterno/export/sites/default/it/temi/immigrazione/sottotema002. html.

Ministero dell'Interno 2007b. *Nel 2006 diminuiscono gli sbarchi dei clandestini rispetto all'anno precedente*. www.interno.it/mininterno/export/sites/ default/it/sezioni/sala_stampa/notizie/immigrazione/notizia_23488.html.

Ministero dell'Interno. 2007c. "Notizie: Immigrazione." In *Lotta all'immigrazione irregulare, Amato: Coinvolgere la Libia nel pattugliamento del Mediterraneo*. www.interno.it/mininterno/export/sites/default/it/sezioni/sala_stampa/ notizie/immigrazione/0993_2007_06_11_Amato_a_bruxelles_auspica_ coinvolgimento_Libia.html_631041316.html.

Ministero dell'Interno. 2007d. "Notizie: Immigrazione." In *Cooperazione Italia– Libia, le Autoritá libiche bloccano la partenza di 190 clandestini*. www.interno.it/ mininterno/export/sites/default/it/sezioni/sala_stampa/notizie/ immigrazione/notizia_23541.html_1901981482.html.

Mitchell, W. J. T. 1983. *Articulate Images: The Sisters Arts from Hogarth to Tennison*. Minneapolis: University of Minnesota Press.

Nigro, Vicenzo. 2008a. "Immigrazione e petrolio le minacce della Libia." *La Repubblica*. May 9. www.repubblica.it/2008/05/sezioni/esteri/libia-italia/ gheddafi-ritorsioni/gheddafi-ritorsioni.html.

Nigro, Vicenzo. 2008b. "Firma per risarcimento Italia–Libia 'Saremo uniti sull'immigrazione.'" *La Repubblica*. August 30. www.repubblica.it/2008/05/ sezioni/esteri/libia-italia/berlusconi-gheddafi/berlusconi-gheddafi.html.

Nukunya, G. K. 1992. *Tradition and Change in Ghana: An Introduction to Sociology*. Accra: Ghana University Press.

Odotei, I. K. 1992. "The Migration of Ghanaian Women in the Canoe Fishing Industry." *MAST* 5 (2): 88–95.

Onishi, Norimitsu. 2001. "Out of Africa, or Bust, with a Desert to Cross." *New York Times*. January 4. www.nytimes.com/2001/01/04/world/out-of-africa-or-bust-with-a-desert-to-cross.html.

Owen, Richard. 2008. "Berlusconi Sends the Troops against Caserta Mafia after Anti-immigrant Violence." *The Times*. September 23. www.timesonline.co. uk/tol/news/world/europe/article4810085.ece

Owen, Richard. 2009. "New 'Blackshirts' Fear Prompts Inquiry into Italian National Guard." *The Times*. June 15. www.timesonline.co.uk/tol/news/ world/europe/article6499352.ece.

Overå, Ragnhild. 1993. "Wives and Traders: Women's Careers in Ghanaian Canoe Fisheries." *MAST* 6 (1–2): 110–135.

Pardo, Italo. 1996. *Managing Existence in Naples: Morality, Action and Structure*. Cambridge Studies in Social and Cultural Anthropology. Cambridge: Cambridge University Press.

Popham, Peter. 2007. "Europe's Shame." *The Independent*. May 27. http://
news.independent.co.uk/europe/article2588985.ece.

Pratt, Jeff. 2002. "Italy: Political Unity and Cultural Diversity." In *The Politics of
Recognizing Difference: Multiculturalism Italian-Style*. Ed. Ralph Grillo and Jeff
Pratt, 25–39. Aldershot, UK: Ashgate.

Reyneri, Emilio. 2001. *Migrants' Involvement in Irregular Employment in the
Mediterranean Countries of the European Union*. International Labour
Organization Working Paper 41. Geneva: IMO.

Reyneri, Emilio. 2004. "Immigration in a Segmented and Often Undeclared
Labour Market." *Journal of Modern Italian Studies* 9 (1): 71–93.

Riccio, Bruno. 2001. "From 'Ethnic Group' to 'Transnational Community'?
Senegalese Migrants' Ambivalent Experiences and Multiple Trajectories."
Journal of Ethnic and Migration Studies 27 (4): 583–599.

Riccio, Bruno. 2002. "Toubab and Vu Cumpra: Italian Perceptions of Senegalese
Transmigrants and the Senegalese Afro–Muslim Critique of Italian Society."
In *The Politics of Recognizing Difference: Multiculturalism Italian–style*. Ed.
Ralph Grillo and Jeff Pratt, 176–196. Aldershot, UK: Ashgate.

Riccio, Bruno. 2008. "West African Transnationalisms Compared: Ghanaians
and Senegalese in Italy." *Journal of Ethnic and Migration Studies* 34 (2):
217–234.

Ridler, Keith. 1996. "If Not the Words: Shared Practical Activity and
Friendship in Fieldwork." In *Things As They Are: New Directions in
Phenomenological Anthropology*. Ed. Michael Jackson, 238–258. Bloomington
and Indianapolis: Indiana University Press.

Rouse, Roger. 1991. "Mexican Migration and the Social Space of
Postmodernism." *Diaspora* 1 (1): 8–23.

Sahlins, Marshall. 1972. *Stone Age Economics*. London: Tavistock.

Sartre, Jean-Paul. 2005. *Being and Nothingness*. London: Routledge.

Segre, Andrea, Dagmawi Yimer, and Riccardo Biadene. 2009. *Come un uomo
sulla terra*. DVD. Roma: Infinito Edizioni.

Seneca, Lucius Annaeus. 1964. *On Benifits [De Beneficiis]*. Trans. John W. Basore.
London: William Heinemann.

Scheper–Hughes, Nancy. 1996. "Theft of Life: The Globalization of Organ
Stealing Rumors." *Anthropology Today* 12 (3): 3–11.

Schutz, Alfred, and Thomas Luckmann. 1973. *The Structures of the Life-World*.
Vol. 1. Evanston, IL: Northwestern University Press.

Sciortino, G., and A. Colombo. 2004. "The Flows and the Flood: The Public
Discourse on Immigration in Italy, 1969–2001." *Journal of Modern Italian
Studies* 9 (1): 94–113.

Simon, Julien. 2006. "Irregular Transit Migration in the Mediterranean: Facts,
Figures, and Insight." In *Mediterranean Transit Migration*. Ed. Ninna N.
Sørensen, 25–66. Copenhagen: Danish Institute for International Studies.

Statewatch Bulletin. 2005. "EU: European Commission Technical Mission to Libya; Exporting Fortress Europe." *Statewatch Bulletin* 15 (2). www. statewatch.org/news/2006/jul/libya.pdf.

Steegstra, Marijke. 2006. "'White Chiefs' and Queens in Ghana: Personification of 'Development.'" In *Chieftaincy in Ghana: Culture, Governance, and Development*. Ed. K. I. Odotei and A. K. Awedoba, 603–620. Accra: Sub-Saharan Publishers.

Sørensen, Villy. 1995. *Seneca: Humanisten ved Neros hof.* Copenhagen: Gyldendal.

Takyi, B. K., and Addai, I. 2003. "Demographic Processes, Economic Growth, and Socio-economic Developments in Ghana, 1960–2000." In *Critical Perspectives in Politics and Socio-economic Development in Ghana*. Ed. W. J. Tettey et al., 223–237. Leiden, The Netherlands: Brill.

Tettey, Wisdom J. 2006. "Globalization, the Economy of Desire, and Cybersexual Activity among Ghanaian Youth." *Studies in Political Economy* 77: 33–55.

Tortzen, Chr. Gorm. 2005. *Antik mytologi.* Copenhagen: Høst & Søn.

Turner, Victor. 1967. *The Forest of Symbols: Aspects of Ndembu Ritual.* Ithaca, NY: Cornell University Press.

UNDP. *See* United Nations Development Programme.

UNEP. *See* United Nations Environment Programme.

UNHCR. *See* United Nations High Commissioner for Refugees.

United Nations Development Programme. 2005. *Policy Incoherence: EU Fisheries Policy in Senegal.* Human Development Report Office occasional paper (29).

United Nations Environment Programme. 2002. Press Releases March. www. unep.org/Documents/Default.asp?/DocumentID=241&ArticleI D=3026.

United Nations High Commissioner for Refugees. 2006. "As Thousands Risk Their Lives at Sea to Reach Europe, UNHCR Calls for a Broad Joint Response to Deal with the Challenge." www.unhcr.org/cgi-bin/texis/vtx/news/opendoc.htm?tbl=NEWS&id=447489cf2.

United Nations High Commissioner for Refugees. 2009. "UNHCR Interviews Asylum Seekers Pushed Back to Libya." www.unhcr.org/4a5c638b6.html.

Van Dalen, Hendrik P., et al. 2005. "Out of Africa: What Drives the Pressure to Emigrate." *Journal of Population Economy* 18 (4): 741–778.

Van der Geest, Sjaak. 2006. "Between Death and Funeral: Mortuaries and the Exploitation of Liminality in Kwahu, Ghana." *Africa.* 76 (4): 485–501.

Van Velsen, J. 1967. "The Extended-Case Method and Situational Analysis." In *The Craft of Social Anthropology*. Ed. A. L. Epstein, 129–149. London: Tavistock.

Vigh, Henrik. 2009. "Wayward Migration: On Imagined Futures and Technological Voids." *Ethnos* 74 (1):91–109.

Ventresca, Robert. 2006. "Debating the Meaning of Fascism in Contemporary Italy." *Modern Italy* 11 (2): 189–209.

Venturi, A., and C. Villosio. 2006. "Labour Market Effects of Immigration into Italy: An Empirical Analysis." *International Labour Review* 145 (1–2): 91–118.

Vercruijsse, E. 1983. "Fishmongers, Big Dealers and Fishermen: Co-operation and Conflict Between the Sexes in Ghanaian Canoe Fishing." In *Female and male in West Africa*. Ed. C. Oppong, 62–77. London: George Allen & Unwin.

Walker, B. L. E. 2002. "Engendering Ghana's Seascape: Fanti Fishtraders and Marine Property in Colonial History." *Society and Natural Resources*. 15: 389–407.

Ward, A. R., et al. 2004. *Poverty and Post-harvest Fishery Livelihoods in Ghana: Output from the Post-harvest Fisheries Research Program*. Project R8111. Exeter: University of Exeter.

Weiner, Annette B. 1992. *Inalienable Possessions: The Paradox of Keeping-While-Giving*. Berkeley: University of California Press.

Winnicott, D. W. 1962. *The Child and the Outside World*. London: Tavistock.

Whyte, William F. 1964. "The Slum: On the Evolution of Street Corner Society." In *Reflections on Community Studies*. Ed. A. Vidich and J. Bensman, 3–29. New York: Harper Torchbooks.

Wyllie, Robert W. 1967. "The "Aboakyer" of the Effutu: A Critique of Meyerowitz's Account." *Africa: Journal of the International African Institute*. 37 (1): 81–85.

Zahavi, Dan. 2003. *Fænomenologi*. Frederiksberg, Denmark: Roskilde Universitetsforlag.

Zarro, Angela. 2007. "Sahara There and Back: A Photo Essay." *Development* 50 (4): 123–126.

Zizek, Slavoj. 1994. *For They Know Not What They Do: Enjoyment as a Political Factor*. London: Verso.

Text: 10/14 Palatino
Display: Univers Condensed Light 47 and Bauer Bodoni
Compositor: Toppan Best-set Premedia Limited
Printer and binder: IBT Global